TEXT BOOK OF CLINICAL RESEARCH FOR M.PHARM PHARMACY PRACTICE

AS PER PCI SYLLABUS

DR. SHAIMA K A

Made with ♥ on the Notion Press Platform
www.notionpress.com

To all those who matter so much to me:

My family- husband Roopesh and parents and

All students and colleagues - former and present with whom

i had occasion to share and interact

Contents

Foreword

It is common knowledge that books play a major complementary and contributing role in any educational process. While they are envisioned to facilitate self-learning beyond class room exercises, not all of them promote learning; some, indeed, hinder it. The contents of Text Book of Clinical Research for M. Pharm Pharmacy Practice will enable students an opportunity to learn drug development process especially the phases of clinical trials and also the ethical issues involved in the conduct of clinical research.

Iam confident that this well thought out & well-planned book. Text Book of Clinical Research for M. Pharm Pharmacy Practice by Dr.Shaima K A will be tremendous use to the students.

With Pleasure, I compliment Dr.Shaima, friend of mine, for such a fine piece of work

Dr. Akshailekshmi. P
Associate Professor
Mariya Group of Institutions, Atoor,
Thiruvananthapuram ,Kerala, India

Preface

There are many good text books on Clinical Research. However no seperate book for M.Pharm Pharmacy Practice students. Thus the necessity of a book on Text Book of Clinical Research for M. Pharm Pharmacy Practice was observed. This book provides the students an opportunity to learn drug development process especially the phases of clinical trials and also the ethical issues involved in the conduct of clinical research. Also, it aims to imparts knowledge and develop skills on conceptualizing, designing, conducting and managing clinical trials. Objectives of this book is expected that students shall be able to Know the new drug development process., Understand the regulatory and ethical requirements., Appreciate and conduct the clinical trials activities, know safety monitoring and reporting in clinical trials and to Manage the trial coordination process. This book is specially designed for Pharm, Pharmacy Practice students, As per PCI Syllabus.

I feel that this book will be found interesting by students and faculty of Pharmacy and also of other allied science field. Critical comments are welcome.

Dr.Shaima K A
Associate Professor
Department of Pharmacy Practice
Shambhunath Institute of Pharmacy, Jalwa,
Prayagraj,Uttarpredesh, India

Acknowledgements

It is with a sense of pleasure when I look back to acknowledge those who have been the source of encouragement in my entire endeavor. The protection of your anonymity, require me to leave out your names even if I should remember them. Still, without your participation, no part of this work would have been possible.God is my provider, and we thank him, for the wisdom and perseverance that he has been bestowed upon us during this book writing and indeed, throughout our life. We bow our head in front of him, thanking him for all the positive energy we have in us and giving us his blessings in form of people we always look up to and inspire from. I woluld like to thank my parents, teachers, friends and fellow members without whom it was almost impossible for me to complete this work.

Prologue

Pharmacy is the branch of pharmacy in which clinical pharmacists provide direct patient care that optimizes the use of medication and promotes health, wellness, and disease prevention. Clinical pharmacists care for patients in all health care settings but the clinical pharmacy movement initially began inside hospitals and clinics. Clinical pharmacists often work in collaboration with physician and other healthcare professionals.Clinical pharmacists can enter into a formal collaborative practice agreement with another healthcare provider, generally one or more physicians, that allows pharmacists to prescribe medications and order laboratory tests.Text Book of Clinical Research for M. Pharm Pharmacy Practice book provides the students an opportunity to learn drug development process especially the phases of clinical trials and also the ethical issues involved in the conduct of clinical research. Also, it aims to imparts knowledge and develop skills on conceptualizing, designing, conducting and managing clinical trials. Objectives of this book is expected that students shall be able to Know the new drug development process., Understand the regulatory and ethical requirements., Appreciate and conduct the clinical trials activities, know safety monitoring and reporting in clinical trials and to Manage the trial coordination process. This book is specially designed for Pharm, Pharmacy Practice students, As per PCI Syllabus.

CHAPTER ONE

Drug development process

Drug development process

Drug development process mainly involves 5 steps

Step 1: Discovery and Development

Step 2: Preclinical Research

Step 3: Clinical Research

Step 4: FDA Drug Review

Step 5: FDA Post-Market Drug Safety Monitoring

1. DISCOVERY AND DEVELOPMENT

Discovery

Typically, researchers discover new drugs through:

• New insights into a disease process that allow researchers to design a product to stop or reverse the effects of the disease.

• Many tests of molecular compounds to find possible beneficial effects against any of a large number of diseases.

• Existing treatments that have unanticipated effects.

• New technologies, such as those that provide new ways to target medical products to specific sites within the body or to manipulate genetic material.

At this stage in the process, thousands of compounds may be potential candidates for development as a medical treatment. After early testing, however, only a small number of compounds look promising and call for further study.

Development

Once researchers identify a promising compound for development, they conduct experiments to gather information on:

• How it is absorbed, distributed, metabolized, and excreted.

• Its potential benefits and mechanisms of action.

• The best dosage.

• The best way to give the drug (such as by mouth or injection).

• Side effects or adverse events that can often be referred to as toxicity.

• How it affects different groups of people (such as by gender, race, or ethnicity) differently.

• How it interacts with other drugs and treatments.

• Its effectiveness as compared with similar drugs.

PRECLINICAL RESEARCH

Before testing a drug in people, researchers must find out whether it has the potential to cause serious harm, also called toxicity. The two types of preclinical research are:

- **In Vitro**
- **In Vivo**

FDA requires researchers to use good laboratory practices (GLP), defined in medical product development regulations, for preclinical laboratory studies. The GLP regulations are found in 21 CFR Part 58.1: Good Laboratory

Practice for Nonclinical Laboratory Studies. These regulations set the minimum basic requirements for:

- study conduct
- personnel
- facilities
- equipment
- written protocols
- operating procedures
- study reports and a system of quality assurance oversight for each study to help assure the safety of FDA-regulated product.

Usually, preclinical studies are not very large. However, these studies must provide detailed information on dosing and toxicity levels. After preclinical testing, researchers review their findings and decide whether the drug should be tested in people.

CLINICAL RESEARCH

While preclinical research answers basic questions about a drug's safety, it is not a substitute for studies of ways the drug will interact with the human body. "Clinical research" refers to studies, or trials, that are done in people. As the developers design the clinical study, they will consider what they want to accomplish for each of the different Clinical Research Phases and begin the Investigational New Drug Process (IND), a process they must go through before clinical research begins.

On this page you will find information on:

- Designing Clinical Trials
- Clinical Research Phase Studies
- The Investigational New Drug Process
- Asking for FDA Assistance
- FDA IND Review Team
- Approval

Designing Clinical Trials

Researchers design clinical trials to answer specific research questions related to a medical product. These trials follow a specific study plan, called a protocol, that is developed by the researcher or manufacturer. Before a clinical trial begins, researchers review prior information about the drug to develop research questions and objectives. Then, they decide:

- Who qualifies to participate (selection criteria)
- How many people will be part of the study
- How long the study will last
- Whether there will be a control group and other ways to limit research bias
- How the drug will be given to patients and at what dosage
- What assessments will be conducted, when, and what data will be collected
- How the data will be reviewed and analyzed

Clinical trials follow a typical series from early, small-scale, Phase 1 studies to late-stage, large scale, Phase 3 studies.

The Investigational New Drug Process

Drug developers, or sponsors, must submit an Investigational New Drug (IND) application to FDA before beginning clinical research.

In the IND application, developers must include:

- Animal study data and toxicity (side effects that cause great harm) data
- Manufacturing information
- Clinical protocols (study plans) for studies to be conducted
- Data from any prior human research
- Information about the investigator

Phase 1

Study Participants: 20 to 100 healthy volunteers or people with the disease/condition.

Length of Study: Several months

Purpose: Safety and dosage

Approximately 70% of drugs move to the next phase

Phase 2

Study Participants: Up to several hundred people with the disease/condition.

Length of Study: Several months to 2 years

Purpose: Efficacy and side effects

Approximately 33% of drugs move to the next phase

Phase 3

Study Participants: 300 to 3,000 volunteers who have the disease or condition

Length of Study: 1 to 4 years

Purpose: Efficacy and monitoring of adverse reactions

Approximately 25-30% of drugs move to the next phase

Phase 4

Study Participants: Several thousand volunteers who have the disease/condition

Purpose: Safety and efficacy

Drug developers are free to ask for help from FDA at any point in the drug development process, including:

- Pre-IND application, to review FDA guidance documents and get answers to questions that may help enhance their research
- After Phase 2, to obtain guidance on the design of large Phase 3 studies
- Any time during the process, to obtain an assessment of the IND application

Even though FDA offers extensive technical assistance, drug developers are not required to take FDA's suggestions. As long as clinical trials are thoughtfully designed, reflect what developers know about a product, safeguard participants, and otherwise meet Federal standards, FDA allows wide latitude in clinical trial design.

FDA IND Review Team

The review team consists of a group of specialists in different scientific fields. Each member has different responsibilities.

- Project Manager: Coordinates the team's activities throughout the review process, and is the primary contact for the sponsor.
- Medical Officer: Reviews all clinical study information and data before, during, and after the trial is complete.
- Statistician: Interprets clinical trial designs and data, and works closely with the medical officer to evaluate protocols and safety and efficacy data.
- Pharmacologist: Reviews preclinical studies.
- Pharmakineticist: Focuses on the drug's absorption, distribution, metabolism, and excretion processes.Interprets blood-level data at different time intervals from clinical trials, as a way to assess drug dosages and administration schedules.
- Chemist: Evaluates a drug's chemical compounds. Analyzes how a drug was made and its stability, quality control, continuity, the presence of impurities, etc.
- Microbiologist: Reviews the data submitted, if the product is an antimicrobial product, to assess response across different classes of microbes.

Approval

The FDA review team has 30 days to review the original IND submission. The process protects volunteers who participate in clinical trials from unreasonable and significant risk in clinical trials. FDA responds to IND applications in one of two ways:

- Approval to begin clinical trials.
- Clinical hold to delay or stop the investigation. FDA can place a clinical hold for specific reasons, including:

o Participants are exposed to unreasonable or significant risk.

o Investigators are not qualified.

o Materials for the volunteer participants are misleading.

o The IND application does not include enough information about the trial's risks.

A clinical hold is rare; instead, FDA often provides comments intended to improve the quality of a clinical trial. In most cases, if FDA is satisfied that the trial meets Federal standards, the applicant is allowed to proceed with the proposed study.

The developer is responsible for informing the review team about new protocols, as well as serious side effects seen during the trial. This information ensures that the team can monitor the trials carefully for signs of any problems. After the trial ends, researchers must submit study reports.

This process continues until the developer decides to end clinical trials or files a marketing application. Before filing a marketing application, a developer must have adequate data from two large, controlled clinical trials.

FDA Post-Market Drug Safety Monitoring

Even though clinical trials provide important information on a drug's efficacy and safety, it is impossible to have complete information about the safety of a drug at the time of approval. Despite the rigorous steps in the process of drug development, limitations exist. Therefore, the true picture of a product's safety actually evolves over the months and even years that make up a product's lifetime in the marketplace. FDA reviews reports of problems with prescription and over-the-counter drugs, and can decide to add cautions to the dosage or usage information, as well as other measures for more serious issues.

On this page you will find information on:

- Supplemental Applications
- INDs for Marketed Drugs
- Manufacturer Inspections
- Drug Advertising
- Generic Drugs
- Reporting Problems
- Active Surveillance

Supplemental Applications

Developers must file a supplemental application if they wish to make any significant changes from the original NDA. Generally, any changes in formulation, labeling, or dosage strength must be approved by FDA before they can be made.

INDs for Marketed Drugs

If sponsors want to further develop an approved drug for a new use, dosage strength, new form, or different form (such as an injectable or oral liquid, as opposed to tablet form), or if they want to conduct other clinical research or a post-market safety study, they would do so under an IND.

Manufacturer Inspections

FDA officials conduct routine inspections of drug manufacturing facilities across the United States, and abroad if approved products are manufactured overseas. Manufacturers may be informed of inspections in advance, or the inspections may be unannounced. Inspections may be routine or caused by a particular problem or concern. The purpose of these inspections is to make sure that developers are following good manufacturer practice. FDA can shut down a facility if minimum standards are not met.

Drug Advertising

FDA regulates prescription drug advertisements and promotional labeling. By law, a developer is prohibited from advertising unapproved uses of their product.

All advertisements, such as product claims or reminder ads, cannot be false or misleading. They must contain truthful information about a drug's effectiveness, side effects, and prescribing information. These advertisements can be found in medical journals, newspapers, and magazines, and on the Internet, television, or radio.

Promotional labeling differs from drug advertisements in the way it is distributed. Pharmaceutical companies give out brochures or other promotional materials to physicians or consumers. The drug's prescribing information must accompany promotional labeling. Learn more at Prescription Drug Advertising.

Generic Drugs

New drugs are patent protected when they are approved for marketing. This means that only the sponsor has the right to market the drug exclusively. Once the patent expires, other drug manufacturers can develop the drug, which will be known as a generic version of the drug. Generic drugs are comparable to brand name drugs and must have the same:

- Dosage form
- Strength
- Safety
- Quality
- Performance characteristics
- Intended use

Because generic drugs are comparable to drugs already on the market, generic drug manufacturers do not have to conduct clinical trials to demonstrate that their product is safe and effective. Instead, they conduct bio-equivalence studies and file an Abbreviated New Drug Application. Learn more at Generic Drugs: Questions and Answers.

Reporting Problems

FDA has several programs that allow manufacturers, health professionals, and consumers to report problems associated with approved drugs.

- MedWatch is a gateway for reporting problems with medical products (drugs and devices) and learning about new safety information. You can subscribe to regular MedWatch safety alerts.
- Medical Product Safety Network (MedSun) monitors the safety and effectiveness of medical devices. FDA recruits 350 healthcare providers throughout the United States to report any medical device problems that result in serious injury or death. Each month, FDA publishes the MedSun newsletter. The newsletter gives consumers important information about medical device safety.

Active Surveillance

Under the Sentinel Initiative, FDA is developing a new national system to more quickly spot possible safety issues. The system will use very large existing electronic health databases—like electronic health records systems, administrative and insurance claims databases, and registries—to keep an eye on the safety of approved medical products in real time. This tool will add to, but not replace, FDA's existing postmarket safety assessment tools. Learn more about the Sentinel Initiative and its major activities.

Investigational New Drug (IND) Application

Introduction

Current Federal law requires that a drug be the subject of an approved marketing application before it is transported or distributed across state lines. Because a sponsor will probably want to ship the investigational drug to clinical investigators in many states, it must seek an exemption from that legal requirement. The IND is the means through which the sponsor technically obtains this exemption from the FDA.

During a new drug's early preclinical development, the sponsor's primary goal is to determine if the product is reasonably safe for initial use in humans, and if the compound exhibits pharmacological activity that justifies commercial development. When a product is identified as a viable candidate for further development, the sponsor then focuses on collecting the data and information necessary to establish that the product will not expose humans to unreasonable risks when used in limited, early-stage clinical studies.

FDA's role in the development of a new drug begins when the drug's sponsor (usually the manufacturer or potential marketer), having screened the new molecule for pharmacological activity and acute toxicity potential in animals, wants to test its diagnostic or therapeutic potential in humans. At that point, the molecule changes in legal status under the Federal Food, Drug, and Cosmetic Act and becomes a new drug subject to specific requirements of the drug regulatory system.

There are three IND types:

- **An Investigator IND** is submitted by a physician who both initiates and conducts an investigation, and under whose immediate direction the investigational drug is administered or dispensed. A physician might submit a research IND to propose studying an unapproved drug, or an approved product for a new indication or in a new patient population.
- **Emergency Use IND** allows the FDA to authorize use of an experimental drug in an emergency situation that does not allow time for submission of an IND in accordance with 21CFR, Sec. 312.23 or Sec. 312.20. It is also used for patients who do not meet the criteria of an existing study protocol, or if an approved study protocol does not exist.
- **Treatment IND** is submitted for experimental drugs showing promise in clinical testing for serious or immediately life-threatening conditions while the final clinical work is conducted and the FDA review takes place.

There are two IND categories:

- Commercial
- Research (non-commercial)

The IND application must contain information in three broad areas:

- **Animal Pharmacology and Toxicology Studies –**

Preclinical data to permit an assessment as to whether the product is reasonably safe for initial testing in humans. Also included are any previous experience with the drug in humans (often foreign use).

- **Manufacturing Information –**

Information pertaining to the composition, manufacturer, stability, and controls used for manufacturing the drug substance and the drug product. This information is assessed to ensure that the company can adequately produce and supply consistent batches of the drug.

- **Clinical Protocols and Investigator Information –**

Detailed protocols for proposed clinical studies to assess whether the initial-phase trials will expose subjects to unnecessary risks. Also, information on the qualifications of clinical investigators--professionals (generally physicians) who oversee the administration of the experimental compound--to assess whether they are qualified to fulfill their clinical trial duties. Finally, commitments to obtain informed consent from the research subjects, to obtain review of the study by an institutional review board (IRB), and to adhere to the investigational new drug regulations.

Once the IND is submitted, the sponsor must wait 30 calendar days before initiating any clinical trials. During this time, FDA has an opportunity to review the IND for safety to assure that research subjects will not be subjected to unreasonable risk.

Resources for IND Applications

The following resources include the legal requirements of an IND application, assistance from CDER to help you meet those requirements, and internal IND review principles, policies and procedures.

Pre-IND Consultation Program

CDER's (Center for Drug Evaluation and Research) Pre-Investigational New Drug Application (IND) Consultation Program fosters early communications between sponsors and new drug review divisions to provide guidance on the data necessary to warrant IND submission. The review divisions are organized generally along therapeutic class.

Guidance Documents for INDs

Guidance documents represent the Agency's current thinking on a particular subject. These documents provide FDA review staff and applicants/sponsors with guidelines to the processing, content, and evaluation/approval of applications and also to the design, production, manufacturing, and testing of regulated products. They also establish policies intended to achieve consistency in the Agency's regulatory approach and establish inspection and enforcement procedures.

Because guidances are not regulations or laws, they are not enforceable, either through administrative actions or through the courts. An alternative approach may be used if it satisfies the requirements of the applicable statute, regulations, or both. For information on a specific guidance document, please contact the originating office.

To find guidance documents to help prepare INDs, go to Guidances (Drugs) and use "investigational" in the search box.

Laws, Regulations, Policies and Procedures

The mission of FDA is to enforce laws enacted by the U.S. Congress and regulations established by the Agency to protect the consumer's health, safety, and pocketbook. The Federal Food, Drug, and Cosmetic Act is the basic food and drug law of the U.S. The law is intended to assure consumers that foods are pure and wholesome, safe to eat, and produced under sanitary conditions; that drugs and devices are safe and effective for their intended uses; that cosmetics are safe and made from appropriate ingredients; and that all labeling and packaging is truthful, informative, and not deceptive.

Code of Federal Regulations (CFR)

The final regulations published in the Federal Register (daily published record of proposed rules, final rules, meeting notices, etc.) are collected in the Code of Federal Regulations (CFR). The CFR is divided into 50 titles that represent broad areas subject to Federal regulations. The FDA's portion of the CFR interprets the The Federal Food, Drug, and Cosmetic Act and related statutes. Section 21 of the CFR contains most regulations pertaining to food and drugs. The regulations document all actions of all drug sponsors that are required under Federal law.

The following regulations apply to the IND application process:

21CFR Part 201 : Drug Labeling

21CFR Part 312 : Investigational New Drug Application

21CFR Part 314: INDA and NDA Applications for FDA Approval to Market a New Drug (New Drug Approval)

21CFR Part 316: Orphan Drugs

21CFR Part 50: Protection of Human Subjects

21CFR Part 54: Financial Disclosure by Clinical Investigators

21CFR Part 56:Institutional Review Boards

21CFR Part 58:Good Lab Practice for Nonclinical Laboratory [Animal] Studies

Manual of Policies and Procedures (MaPPs)

CDER's Manual of Policies and Procedures (MaPPs) are approved instructions for internal practices and procedures followed by CDER staff to help standardize the new drug review process and other activities. All MAPPs are available for the public to review for a better understanding of office policies, definitions, staff responsibilities and procedures.

Emergency Use of an Investigational Drug or Biologic

- Emergency Use of an Investigational Drug or Biologic - Information Sheet
- The Guidance for Institutional Review Boards and Clinical Investigators contains information on: Obtaining an Emergency IND, Emergency Exemption from Prospective IRB, Approval Exception from Informed Consent, and Requirement Planned Emergency Research, Informed Consent Exception.
- Physician Request for a Single Patient IND for Compassionate or Emergency Use
- Instructions for Sponsors of Emergency Investigational New Drug (EIND) Applications for Antimicrobial Products. From the Office of Antimicrobial Products, Division of Antiviral Products

Emergency use requests:

For investigational biological products regulated by CBER, call 800-835-4709 or 240-402-8020.
For all other investigational drugs, call 301-796-3400.
After working hours, call FDA's Office of Emergency Operations at 1-866-300-4374 or 301-796-8240.

CDERLearn Courses

- Chemistry, Manufacturing, and Controls (CMC) Perspective of the IND course
- Courses for Industry on drug development

Guidance documents to help prepare INDs include:

1. Bioavailability and Bioequivalence Studies Submitted in NDAs or INDs — General Considerations
2. Content and Format of INDs for Phase 1 Studies of Drugs, Including Well-Characterized, Therapeutic, Biotechnology-Derived Products. Questions and Answers
3. Content and Format of Investigational New Drug Applications (INDs) for Phase 1 Studies of Drugs, Including Well-Characterized, Therapeutic, Biotechnology-derived Products
4. Current Good Manufacturing Practice for Phase 1 Investigational Drugs.
5. Drug Master Files: Guidelines
6. Exploratory IND Studies
7. FDA IND, NDA, ANDA, or Drug Master File Binders
8. Immunotoxicology Evaluation of Investigational New Drugs
9. IND Exemptions for Studies of Lawfully Marketed Drug or Biological Products for the Treatment of Cancer.
10. Safety Assessment for IND Safety Reporting Guidance for Industry
11. Safety Reporting Requirements for INDs (Investigational New Drug Applications) and BA/BE (Bioavailability/ Bioequivalence) Studies.

Manuals of Policies and Procedures (MAPP)

1. Consulting the Controlled Substance Staff on INDs and Protocols That Use Schedule I Controlled Substances and Drugs.
2. Consulting the Controlled Substance Staff on INDs and Protocols That Use Schedule I Controlled Substances and Drugs.
3. IND Clinical Holds
4. IND Clinical Holds
5. INDs: Exception from Informed Consent Requirements for Emergency Research
6. INDs: Exception from Informed Consent Requirements for Emergency Research.
7. INDs: Processing Treatment INDs and Treatment Protocols.
8. INDs: Processing Treatment INDs and Treatment Protocols.
9. INDs: Review of Informed Consent Documents
10. INDs: Review of Informed Consent Documents
11. Review of Investigational New Drug Applications (Bio-INDs) by the Office of Generic Drugs
12. Review of Investigational New Drug Applications (Bio-INDs) by the Office of Generic Drugs

IND Forms and Instructions

Information for Sponsor-Investigators Submitting Investigational New Drug Applications (INDs), including:

1. Mailing addresses
2. Instructions for forms
3. FDA's receipt of the IND

Forms:

- Form FDA 1571 (PDF - 221KB): Investigational New Drug Application (IND)
- Form FDA 1572 (PDF - 208KB): Statement of Investigator
- Form FDA 3674 (PDF - 3MB): Certification of Compliance
- Form FDA 3454 (PDF - 47KB): Certification: Financial Interests and Arrangements of Clinical Investigators
- Form FDA 3455 (PDF - 56KB): Disclosure: Financial Interest and Arrangements of Clinical Investigators
- Form FDA 3500 (PDF - 1MB): MedWatch Medical Product Reporting Program – Voluntary
- Form FDA 3500A (PDF - 903KB): Medwatch Medical Products Reporting Program – Mandatory
- Form FDA 3926 (PDF - 473KB) : Individual Patient Expanded Access Applications

INSTRUCTIONS FOR FILLING OUT FORM FDA 3926 – INDIVIDUAL PATIENT EXPANDED ACCESS, INVESTIGATIONAL NEW DRUG APPLICATION (IND)

(The field numbers below correspond to the numbered boxes on the Form FDA 3926.)

Do not attempt to fill out this form after opening in your Internet Browser. To enable field fillable functionality,first save the file to your local computer, close the file and re-open the Form. Checking either box 3a or 3b will enable the appropriate fields to be fillable. Form should be completed electronically, i.e., not hand-written.

Field 1: PATIENT'S INITIALS

Enter the patient's initials (not the full name, to preserve confidentiality). The patient need not initial the form.

Field 2: DATE OF SUBMISSION

Provide the date of the submission in the following format: mm/dd/yyyy.

Field 3: TYPE OF SUBMISSION

(3.a.) Initial Submission: If the submission is an initial (original) submission for an individual patient expanded access IND (including for emergency use), select the box provided in field 3.a.and complete only fields 4 through 8, and fields 10 and 11.

(3.b.) Follow-Up Submission: If this is a follow-up submission to an existing individual patient expanded access IND, select the box provided in field 3.b. and complete the items to the right of the checkbox in field 3.b. (Investigational Drug Name and the physician's existing IND Number), and fields 8 through 11. Do not include the commercial sponsor's IND number.

Field 4: CLINICAL INFORMATION

Provide the indication (proposed treatment use) and a brief clinical history of the patient. The clinical history includes age, gender, weight, allergies, diagnosis, prior therapy, response to prior therapy, and the reason for requesting the proposed treatment, including an explanation of why the patient lacks other therapeutic options.

Field 5: TREATMENT INFORMATION

Provide treatment information, including the investigational drug's name and the name of the entity supplying the drug (generally the manufacturer), the applicable FDA review division (if known), and a concise statement regarding the treatment plan. This includes the planned dose, route and schedule of administration, planned duration of treatment, monitoring procedures, and planned modifications to the treatment plan in the event of toxicity. The information should be entered within the space provided.

Field 6: LETTER OF AUTHORIZATION (LOA), IF APPLICABLE

An LOA grants FDA the right to reference another application (IND) for information to satisfy submission requirements, such as a description of the manufacturing facility, chemistry, manufacturing and controls information, and pharmacology and toxicology information.

How to obtain an LOA: The physician is responsible for obtaining the LOA in advance from the entity that is the sponsor of the IND (e.g., commercial sponsor/drug manufacturer) being referenced. Physicians should attach the LOA to Form FDA 3926. The LOA should include the IND number for the application being referenced.

If the LOA is unavailable: In cases where it is not possible to obtain an LOA (e.g., the entity supplying the drug does not have an IND already filed with FDA), physicians should contact the applicable FDA review division

(http://www.fda.gov/NewsEvents/PublicHealthFocus/ExpandedAccessCompassionateUse/ucm429610.htm) to determine what other sources of information may satisfy the regulatory requirements. For emergency individual patient expanded access INDs, the physician must submit the LOA (if applicable) and all other paperwork (including Form FDA 3926) to FDA within 15 working days of FDA's initial authorization.

Field 7: PHYSICIAN'S QUALIFICATION STATEMENT

Provide a statement of the physician's qualifications. An appropriate qualification statement includes the medical school attended, year of graduation, medical specialty, state medical license number, current employment, and job title. Alternatively, the relevant portion of the physician's curriculum vitae that includes this information (usually the first few pages) may be attached.

Field 8: PHYSICIAN'S NAME, ADDRESS, AND CONTACT INFORMATION

Enter the physician's name and contact information, including the physical address, email address, telephone number, facsimile (FAX) number, and physician's IND number, if previously issued by the FDA. Do not include the commercial sponsor's IND number here.

Field 9: CONTENTS OF SUBMISSION (FOLLOW-UP/ADDITIONAL SUBMISSIONS ONLY)

This field should only be completed for follow-up/additional submissions to an existing individual patient

expanded access IND. Select the appropriate box (or boxes, if more than one apply) and attach the materials indicated for the following categories of follow-up/additional submissions (the relevant FDA regulations are provided in parentheses for additional details).

If none of the following apply to the follow-up/additional communications, use Form FDA 1571 for your submission.

• Initial Written IND Safety Report: A report of potential serious risks to be submitted as soon as possible but no later than 15 calendar days after the sponsor (i.e., the physician, who is considered a sponsorinvestigator) determines that information qualifies for reporting, or, a report of unexpected fatal or lifethreatening suspected adverse reactions, submitted no later than 7 calendar days after the sponsor's

initial receipt of the information (21 CFR 312.32(c))

• Follow-up to a Written Safety Report: A follow-up report to an IND safety report, to be made as soon as the information is available but no later than 15 calendar days after the sponsor receives the information (21 CFR 312.32(d))

• Annual Report: A brief report of the progress of the investigation, submitted within 60 days of the anniversary date that the IND went into effect (21 CFR 312.33)

• Summary of Expanded Access Use (treatment completed): A written summary of the results of the expanded access use, including adverse effects, at the conclusion of treatment (21 CFR 312.310(c)(2))

• Change in Treatment Plan: Also known as protocol amendments; a submission describing changes in the IND, including changes of investigators (21 CFR 312.30)

• General Correspondence: Any other communication between the sponsor and FDA pertinent to the investigation (21 CFR 312.41)

• Response to FDA Request for Information: A submission containing responses to clinical information requests (21 CFR 312.41)

• Response to Clinical Hold: A submission correcting deficiencies previously cited in a FDA Clinical Hold letter (21 CFR 312.42(e))

Field 10.a: REQUEST FOR AUTHORIZATION TO USE FORM FDA 3926 FOR INDIVIDUAL PATIENT EXPANDED ACCESS

Select this box to request under 21 CFR 312.10, that FDA accept the completed Form FDA 3926 to satisfy FDA's requirements for submitting an individual patient expanded access IND.

Field 10.b: REQUEST FOR AUTHORIZATION TO USE ALTERNATIVE IRB REVIEW PROCEDURES

Select this box to request under 21 CFR 56.105, authorization to obtain concurrence by the IRB chairperson or by a designated IRB member, instead of at a convened IRB meeting, before the treatment use begins, in order to comply with FDA's requirements for IRB review and approval.

Field 11: CERTIFICATION STATEMENT AND SIGNATURE OF THE PHYSICIAN

The licensed physician identified in Field 8 must sign this field. By signing this field, the physician certifies that treatment will not begin until 30 days after FDA receives the completed application and all required materials unless the submitting physician receives earlier notification from FDA that the treatment may proceed. The physician agrees not to begin or continue clinical investigations covered by the IND if those studies are placed on clinical hold. The physician also certifies that informed consent will be obtained in compliance with FDA requirements (see 21 CFR part 50) and that an Institutional Review Board (IRB)will be responsible for initial and continuing review and approval of the expanded access use, consistent with applicable FDA requirements (see 21 CFR part 56). The physician also acknowledges that in the case of an emergency request, treatment may begin without prior IRB approval provided the IRB is notified of the emergency treatment within 5 working days of treatment. The physician agrees to conduct the investigation in accordance with all other applicable regulatory requirements

For electronic form submissions, see Electronic Regulatory Submissions.

The Electronic Common Technical Document (eCTD) is the standard, accepted electronic format for the following submission types:

• New Drug Application (NDA)

• Abbreviated New Drug Application (ANDA)

• Investigational New Drug Application (IND)

• Biologics License Application (BLA)

• Master files: Drug Master File (DMF) and Biologics Master File (BMF)

• Emergency Use Authorization (EUA)

Please visit the Electronic Common Technical Document (eCTD) web page to access a wide variety of resources and support regarding eCTD submissions.

Instruction for Guidance Compliant Test Submission:

(Use WebTrader test account. See Setting up a Web Trader Account Checklist for details)

CDER requests the Guidance Compliant Test Submission in order to validate the format of your submission, your understanding of entire submission process, and to make sure FDA systems can receive and load your submissions.

• NDA, BLA, ANDA, DMF, and Commercial IND guidance compliant test submissions must be in eCTD format:

o Select "CDER" as the Center

o Select "ECTD" as Submission Type

o Use any 6-digit number as the test application number

o Select an eCTD sequence folder. Do not submit a single file as this will not pass validation. Do not include .exe, zip files, RAR files or other archives as this will not pass validation.

o The test submission must contain at least Module 1, FDA Form (356h for NDA/BLA/ANDA or 1571 for IND, no form for DMF), cover letter, and all XML components *

• Non-commercial/Research IND guidance compliant test submissions must be either eCTD or a folder containing the non-eCTD file(s)

o For eCTD test submissions, follow instructions above

o For non-eCTD Submissions (only for Non-commercial IND submissions), select "CDER" as the Center and select "EIND" as Submission Type

o Select a folder with eIND documents. Do not submit a single file as this will not pass validation. Do not include .exe, zip files, RAR files or other archives as this will not pass validation.

* An eCTD publishing tool is recommended to automatically create the eCTD sequence folder and file structure. FDA does not recommend specific tool vendors; however, they can be located via internet search.

For information on eCTD format, please see www.fda.gov/ectd

Questions and general information regarding the preparation of submissions in electronic format may be directed to CDER at esub@fda.hhs.gov or CBER at esubprep@cber.fda.gov. Questions regarding submission of datasets to CDER may be sent to edata@fda.hhs.gov.

Pre-IND Consultation Program

In 1988, the Office of Antimicrobial Products (OAP), which is now the Office of Infectious Diseases (OID), established the Pre-Investigational New Drug Application (Pre-IND) Consultation Program. This program is designed to facilitate and foster early communications between the divisions of OID and potential sponsors of new therapeutics (drugs, monoclonal antibodies, and therapeutic proteins) for the treatment of bacterial, fungal, and viral infections, opportunistic infections, emerging infections (including naturally emerging diseases and potential biothreat agents), and topical microbicides directed at prevention of HIV transmission. (21 CFR 312.82(a)).

Pre-IND advice may be requested for issues related to data needed to support the rationale for testing a drug in humans; the design of nonclinical pharmacology, toxicology, and drug activity studies, including design and potential uses of any proposed treatment studies in animal models; data requirements for an Investigational New Drug (IND) application; initial drug development plans, and regulatory requirements for demonstrating safety and efficacy.

We encourage all potential drug sponsors or investigators to examine the information available from this site and to initiate contact with us as early in the drug development process as possible, so that they will have the opportunity to consider our recommendations in planning preclinical and clinical development programs.

How Do I Obtain Further Information Regarding the Program?

Please contact the appropriate Division for further information and specific contact information.

The Division of Antivirals (DAV) is responsible for:

- HIV, AIDS and prevention of HIV transmission
- Viral hepatitis
- Herpesviruses
- Topical microbicides
- Emerging viral infections (including but not limited to respiratory viruses, zoonoses, and potential biologic threat agents)
- Other non-life-threatening and life-threatening viral infections

For more information, please visit the Office of Infectious Diseases Web page.

The Division of Anti-Infectives (DAI) is responsible for:

- Most systemic and topical antimicrobials
- Topical antiseptics
- Drug products for the adjunctive treatment of sepsis
- Drug products for treatment of Lyme disease

For more information please call 301-796-1400.

Note: Pre-IND interactions should be considered as preliminary communications based on early development information, and will generally take the form of written comments that may be supplemented by teleconferences or meetings as needed and appropriate. Additions or modifications to these communications may arise as additional information becomes available, during follow-up pre-IND interactions or when an IND is established.

Ethics in Biomedical Research

The origin of the principles

In 1947, the International Tribunal of Nuremberg defined a code made up of ten rules, and universally known as the "Nuremberg Code". This Code "recognizes" that experimentation on humans "for the good of society" is admissible and stipulates that "the voluntary consent of the human subject is absolutely essential" (Article 1) and must be prior.

This was followed in 1948 by the Universal Declaration of Human Rights, to which the principles of freedom, security, equality and human dignity are attached, then in 1949, the International Code of Medical Ethics, and in 1964, the Declaration of Helsinki.

The Declaration of Helsinki

Adopted by the World Medical Association in 1964, its objective was to define the bases of ethics in biomedical research and to constitute a guide for the doctors who took part in it. Over the course of the revisions, clarifications have been made concerning the protection of individuals in general, that of vulnerable individuals, or even the use of the placebo.

In the 1975 version the principles stated in the initial version, the primacy of the human being over the interest of science and society, and the collection of the informed consent of the subject to participate in the study. Responsibility for the study rests with the medically qualified person conducting it. An independent ethics committee (EC) must be set up to review study protocols for evaluation and opinion. For vulnerable populations (physical or mental disability) and minors, consent must be obtained from the legal representative. Finally, the subject must benefit from the best diagnostic or therapeutic method.

The 1983 version provides that in the case of minors, the consent of the minor will be obtained in addition to that of his legal representative. In the 1989 version, it is specified that the ethics committee, independent of the sponsor and the investigator, must follow the laws and regulations of the country where the research is conducted. In 1996, it is added that the use of the placebo is possible in certain studies, only if there is no other proven diagnostic or therapeutic method.

Whereas in previous versions it was considered a guide and the law of the land was sovereign, the 1996 version, and then that of 2000, specify that no national regulatory, legal or ethical requirement can eliminate or reduce the level protection of human subjects as defined in the Declaration. This version provides that before giving consent, the participant will also be informed of the objectives and constraints of the research, the sources of funding and the potential conflicts of interest of the researchers. This information is also transmitted to the ethics committee. If consent cannot be obtained in writing, it must be formally documented and witnessed. The specific reasons for involving subjects in research in a condition rendering them incapable of giving consent must be established in the protocol for review and approval by the ethics committee. In this case, the protocol must establish that the consent to remain in the study must be obtained as quickly as possible from the subject or his authorized legal representative (example: case of research carried out in an emergency situation, etc.).

Research involving subjects in whom it is not possible to obtain consent, even by proxy, should be conducted only if the mental or physical condition preventing obtaining consent is a characteristic of the population concerned by the research. Research is only justified if it is likely that the populations participating in it will benefit from it.

The placebo, or the absence of treatment, can only be considered if there is no proven prophylactic, diagnostic or therapeutic method.

Particular attention must be paid to populations that will not directly benefit from the results of the research. As such, the participation of healthy volunteers should not be excluded. The importance of the objective must then exceed the risks and constraints. It is also mentioned that vulnerable populations can only be included if the study can only be conducted in such a population because of its characteristics. Those who are economically and medically disadvantaged must be recognised, providing them with adequate protection.

The ethics committee must not only be independent of the sponsor and the investigator, but free from any outside influence. He monitors the progress of the study and the investigator must inform him of the occurrence of serious adverse events. At the end of the study, the participant must benefit from the best prophylactic, diagnostic or therapeutic method available. Finally, whether the results of the research are positive or negative, they must be published or made public.

The modifications made to the last revised version, resulting from the Edinburgh Conference in October 2000, were the subject of debates, controversies and finally clarifications during the assemblies of 2002 and 2004, at the origin of "notes of clarification" which are now added to the main text.

The details provided concern the use of the placebo. Placebo- controlled trials are ethically acceptable, even if a proven therapy is available, if for compelling scientific or methodological reasons, they are necessary to determine the efficacy and safety of a method, or if the method studied concerns a pathology minor such that the subject does not incur additional or irreversible risks. In 2004, the guarantee for the participant to benefit from the best care at the end of the study was reinforced.

By defining the main ethical principles, the Declaration of Helsinki has had a very strong influence on the creation and evolution of (inter)national ethical laws and regulations for biomedical research.

The institutions

The World Medical Association was established in 1947. The Institutional Review Board (IRB) appeared in the 1970s. The main international ethical bodies date from the 1990s. Dependent on the WHO with the ERC (Research Ethic Review Committee), on UNESCO with the CIB (International Bioethics Committee) or on the Council of Europe with the CAHBI (Ad Hoc Committee of Experts for Bioethics), which became the CDBI in 1992 (Steering Committee for Bioethics), they ensure the harmonization of principles and practices.

Most of the countries where clinical research is conducted currently have their own ethics committees, like the countries of the European community and the United States. But a certain number of developing countries where clinical trials are carried out do not yet have ethics committees or these committees are not sufficiently independent.

In France, the Huriet-Sérusclat law (1988) established the advisory committees for the protection of persons taking part in biomedical research (CCPPRB) in 1991, transformed into Committees for the Protection of Persons (CPP) in 2004. Neither an ethical body nor a regulatory body, their objective is to verify that the sponsor and the investigators respect, in the construction of their project, the provisions of the law and regulations in terms of biomedical research.

In the scientific field, the first health product authorization systems were created in the 1930s in the United States (with the FDA) and then in the 1950s in Japan.

In Europe, the Council of Europe, the European Commission and the European Medicines Agency (EMEA) oversee clinical trials, standardize practices and comply with regulations. In France, the French Medicines Agency, which became Afssaps (French Health Products Safety Agency) in 1998, oversees the conduct of biomedical research subject to its prior authorization.

Reference texts

The main guidelines governing biomedical research activities were published during the 1990s and 2000s. These include: the guidelines for biomedical research involving human subjects in 1993 (UNESCO, revision in 2002); the Convention on Human Rights and Biomedicine of the Council of Europe in 1997); the WHO guidelines on ethics committees established in 2000, the statement of research ethics policy in Canada the same year, then the European directives in 2001 and 2004 .

Good practice standards were enacted at the end of the 1980s: good clinical practices (French GCPs published in 1987, European 1990), good laboratory practices and good manufacturing practices in 1989. All the good practices applied at the international level (example: ICH-E6 text on PCBs, applicable in the United States, Europe and Japan since 1996) guides the evaluation, monitoring and ethical and scientific control of activities related to drug development. The ICH PCB guide is appended to federal regulations in the United States, while the European Commission has made it a European directive (2001/20/EC) "relating to the application of good clinical practice in the conduct of clinical trials. human drug clinics".

In France, the revision of the Huriet-Sérusclat law and the transposition of European texts is at the origin of the law on patients' rights in 2002 and the modification of the Huriet Law into the Public Health Law (LSP) of August 9, 2004 which organizes the CPPs whose opinion relating to a biomedical research project must be favorable for its implementation.

Principles of ethics in biomedical research

Application of ethical principles ensures the protection of human rights in research situations.

Participant protection

It is based on the following principles.

1. **dignity of the person**

The first is that of the dignity of the person, according to which health, well-being, care, respect for privacy and personal data come before the objectives of the research. From this follows the rule of consent. Consent must be personal, prior to any involvement in a research activity, free, informed and express. Any person agreeing to research must be informed of their rights and the guarantees provided by law for their protection. The participant has a period of reflection between the information stage and the collection in writing of his consent. In certain specific cases, consent may be obtained in the presence of an independent witness who attests in writing to the person's desire to participate in the research. Consent can be freely withdrawn at any time without justification and without this resulting in a loss of opportunity for the patient.

2. Beneficence and that of non-maleficence

The second principle is that of beneficence and that of non-maleficence, from which derives the rule of the evaluation of the risk-benefit ratio. Their distribution must be equitable among all groups and classes of society. The research should not involve risks or burdens disproportionate to the potential benefits. The risks must be satisfactorily assessed and controllable for a study to be undertaken.

3. **principle of justice**

Finally, the third is the principle of justice from which stems the rule of equity which prohibits exploitation for the benefit of research on vulnerable populations when it is possible to do otherwise. Medical research on human beings is only legitimate if the populations in which it is carried out have a real chance of benefiting from it.

Rationale for biomedical research

All research must:

• be scientifically justified on the basis of an in-depth knowledge of the state of the art in the field and by appropriate prior animal experimentation.

It must meet recognized scientific quality criteria:

• be carried out in compliance with applicable professional standards and obligations,

• be conducted by scientifically qualified persons and under the supervision of a competent doctor,

• be approved by the competent bodies after a multidisciplinary and independent examination.

As a corollary to these prerequisites, the responsibilities of the participants (investigator, trial sponsor, monitor, etc.) in a study must be clearly defined, identified and assumed by qualified personnel.

STATEMENT OF GENERAL PRINCIPLES IN BIOMEDICAL RESEARCH INVOLVING HUMAN PARTICIPANTS

The statement of Ethical Guidelines for Biomedical Research on Human participants shall be known as the ICMR Code and shall consist of the following: -

a. Statement of General Principles on Research using Human participants in Biomedical Research
b. Statement of Specific Principles on Research using Human participants in specific areas of Biomedical Research

These statements of General and Specific Principles may be varied, amended, substituted and added from time to time.

GENERAL STATEMENT

Medial and related research using human beings as research participants must necessarily ensurethat -

i. The PURPOSE, of such research is that it should be directed towards the increase of knowledge about the human condition in relation to its social and natural environment, mindful that the human species is one of the many species in a planet in which the wellbeing of all species is under threat, no less from the human species as any other, and that such research is for the betterment of all, especially the least advantaged.

ii. Such research is CONDUCTED under conditions that no person or persons become a mere means for the betterment of others and that human beings who are subject to any medical research or scientific experimentation are dealt with in a manner conductive to and consistent with their dignity and wellbeing, under conditions of professional fair treatment and transparency; and after ensuring that the participant is placed at no greater risk other than such risk commensurate with the wellbeing of the participant in question in the light of the object to the achieved.

iii. Such research must be subjected to a regime of EVALUATION at all stages of the proposal i.e., research design and experimentation, declaration of results and use of the results thereof, and that each such evaluation shall bear in mind the objects to be achieved, the means by which they are sought to be achieved, the anticipated benefits and dangers, the potential uses and abuses of the experiment and its results, and above all, the premium that civilized society places on saving and ensuring the safety of each human life as an end in itself.

STATEMENT OF GENERAL PRINCIPLES

Any research using the human beings as participants shall follow the principles given below -

I. Principles of essentiality whereby the research entailing the use of human participants is considered to be absolutely essential after a due consideration of all alternatives in the light of the existing knowledge in the proposed area of research and after the proposed research has been duly vetted and considered by an appropriate and responsible body of persons who are external to the particular research and who, after careful consideration, come to the conclusion that the said research is necessary for the advancement of knowledge and for the benefit of all members of the human species and for the ecological and environmental wellbeing of the planet.

II. Principle of voluntaries, informed consent and community agreement whereby research participants are fully apprised of the research and the impact and risk of such research on the research participant and others; and whereby the research participants retain the right to abstain from further participation in the research irrespective of any legal or other obligation that may have been entered into by such human participants or someone on their behalf, subject to only minimal restitutive obligations of any advance consideration received and outstanding. Where any such research entails treating any community or group of persons as a research participant, these principles of voluntariness and informed consent shall apply, mutatis mutandis, to the community as a whole and to each individual member who is the participant of the research or experiment. Where the human participant is incapable of giving consent and it is considered essential that research or experimentation be conducted on such a person incompetent to give consent, the principle of voluntariness and informed consent shall continue to apply and such consent and voluntariness shall be obtained and exercised on behalf of such research participants by someone who is empowered and under a duty to act on their behalf. The principles of informed consent and voluntariness are cardinal principles to be observed throughout the research and experiment, including its aftermath and applied use so that research participants are continually kept informed of any and all developments in so far as they affect them and others.

However, without in any way undermining the cardinal importance of obtaining informed consent from any human participant involved in any research, the nature and form of the consent and the evidentiary requirements to prove that such consent was taken, shall depend upon the degree and seriousness of the invasiveness into the concerned human participant's person and privacy, health and life generally, and, the overall purpose and the importance of the research. Ethics committee shall decide on the form of consent to be taken or its waiver based on the degree of risk that may be involved.

III. Principles of non - exploitation whereby as a general rule, research participants are remunerated for their involvement in the research or experiment; and, irrespective of the social and economic condition or status, or educational levels attained by the research

Participants kept fully apprised of all the dangers arising in and out of the research so that they can appreciate all the physical and psychological risks as well as moral implications of the research whether to themselves or others, including those yet to be born. Such human participants should be selected so that the burdens and benefits of the research are distributed without arbitrariness, discrimination or caprice. Each research shall include an in-built mechanism for compensation for the human participants either through insurance cover or any other appropriate means to cover all foreseeable and unforeseeable risks by providing for remedial action and comprehensive aftercare, including treatment during and after the research or experiment, in respect of any effect that the conduct of research of experimentation may have on the human participant and to ensure that immediate recompense and rehabilitative measures are taken in respect of all affected, if and when necessary.

IV. Principles of privacy and confidentiality whereby the identify and records of the human participants of the research or experiment are as far as possible kept confidential; and that no details about identify of said human participants, which would result in the disclosure of their identify, are disclosure without valid scientific and legal reasons which may be essential for the purposes of therapeutics or other interventions, without the specific consent in writing of the human participant concerned, or someone authorized on their behalf; and after ensuring that the said human participant does not suffer from any form of hardship, discrimination or stigmatization as a consequence of having participated in the research or experiment.

V. Principle of precaution and risk minimization whereby due care and caution is taken at all stages of the research and experiment (from its inception as a research idea, its subsequent research design, the conduct of the research or experiment and its applicative use) to ensure that the research participant and those affected by it including community are put to the minimum risk, suffer from no known irreversible adverse effects, and generally, benefit from and by the research or experiment; and that requisite steps are taken to ensure that both professional and ethical reviews of the research are undertaken at appropriate stages so that further and specific.

Guidelines are laid down, and necessary directions given, in respect of the conduct of the research or experiment.

VI. Principle of professional competence whereby the research is conducted at all times by competent and qualified persons who act with total integrity and impartiality and who have been made aware of, and are mindful of, preferably through training, the ethical considerations to be borne in mind in respect of such research or experiment.

VII. Principle of accountability and transparency whereby the research or experiment will be conducted in a fair, honest, impartial and transparent manner after full disclosure is made by those associated with the research or experiment of each aspect of their interest in the research, and any conflict of interest that may exist; and whereby, subject to the principles of privacy and confidentiality and the rights of the researcher, full and complete records of the research inclusive of data and notes are retained for such reasonable period as may be prescribed or considered

Necessary for the purposes of post-research monitoring, evaluation of the research, conducting further research (whether by the initial researcher or otherwise) and in order to make such records available for scrutiny by the appropriate legal and administrative authority, if necessary.

VIII. Principle of the maximization of the public interest and of distributive justice whereby the research or experiment and its subsequent applicative use are conducted and used to benefit all human kind and not just those who are socially better off but also the least advantaged; and in particular, the research participants themselves and or the community from which they are drawn.

IX. Principle of institutional arrangements whereby there shall be a duly on all persons connected with the research to ensure that all the procedures required to be complied with and all institutional arrangements required to be made in respect of the research and its subsequent use or application are duly made in a Bonafede and transparent manner; and to take all appropriate steps to ensure that research reports, materials and data connected with the research are duly preserved and archived.

X. Principle of public domain whereby the research and any further research, experimentation or evaluation in response to, and emanating from such research is brought into the public domain so that its results are generally made known through scientific and other publications subject to such rights as are available to the researcher and those associated with the research under the law in force at that time.

XI. Principle of totality of responsibility whereby the professional and moral responsibility, for the due observance of all the principles, guidelines or prescription laid down generally or in respect of the research or experiment in question, devolves on all those directly or indirectly connected with the research or experiment inducing the researchers, those responsible for funding or contributing to the funding of the research, the institution or institutions where the research is conducted and the various persons, groups or undertakings who sponsor, use or derive benefit from the research, market the product (if any) or prescribe its use so that, inter alia, the effect of the research or experiment is duly monitored and constantly subject to review and remedial action at all stages of the research and experiment and its future use.

XII. Principles of compliance whereby, there is a general and positive duly on all persons, conducing, associated or connected with any research entailing the use of a human participant to ensure that both the letter and the spirit of these guidelines, as well as any other norms, guidelines which have been specifically laid down or prescribed and which are applicable for that area of research or experimentation, are scrupulously observed and duly complied with. There 12 principles laid down under statement on general principles are common to all areas of biomedical research. The specific issues are mentioned under relevant topics.

Ethical committee [institutional review board]

An ethics committee is an "independent, multidisciplinary and pluralistic body, responsible for safeguarding the rights, safety and well-being of trial participants".

Amendments to Drugs and Cosmetics Rules were published vide G.S.R.72 (E) dated 08.02.2013 specifying the requirements and guidelines for registration of Ethics Committee and re-registration under Rule 122DD to the Drugs and Cosmetics Rules 1945.

For the purpose of the Rule 122DD, an Ethics Committee is a committee comprising of medical, scientific, non-medical and nonscientific members, whose responsibility is to ensure the protection of the rights, safety and well-being of human subjects involved in a clinical trial and it shall be responsible for reviewing and approving the protocol, the suitability of the investigators, facilities, methods and adequacy of information to be used for obtaining and documenting informed consent of the study subjects and adequacy of confidentiality safeguards. In the case of any serious adverse event occurring to the clinical trial subjects during the clinical trial, the Ethics Committee shall analyze and forward its opinion as per procedure specified under APPENDIX XII of Schedule Y.

The Ethics Committee shall allow inspectors or officials authorized by the Central Drugs Standard Control Organization to enter its premises to inspect any record, data or any document related to clinical trial and provide adequate replies to any query raised by such inspectors or officials, as the case may be in relation to the conduct of clinical trial.

If the Ethics Committee fails to comply with any of the conditions of registration, the Licensing Authority may, after giving an opportunity to show cause why such an order should not be passed, by an order in writing stating the reasons therefor, suspend or cancel the registration of the Ethics Committee for such period as considered necessary.

Functionalities

Ethics Committee division deals with the applications seeking registration, re-registration and post approval changes of Institutional Ethics Committee. No Ethics Committee shall review and accord its approval to a clinical trial protocol without prior registration with the Licensing Authority as defined in clause (b) of Rule 21.

An application for registration of Ethics Committee shall be made to the Licensing Authority in accordance with the requirements as specified in the Appendix VIII of Schedule Y.

The Licensing Authority after being satisfied that the requirements have been complied with, may grant registration to the Ethics Committee subject to such conditions as may be stated therein.

The registration of Ethics Committees is valid for a period of three years. The re-registration applications need to be made within 3 months before the expiry of registration. Registration remains deemed continued unless otherwise orders are passed or until the registration is Suspended or Cancelled. Accordingly, applicant shall apply to CDSCO for re-registration as per checklist.

Note: CDSCO is also encouraging the online applications for registration and re-registration of Ethics Committees through SUGAM - An e-Governance solution for CDSCO. Details of SUGAM registration and subsequent Ethics Committee registration procedure are available on https://cdscoonline.gov.in/CDSCO/homepage

IRB/IEC Responsibilities:

1. An IRB/IEC should safeguard the rights, safety, and well-being of all trial subjects. Special attention should be paid to trials that may include vulnerable subjects.
2. The IRB/IEC should obtain the following documents:

- Trial protocol(s)/amendment(s),
- Written informed consent form(s) and consent form updates that the investigator proposes for use in the trial,
- Subject recruitment procedures (e.g. advertisements),
- Written information to be provided to subjects,
- Investigator's Brochure (IB),
- Information about payments and compensation available to subjects,
- Available safety information, The investigators current curriculum vitae and/or other documentation evidencing qualifications, &
- Any other documents that the IRB/IEC may need to fulfill its responsibilities,
- The IRB/IEC should review a proposed clinical trial within a reasonable time and document its views in writing, clearly identifying the trial, the documents reviewed and the dates for the following:
- Approval/favorable opinion;
- Modifications required prior to its approval/favorable opinion;
- Disapproval/ negative opinion; and
- Termination/suspension of any prior approval/favorable opinion.

3. The IRB/IEC should consider the qualifications of the investigator for the proposed trial, as documented by a current curriculum vitae and/or by any other relevant documentation the IRB/IEC requests.
4. The IRB/IEC should conduct continuing review of each ongoing trial at intervals appropriate to the degree of risk to human subjects, but at least once per year.
5. The IRB/IEC may request more information than be given to subjects when, in the judgment of the IRB/IEC, the additional information would add meaningfully to the protection of the rights, safety and/or well-being of the subjects.
6. When a non-therapeutic trial is to be carried out with the consent of the subject is legally acceptable representative, the IRB/IEC should determine that the proposed protocol and/or other document(s) adequately addresses relevant ethical concerns and meets applicable regulatory requirements for such trials.
7. Where the protocol indicates that prior consent of the trial subject or the subject is legally acceptable representative is not possible, the IRB/IEC should determine that the proposed protocol and/or other

document(s) adequately addresses relevant ethical concerns and meets applicates regulatory requirements for such trials (i.e. in emergency situations).

8. The IRB/IEC should review both the amount and method of payment to subjects to assure that neither presents problems of coerecion or undue influence on the trial subjects. Payment to a subject should be prorated and not wholly contingent on completion of the trial by the subject.
9. The IRB/IEC should ensure that information regarding payment to subjects, including the methods, amounts, and schedule of payment to trial subjects, is set forth in the written informed consent form and any other written information to be provided to subjects. The way payment will be prorated should be specified.

Composition, Functions and Operations:

1. The IRB/IEC should consist of a reasonable number of members, who collectively have the qualifications and experience to review and evaluate the science, medical aspects, and ethics of the proposed trial. It is recommended that the IRB/IEC should include:

- At least five members.
- At least one member whose primary area of interest is in a nonscientific area
- At least one member who is independent of the institution/trial site.
- Only those IRB/IEC members who are independent of the investigator and the sponsor of the trial should vote/ provide opinion on a trial-related matter.
- A list of IRB/IEC members and their qualifications should be maintained.

2. The IRB/IEC should perform its functions according to written operating procedures, should maintain written records of its activities and minutes of its meetings, and should comply with GCP and with the applicable regulatory requirement(s).
3. An IRB/IEC should make its decisions at announced meetings at which at least a quorum, as stipulated in its written operating procedures, is present
4. Only members who participate in the IRB/IEC review and discussion should vote/provide their opinion and/or advise.
5. The investigator may provide information on any aspect of the trial, but should not participate in the deliberations of the IRB/IEC or in the vote/opinion of the IRB/IEC.
6. An IRB/IEC may invite nonmembers with expertise in special areas for assistance.

Procedures

The IRB/IEC should establish, document in writing, and follow its procedures, which should include:

1. Detemining its composition (names and qualifications of the members) and the authority under which it is established
2. Scheduling, notifying its members of, and conducting its meetings.
3. Conducting initial and continuing review of trials.
4. Detemining the frequency of continuing review, as appropriate.
5. Providing, according to the applicable regulatory requirements, expedited review and approval/favourable opinion of minor change(s) in ongoing trials that have the approval/favourable opinion of the IRB/IEC.
6. Specifying that no subject should be admitted to a trial before the IRB/IEC issues its written approval/favourable opinion of the trial.
7. Specifying that no deviations from, or changes of, the protocol should be initiated without prior written IRB/IEC approval/favourable opinion of an appropriate amendment, except when the change(s) involves only logistical or administrative aspects of the trial (e.g., change of monitor(s), telephone number(s))

8. Specifying that the investigator should promptly report to the IRB/IEC :

a. Deviations from, or changes of, the protocol to eliminate immediate hazards to the trial subjects
b. Changes increasing the risk to subjects and/or affecting significantly the conduct of the trial
c. All adverse drug reactions (ADRs) that are both serious and unexpected.
d. New information that may affect adversely the safety of the subjects or the conduct of the trial

9. Ensuring that the IRB/IEC promptly notify in writing the investigator/institution concerning:
10. Its trial-related decisions/opinions
11. The reasons for its decisions/opinions.
12. Procedures for appeal of its decisions/opinions.

Records

- The IRB/IEC should retain all relevant records (e.g., written procedures, membership lists, lists of occupations/affiliations of members, submitted documents, minutes of meetings, and correspondence) for a period of at least 3 years after completion of the trial and make them available upon request from the regulatory authority (ies).

The IRB/IEC may be asked by investigators, sponsors or regulatory authorities to provide its written procedures and membership lists.

Ethical Issues in Biomedical Research

Bioethics is the discipline of ethics dealing with moral problems arising in the practice of medicine and the pursuit of biomedical research.

Physicians may confront ethical dilemmas regularly in their individual relationships with patients and in institutional and societal decisions on health care policy.

Human subjects research has been the focus of numerous controversies over the years. The dilemma lies between the potential harm to individuals who participate in research and the knowledge to be gained from the research study that might benefit society.

Some of the ethical issues that arise in clinical practice, including informed consent, do-not-resuscitate orders, non-initiation and termination of medical therapy, genetic intervention, allocation of scarce health resources, and infection with the human immunodeficiency virus (HIV). Some of these problems require ethical analysis at the bedside; others require physician involvement on a broader level.

CHALLENGES IN THE IMPLEMENTION OF ETHICAL GUIDELINES

Someof the challenges in the implementation of GCP guidelines:

1. Professional Training on GCP
2. Infrastructure
3. Regulatory Environment
4. ERB/IRB/IEC
5. ICD Administration
6. Safety Reporting
7. Investigational Product
8. Record Keeping/Source Document(s)
9. Grants & Payments

10. Trial Report/Publication

1. Professional Training on GCP

- The scarcity of GCP trained competent professionals.
- Lack of professional training on GCP across various stroke holders (sponsor, investigator, ERB, patient, regulators etc.).
- No Indian university offers a curriculum in this
- Discipline.

2. Infrastructure

- Most of the hospitals in India do not meet the infrastructure requirements as per GCP guidelines.
- Lack of supportive infrastructure like labs and diagnostics up to the standards of international accreditation.

3. **Regulatory Environment**

- Biggest challenge is their implementation and adherence.
- Do not have a regulatory inspection system in place to monitor and adherence and compliance to these guidelines.
- Mostly the adherence to GCP guidelines is a matter of self-discipline at the part of sponsor(s), investigator(s) and ERB(s).

4. **ERB/IRB/IEC**

- GCP requires written standard operating procedures (SOP) for ERB/IRB/IEC
- No standard guidelines on what should be the content of an ideal SOP.
- Many of the hospitals either do not have the written SOP for ERB or have improper guidelines not about all the critical elements of GCP.
- No provision to check whether the sop is being followed during each meeting or not.

5. **ICD Administration**

- In India, the patient/legal representatives have an immense faith on treating doctor that they insist on signing the documents without even reading or after reading it superficially.
- A layman cannot understand the wording and contents of the majority of documents.
- Situation becomes even grim when transiations are used, which leads to varied interpretations due to lack of authentic validation.
- Lack of patients advocacy group who can be a guardian to the patients' rights and safety, makes poor uneducated masses susceptible to abuse in clinical trials in the name of treatment.

6. **Safety Reporting**

- Investigator and sponsor have joint responsibility to report all the serious and un-expected adverse events to ERB/IRB and regulatory authority(ies).
- The regulatory pharmacovigilance presently is not optionally implemented for adverse event handing and review.
- In majority of cases sponsor does not even comply with the expedited safety reporting to local regulatory authority and regulators often remain unaware of this fact.

7. **Investigational Product**

- Investigational product storage, handling and access control is a major challenge.
- It is difficult to produce an evidence of temperature chain being maintained during shipment of investigational product(s) from sponsor's facility to investigator site(s).
- Eg; courier, custom clearance etc.
- There is no validation and regular standardization of thermometers provided by the sponsor.
- No standardized solutions are available for storing investigational product(s) requiring

8. **Record keeping/Source Document(s)**

- Record retention and retrieval is always a major challenge in majority of hospitals.
- The documentation of patient disease, treatment and progress notes is not adequate to meet the standards of good documentation practices that ensure data completeness and correctness.
- Hospitals using electronic records as source data / document compliance to CRF part 11 is a major hurdle.
- Archival of trial documents for the stipulated time frame and under proper environmental

9. **Grants & Payments**

- Trials agreements are based on the institutional practices where the research grants go to a centralized research account, which in majority of the cases remains un- utilized.
- No incentive to the investigator(s) for investing extra-time, efforts and intellectual capital.

10. **Trial Report/Publication**

- Negative trials or trials that get terminated prematurely are rarely published.
- This is a major threat towards validity of Evidence Based medicine as one gets to know the positive results only.
- India, no doubt has a talented pool of clinical research professional(s) but the above-mentioned challenges need to be addressed in order to perform the world- class clinical trials in compliance with GCP guidelines.

ICH-GCP GUIDELINES

The International Conference on Harmonisation of Technical Requirements for Registration of Pharmaceuticals for Human use (ICH) is a project that brings together the Regulatory authorities of Europe, Japan and the United States and experts from the pharmaceuticals industry in the three regions to discuss scientific and technical aspects of pharmaceutical product registration.

The purpose of ICH is to reduce or obviate the Need to duplicate the testing carried out during the research and development of new medicines by recommending ways to achieve greater Harmonisation in the interpretation and application of technical guidelines and requirements for product registration. Harmonisation would lead to a more economical use of Human, animal and material resources, and the elimination of unnecessary delay in the global development and availability of new medicines While maintaining safeguards on quality, safety, and Efficacy, and regulatory Obligations to protect public health.

ICH guidelines have been adopted as law in several countries, but are only used as guidance For the U.S. food and Drug Administration.

In the 1980s, what is today the European Union began harmonising regulatory requirements. In 1989, Europe, Japan, and United States began creating plans for harmonisation; ICH was created in April 1990 at a meeting in Brussels.

There are 4 categories of ICH Guidelines

- Quality(Q)
- Safety(S)
- Efficacy(E)
- Multidisciplinary(M)

QUALITY GUIDELINES (Q):

Q1A - Q1F Stability

- Q1A (R2) - Stability Testing of New Drug Substances and Products.
- Q1B Stability Testing - Photostability Testing of New Drug Substances and Products
- Q1C Stability Testing for New Dosage Forms
- Q1D Bracketing and Matrixing Designs for stability Testing of New Drug Substances and Products
- Q1E Evaluation of Stability Data
- Q1F Stability Data Package for Registration Application in Climatic Zones III and IV

Q2 Analytical validation

- Q2(R1) validation of Analytical Procedures: Text and Methodology
- Q3A- Q3D Impurities
- Q3A(R2) Impurities in New Drug Substances
- Q3B(R2) Impurities in New Drug Products
- Q3C(R5) Impurities : Guideline for Residual Solvents
- Q3D Guidelines for Elemental Impurities – NEW
- Q3D Implementation of Guideline for Elemental Impurities

Q4 - Q4B Pharmacopoeias

Q4 Pharmacopoeias

- Q4A Pharmacopoeial Harmonisation
- Q4B Evaluation and Recommendation of Pharmacopoeial Texts for Use in the ICH Regions

Q5A - Q5E Quality of Biotechnological Products

- Q5A(R1) Viral Safety Evaluation of Biotechnology Products Derived from Cell Lines of Human or Animal Origin Q5A
- Q5B Analysis of the Expression Construct in cells Used for Production of r-DNA Derived Protein Products
- Q5C Stability Testing of Biotechnological/Biological Products
- Q5D Derivation and Characterisation of Cell Substrates Used for Production of Biotechnological/ Biological Products
- Q5E Comparability of Biotechnological/Biological Products Subject to Changes in their Manufacturing Process

Q6A – Q6B Specifications

- Q6A Specifications : Test Procedures and Acceptance Criteria for New Drug Substances and New Drug Products: Chemical Substances
- Q6B Specifications : Test Procedures and Acceptance Criteria for Biotechnological/Biological Products

Q7 Good Manufacturing Practice

- Q7 Good Manufacturing Practice Guide for Active Pharmaceutical Ingredients Q7A
- Q7 Q&As Questions and Answers: Good Manufacturing Practice Guide for Active Pharmaceutical Ingredients

Q8Pharmaceutical Development

- Q8(R2) Pharmaceutical Development

Q9 Quality Risk Management

- Q9 Quality Risk Management

Q10 Pharmaceutical Quality System

- Q10 Pharmaceutical Quality System

Q11 Development and Manufacture of Drug Substances

- Q11 Development and Manufacture of Drug Substances (Chemical Entities and Biotechnological/Biological Entities)

Q12 Lifecycle Management

- Q12 Technical and Regulatory Considerations for Pharmaceutical Product Lifecycle Management.

SAFETY GUIDELINES (S)

S1A –S1C Carcinogenicity Studies

- S1 Rodent Carcinogenicity Studies for Human Pharmaceuticals
- S1A Need for Carcinogenicity Studies of Pharmaceuticals
- S1B Testing for Carcinogenicity of Pharmaceuticals
- S1C (R2) Dose Selection for Carcinogenicity Studies of Pharmaceuticals

S2 Genotoxicity Studies

- S2(R1) Guidance on Genotoxicity Testing and Data Interpretation for Pharmaceuticals Intended for Human Us

S3A – S3B Toxicokinetic and Pharmacokinetics

- S3A Note for Guidance on Toxicokinetic: The Assessment of Systemic Exposure in Toxicity Studies
- S3A Q & As Questions and Answers: Note for Guidance on Toxicokinetic: The Assessment of Systemic Exposure – Focus on Micro sampling
- S3B Pharmacokinetics: Guidance for Repeated Dose Tissue Distribution Studies

S4 Toxicity Testing

- S4 Duration of Chronic Toxicity Testing in Animals (Rodent and Non Rodent Toxicity Testing)

S5 Reproductive Toxicology

- S5(R2) Detection of Toxicity to Reproduction for Medicinal Products & Toxicity to Male Fertility
- S6 Biotechnological Products
- S6(R1) Preclinical Safety Evaluation of Biotechnology - Derived Pharmaceuticals
- S7A –S7B Pharmacology Studies
- S7A Safety Pharmacology Studies for Human Pharmaceuticals
- S7B The Non-Clinical Evaluation of the Potential for Delayed Ventricular Repolarization (QT Interval
- Prolongation) by Human Pharmaceuticals
- S8 Immunotoxicology Studies
- S8 Immunotoxicity Studies for Human Pharmaceuticals
- S9 Nonclinical Evaluation for Anticancer Pharmaceuticals
- S9 Nonclinical Evaluation for Anticancer Pharmaceuticals
- S10 Photo safety Evaluation
- S10 Photo safety Evaluation of Pharmaceuticals
- S11 Nonclinical Safety Testing
- S11 Nonclinical safety Testing in support of Development of paediatric Medicines

EFFICACY GUIDELINES(E):

E1 Clinical safety for Drugs used in Long – Term Treatment

- E1 The Extent of Population Exposure to Assess clinical safety for Drugs Intended for Long – Term Treatment of Non – Life Threatening Conditions

E2A –E2F Pharmacovigilance

- E2A Clinical Safety Data Management : Definitions and Standards for Expedited Reporting
- E2B(R3) Clinical safety Data Management: Data Elements for Transmission of Individual case safety Reports
- E2B(R3) IWG Implementation: Electronic Transmission of Individual Case Safety Reports
- E2C(R2) Periodic Benefit – Risk Evaluation Report E2C, E2CA
- E2C(R2) Q & As Questions & Answers: Periodic Benefit - Risk Evaluation Report
- E2D Post – Approval Safety Data Management: Definitions and Standards for Expedited Reporting
- E2E Pharmacovigilance Planning
- E2F Development Safety Update Report

E3 Clinical Study Reports

- E3 Structure and Consent of Clinical Study Reports

E4 Dose - Response Studies

- E4 Dose - Response Information to support Drug Registration

E5 Ethic Factors

- E5(R1) Ethic Factors in the Acceptability of Foreign Clinical Data

E6 Good Clinical Practice

- E6(R1) Good Clinical Practice
- E6 (R2) Addendum: Good Clinical Practice

E7 Clinical Trials in Geriartic Population

- E7 Studies in support of special Populations: Geriatics

E8 General Considerations for Clinical Trials

- E8 General Consideration for Clinical Trials

E9 Statistical priniciples for Clinical Trials

- E9 Statistical Priniciples for Clinical Trials

E10 Choice of Control Group in Clinical Trials

- Choice of Control Group and Related Issues in Clinical Trials

E11 Clinical Trials in Pediatric Population

- E11 Clinical Investigation of Medicinal Products in the Pediatric Population

E12 clinical Evaluation by Therapeutic Category

- E12 Principles for Clinical Evaluation of New Antihypertensive Drugs

E14 Clinical Evaluation

- E14 The Clinical Evaluation of QT/QTc Interval Prolongation and Pro –arrhythmic Potential for Non – Anti – arrhythmic Drug

E15 Definitions in Pharmacogenetics / Pharmacogenomics

- E15 Definitions for Genomic Biomarkers, Pharmacogenomics, Pharmacogenetics , Genomic Data and Sample Coding Categories

E16 Qualification of Genomic Biomarkers

- E16 Biomarkers Related to Drug or Biotechnology Product Development: Context, Structure and Format of Qualification Submissions

E17 Multi - Regional Clinical Trials

- E17 General principle on planning / designing Multi – Regional Clinical Trials

E18 Genomic Sampling Methodologies

- E18 Genomic Sampling Mythologies for Future Use

MULTIDISCIPLINARY GUIDELINES(M)

M1 MedDRA Terminology

- MedDRA Medical Dictionary for Regulatory Activities

M2 Electronic Standards

- ESTRI Electronic Standards for the Transfer of Regulatory Information

M3 Nonclinical Safety Studies

- M3(R2) Guidance on Nonclinical Safety Studies for the conduct of Human Clinical Trials and Marketing Authorization for Pharmaceuticals

M4 Common Technical Document

- CTD The common Technical Document

M5 Data Elements and Standards for Drug Dictionaries

- M5 Data Elements and Standards for Drug Dictionaries

M6 Gene Therapy

- M6 virus and Gene Therapy Vector Shedding and Transmission

M7 Genotoxic Impurities

- M7 Assessment and Control of DNA Reactive (Mutagenic) Impurities in Pharmaceuticals to limit potential Carcinogenic

M8 Electronic Common Technical Document (eCTD)

- Electronic Common Technical Document (eCTD)

International council for harmonisation of technical requirements for pharmaceuticals for human use ICH harmonised guideline general considerations for clinical studies E8(R1). E8 Approval by the Steering Committee under Step 4 and recommendation for adoption by ICH regulatory bodies.By 17 July 1997

Revision of E8

E8(R1) Adoption by the Regulatory Members of the ICH. Assembly under Step 4 by 6 October 2021. E8(R1) Minor editorial correction approved by the E8(R1) Topic Leaders within the core text (page 19) by 4 August 2022.

1. OBJECTIVES OF THIS DOCUMENT

Clinical studies of medicinal products are conducted to provide information that can ultimately improve access to safe and effective products with meaningful impact on patients, while protecting those participating in the studies.

This document provides guidance on the clinical development lifecycle, including designing quality into clinical studies, considering the broad range of clinical study designs and data sources used.

The ICH document "General Considerations for Clinical Studies" is intended to:

1. Describe internationally accepted principles and practices in the design and conduct of clinical studies that will ensure the protection of study participants and facilitate acceptance of data and results by regulatory authorities

2. Provide guidance on the consideration of quality in the design and conduct of clinical studies across the product lifecycle, including the identification, during study planning,

of factors that are critical to the quality of the study, and the management of risks to those factors during study conduct

3. Provide an overview of the types of clinical studies performed during the product lifecycle, and describe study design elements that support the identification of quality factors critical to ensuring the protection of study participants, the integrity of the data, the reliability of results, and the ability of the studies to meet their objectives

4. Provide a guide to the ICH efficacy documents to facilitate user's access General principles are described in Section 2 of this document, followed by a discussion of designing quality into clinical studies in Section 3. A broad overview of drug development planning and the information provided by different types of studies needed to progress development through the lifecycle of the product is given in Section 4. In Section 5, important elements of clinical study design are described that reflect the variety of designs used in drug development as well as the range of data sources available. Section 6 addresses study conduct, ensuring the safety of study participants, and study reporting. Some considerations for identifying factors that are critical to the quality of a study are provided in Section 7.

The ICH Efficacy guidelines are an integrated set of guidance covering the planning, design, conduct, safety, analysis, and reporting of clinical studies. ICH E8 provides an overall introduction to clinical development, designing quality into clinical studies and focusing on those factors critical to the quality of the studies. The guidelines should be considered and used in an integrated, holistic way rather than focusing on only one guideline or subsection.

For the purposes of this document, a clinical study is meant to refer to a study of one or more medicinal products in humans, conducted at any point in a product's lifecycle, both prior to and following marketing authorisation. The focus is on clinical studies to support regulatory decisions, recognizing these studies may also inform health policy decisions, clinical practice guidelines, or other actions. The term "drug" should be considered synonymous with therapeutic, preventative, or diagnostic medicinal products. The term "drug approval" refers to obtaining marketing authorisation for the drug

2. GENERAL PRINCIPLES

2.1 Protection of Clinical Study Participants

Important principles of ethical conduct of clinical studies and the protection of participants, including special populations, have their origins in the Declaration of Helsinki and should be

observed in the conduct of all human clinical investigations. These principles are stated in other ICH guidelines, in particular, ICH E6-Good Clinical Practice.

As further described in the E6 guideline, the investigator and sponsor have responsibilities for the protection of study participants together with the Institutional Review Board/Independent Ethics Committee.

The confidentiality of information that could identify participants should be protected in accordance with the applicable regulatory and legal requirement(s).

Before initiating a clinical study, sufficient information should be available to ensure that the drug is acceptably safe for the planned study in humans. Emerging non-clinical, clinical, and

pharmaceutical quality data should be reviewed and evaluated, as they become available, by qualified experts to assess the potential implications for the safety of study participants.

Ongoing and future studies should be appropriately adjusted as needed, to take new knowledge into consideration and to protect study participants. Throughout drug development, care should be taken to ensure all study procedures and assessments are necessary from a scientific viewpoint and do not place undue burden on study participants.

2.2 Scientific Approach in Clinical Study Design, Planning, Conduct, Analysis, and Reporting

The essence of clinical research is to ask important questions and answer them with appropriate studies. The primary objectives of any study should reflect the research questions and be clear and explicitly stated. Clinical studies should be designed, planned, conducted, analysed, and reported according to sound scientific principles to achieve their objectives.

Quality of a clinical study is considered in this document as fitness for purpose. The purpose of a clinical study is to generate reliable information to answer the research questions and support decision making while protecting study participants. The quality of the information generated should therefore be sufficient to support good decision making.

Quality by design in clinical research sets out to ensure that the quality of a study is driven proactively by designing quality into the study protocol and processes. This involves the use of a prospective, multidisciplinary approach to promote the quality of protocol and process design in a manner proportionate to the risks involved, and clear communication of how this will be achieved.

Across the product lifecycle, different types of studies will be conducted with different objectives and designs and may involve different data sources. For purposes of this guideline,

development planning is considered to cover the entire product lifecycle (Section 4). The Annex provides a broad categorisation of study type by objective within the different stages of drug development. Studies should be rigorously designed to address the study objectives with careful attention to the design elements, such as the choice of study population and response variables and the use of methods to minimize biases in the findings (Section 5).

The cardinal logic behind serially conducted studies is that the results of prior studies should inform the plan of later studies. Emerging data will frequently prompt a modification of the development strategy. For example, results of a confirmatory study may suggest a need for additional human pharmacology studies.

The availability of multi-regional data as a result of the increased globalisation of drug development programmes, facilitated by the harmonisation of ICH Guidelines, minimises the need to conduct individual studies in different regions. The results of a study are often used in regulatory submissions in multiple regions, and the design should also consider the relevance of the study results for regions other than the one(s) in which the study is conducted. Further guidance is provided by ICH E5 Ethnic Factors, ICH E6, and ICH E17 Multi-Regional Clinical Trials.

Early engagement with regulatory authorities to understand local/regional requirements and expectations is encouraged and will facilitate the ability to design quality into the study.

2.3 Patient Input into Drug Development

Consulting with patients and/or patient organisations during drug development can help to ensure that patients' perspectives are captured. The views of patients (or of their caregivers/parents) can be valuable throughout all phases of drug development. Involving patients early in the design of a study is likely to increase trust in the study, facilitate recruitment, and promote adherence. Patients also provide their perspective of living with a condition, which may contribute to the determination, for example, of endpoints that are meaningful to patients, selection of the appropriate population and duration of the study, and use of acceptable comparators. This ultimately supports the development of drugs that are

better tailored to patients' needs.

3. DESIGNING QUALITY INTO CLINICAL STUDIES

The quality by design approach to clinical research (Section 3.1) involves focusing on critical to quality factors to ensure the protection of the rights, safety, and wellbeing of study participants, the generation of reliable and meaningful results, and the management of risks to those factors using a risk-proportionate approach (Section 3.2). The approach is supported by the establishment of an appropriate framework for the identification and review of critical to quality factors (Section 3.3) at the time of design and planning of the study, and throughout its conduct, analysis, and reporting.

3.1 Quality by Design of Clinical Studies

Quality is a primary consideration in the design, planning, conduct, analysis, and reporting of clinical studies and a necessary component of clinical development programmes. The likelihood that a clinical study will answer the research questions while preventing important errors can be dramatically improved through prospective attention to the design of all components of the study protocol, procedures, associated operational plans and training.

Activities such as document and data review and monitoring, where conducted retrospectively, are an important part of a quality assurance process; but, even when combined with audits, they are not sufficient to ensure quality of a clinical study.

Good planning and implementation of a clinical study also derive from attention to the design elements of clinical studies as described in Section 5, such as:

- the need for clear pre-defined study objectives that address the primary scientific question(s);
- selection of appropriate participants that have the disease, condition, or molecular/genetic profile that is being studied;
- use of approaches to minimise bias, such as randomisation, blinding or masking, and/or control of confounding;
- endpoints that are well-defined, measurable, clinically meaningful, and relevant to patients.

Operational criteria are also important, such as ensuring a clear understanding of the feasibility of the study, selection of suitable investigator sites, quality of specialised analytical and testing facilities and procedures, and processes that ensure data integrity.

3.2 Critical to Quality Factors

A basic set of factors relevant to ensuring study quality should be identified for each study. Emphasis should be given to those factors that stand out as critical to study quality. These critical to quality factors are attributes of a study whose integrity is fundamental to the protection of study participants, the reliability and interpretability of the study results, and the decisions made based on the study results. These quality factors are considered to be critical because, if their integrity were to be undermined by errors of design or conduct, the reliability or ethics of decision-making based on the results of the study would also be undermined.

Critical to quality factors should also be considered holistically, so that dependencies among them can be identified. Section 7 of this document provides considerations that can help identify critical to quality factors for a study.

The design of a clinical study should reflect the state of knowledge and experience with the drug; the condition to be treated, diagnosed or prevented; the underlying biological mechanism (of both the condition and the treatment); and the population for which the drug is intended. As research progresses, knowledge increases and uncertainties about the pharmacology, safety and efficacy of a drug decrease. Knowledge of the drug at any point in development will continually inform the identification of critical to quality factors and control processes used to manage them.

The sponsor and other parties designing quality into a clinical study should identify the critical to quality factors. Having identified those factors, it is important to determine the risks that threaten their integrity and decide whether they can be accepted or should be mitigated, based on their probability, detectability and impact. Where it is decided that risks should be mitigated, the necessary control processes should be put in place and communicated, and the necessary actions taken to mitigate the risks. The term risk is used here in the context of general risk management methodology applicable to all factors of a study.

Proactive communication of the critical to quality factors and risk mitigation activities will support understanding of priorities and resource allocation by the sponsor and investigator sites. Proactive support (e.g., training to site staff, relevant to their role, and description of critical to quality factors and potential mitigation measures in the protocol) will enhance correct implementation of study protocol, procedures, and associated operational plans and process design.

Perfection in every aspect of an activity is rarely achievable or can only be achieved by use of resources that are out of proportion to the benefit obtained. The quality factors should be prioritised to identify those that are critical to the study, at the time of the study design, and study procedures should be proportionate to the risks inherent in the study and the importance of the information collected. The critical to quality factors should be clear and should not be cluttered with minor issues (e.g., due to extensive secondary objectives or processes/data collection not linked to the proper protection of the study participants and/or primary study objectives).

3.3 Approach to Identifying the Critical to Quality Factors

A key aspect of a quality approach to study design is to ask whether the objectives being addressed by the study are clearly articulated; whether the study is designed to meet the research question it sets out to address; whether these questions are meaningful to patients; and whether the study hypotheses are specific and scientifically valid. The approach to the identification of the critical to quality factors should consider whether those objectives can be met, well and most efficiently, by the chosen design and data sources. Patient consultation early in the study design process can contribute to this approach and ultimately help to identify the critical to quality factors. Study designs should be operationally feasible and avoid unnecessary complexity. Protocols and case report forms/data collection methods should enable the study to be conducted as designed and avoid unnecessary data collection. Identification of critical to quality factors will be enhanced by approaches that include the following elements:

3.3.1 Establishing a Culture that Supports Open Dialogue

Creating a culture that values and rewards critical thinking and open, proactive dialogue about what is critical to quality for a particular study or development programme, going beyond sole reliance on tools and checklists, is encouraged. Open dialogue can facilitate the development of innovative methods for ensuring quality. Inflexible, "one size fits all" approaches should be discouraged. Standardised operating procedures are necessary and beneficial for conducting good quality clinical studies, but study specific strategies and actions are also needed to effectively and efficiently support quality in a study.

Evidence used to inform the study design should be gathered and reviewed, before and during the study, in a transparent manner, while acknowledging gaps in data and conflicting data, where present and known, and anticipating the possible emergence of such gaps or conflicts.

3.3.2 Focusing on Activities Essential to the Study

Efforts should be focused on activities that are essential to the reliability and meaningfulness of study outcomes for patients and public health, and the safe, ethical conduct of the study for participants. Consideration should be given to eliminating nonessential activities and data collection from the study to increase quality by simplifying conduct, improving study efficiency, and targeting resources to critical areas. Resources should be deployed to identify and prevent or control errors that matter.

3.3.3 Engaging Stakeholders in Study Design

Clinical study design is best informed by input from a broad range of stakeholders, including patients and healthcare providers. It should be open to challenge by subject matter experts and stakeholders from outside, as well as within, the sponsor organisation.

The process of building quality into the study may be informed by participation of those directly involved in successful completion of the study such as clinical investigators, study coordinators and other site staff, and patients/ patient organisations. Clinical investigators and potential study participants have valuable insights into the feasibility of enrolling participants who meet proposed eligibility criteria, whether scheduled study visits and procedures may be overly burdensome and lead to early dropouts, and the general relevance of study endpoints and study settings to the targeted patient population. They may also provide insight into the value of a treatment in the context of ethical issues, culture, region, demographics, and other characteristics of subgroups within a targeted patient population.

Early engagement with regulatory authorities is encouraged, particularly when a study has novel elements considered critical to quality (e.g., defining patient populations, procedures, or endpoints).

3.3.4 Reviewing Critical to Quality Factors

Accumulated experience and knowledge, together with periodic review of critical to quality factors should be used to determine whether adjustments to risk control mechanisms are needed, because new or unanticipated issues may arise once the study has begun.

Studies with adaptive features and/or interim decision points need specific attention during proactive planning and ongoing review of critical to quality factors, and risk management (ICH E9 Statistical Principles for Clinical Trials).

3.3.5 Critical to Quality Factors in Operational Practice

The foundation of a successful study is a protocol that is both scientifically sound and operationally feasible. A feasibility assessment involves consideration of study design and implementation elements that could impact the successful completion of clinical development from an operational perspective.

Feasibility considerations also include but are not limited to regional differences in medical practice and patient populations, the availability of qualified investigators/site personnel with experience in conducting a clinical study (ICH E6), availability of equipment and facilities required to successfully conduct the study, availability of the targeted patient population, and ability to enrol a sufficient number of participants to meet the study objectives. The retention and follow up of study participants are also key critical to quality factors. Consideration of these and other critical to quality factors relating to study feasibility can inform study design and enhance quality implementation.

4. DRUG DEVELOPMENT PLANNING

This section provides general principles to consider in drug development planning. Drug development planning adheres to the principles of scientific research and good study design that ensure the reliability and interpretability of results. Efficient drug development includes appropriately planned interactions with regulatory authorities throughout development to ensure alignment with requirements for product quality and to support approval in the condition or disease, including possible post-approval studies to address remaining questions. Throughout this process there is critical attention to the protection of the rights, safety and wellbeing of study participants.

Drug development planning builds on knowledge acquired throughout the investigational process to reduce levels of uncertainty as the process moves from target identification through non-clinical and clinical evaluation. Such planning encompasses quality of medicinal product, includingchemistry, manufacturing and controls (CMC), and non-clinical and clinical studies (pre and post-approval). Modelling and simulation may inform drug development throughout the process. Planning may also include regional considerations for product introduction into the market, such as health technology assessments. It is important to ensure that the experiences, perspectives, needs, and priorities of relevant stakeholders relating to the development and evaluation of the drug throughout its lifecycle are captured and meaningfully incorporated into drug development planning.

Clinical development may also feature requirements for co-development of validated biomarkers, diagnostic testing, or devices that facilitate the safe and effective use of a drug.

The types of studies that may contribute to drug development are described in subsections 4.2 and 4.3 and summarised in the Annex.

4.1 Quality of Investigational Medicinal Product

Ensuring adequate quality and characterisation of physicochemical properties of investigational medicinal product is an important element in planning a drug development programme and is addressed in ICH and regional quality guidelines. More extensive characterisation may be required for complex or biological products. Formulations should be well characterised in the drug development plan, including information on bioavailability,

wherever feasible, and should be appropriate for the stage of drug development and the targeted patient population. Age-appropriate formulation development may be a consideration when clinical studies are planned in paediatric populations (ICH E11- E11A Clinical Trials in Pediatric Population).

Evaluation of the quality of a drug may extend to devices required for its administration or a companion diagnostic to identify the targeted population. Changes in a product during development should be supported by comparability data to ensure the ability to interpret study results across the development programme. This includes establishing links between formulations through bioequivalence studies or other means.

4.2 Non-Clinical Studies

Guidance on non-clinical safety studies is provided in ICH M3 Nonclinical Safety Studies, ICH Safety (S) Guidelines and related Q&A documents, as well as in regional guidance. The nonclinical assessment usually includes toxicology, carcinogenicity, immunogenicity, pharmacology, pharmacokinetics, and other evaluations to support clinical studies (and may encompass evidence generated in in vivo and in vitro models, and by modelling and simulation). The scope of non-clinical studies, and their timing with respect to clinical studies, depend on a variety of factors that inform further development, such as the drug's chemical or molecular properties; pharmacological basis of principal effects (mechanism of action); route(s) of administration; absorption, distribution, metabolism, and excretion (ADME); physiological effects on organ systems; dose/concentration-response relationships; metabolites; and duration of action and use. Use of the drug in special populations (e.g., pregnant or breast-feeding women, children) may require additional non-clinical assessments.

Guidance for non-clinical safety studies to support human clinical studies in special populations should be reviewed (see, e.g., ICH S5 Reproductive Toxicology, S11 Nonclinical Paediatric Safety, and M3).

Assessment of the preclinical characteristics, including physiological and toxicological effects of the drug, serve to inform clinical study design and planned use in humans. Before proceeding to studies in humans there should be sufficient non-clinical information to support initial human

doses and duration of exposure.

4.3 Clinical Studies

Clinical drug development, defined as studying the drug in humans, is conducted in a sequence that builds on knowledge accumulated from non-clinical and previous clinical studies. The structure of the drug development programme will be shaped by many considerations and comprised of studies with different objectives, different designs, and different dependencies.

The Annex provides an illustrative list of example studies and their objectives. Although clinical drug development is often described as consisting of four temporal phases (phases 1- 4), it is important to appreciate that the phase concept is a description and not a requirement, and that the phases of drug development may overlap or be combined.

To develop new drugs efficiently, it is essential to identify their characteristics in the early stages of development and to plan an appropriate development programme based on this profile. Initial clinical studies may be more limited in size and duration to provide an early evaluation of short-term safety and tolerability as well as proof of concept of efficacy. These studies may provide pharmacodynamic, pharmacokinetic, and other information needed to choose a suitable dosage range and/or administration schedule to inform further clinical studies.

As more information is known about the drug, clinical studies may expand in size and duration, may include more diverse study populations, and may include more secondary endpoints in addition to the primary measures of efficacy. Throughout development, new data may suggest the need for additional studies.

The use of biomarkers has the potential to facilitate the availability of safer and more effective drugs, to guide dose selection, and to enhance a drug's benefit-risk profile (see ICH E16

Qualification of Genomic Biomarkers) and may be considered throughout drug development. Clinical studies may evaluate the use of biomarkers to better target patients more likely to benefit and less likely to experience adverse reactions, or as intermediate endpoints that could predict clinical response.

The following subsections describe the types of studies that typically span clinical development from the first studies in humans through late development and post-approval.

4.3.1 Human Pharmacology

The protection of study participants should always be the first priority when designing early clinical studies, especially for the initial administration of an investigational product to humans

(Usually referred to as phase 1). These studies may be conducted in healthy volunteer participants or in a selected population of patients who have the condition or the disease,

depending on drug properties and the objectives of the development programme. These studies typically address one or a combination of the following aspects:

4.3.1.1 Estimation of Initial Safety and Tolerability

The initial and subsequent administration of a drug to humans is usually intended to determine the tolerability of the dose range expected to be evaluated in later clinical studies and to determine the nature of adverse reactions that can be expected. These studies typically include both single and multiple dose administration.

4.3.1.2 Pharmacokinetics

Characterisation of a drug's absorption, distribution, metabolism, and excretion continues throughout the development programme, but the preliminary characterisation is an essential early goal. Pharmacokinetic studies are particularly important to assess the clearance of the drug and to anticipate possible accumulation of parent drug or metabolites, interactions with metabolic enzymes and transporters, and potential drug-drug interactions. Some pharmacokinetic studies are commonly conducted in later phases to answer more specialised questions. For orally administered drugs, the study of food effects on bioavailability is important to inform the dosing instructions in relation to food. Obtaining pharmacokinetic information in sub-populations with potentially different metabolism or excretion, such as patients with renal or hepatic impairment, geriatric patients, children, and ethnic subgroups should be considered (ICH E4 Dose-Response Studies, E7 Clinical Trials in Geriatric Population, E11, and E5, respectively).

4.3.1.3 Pharmacodynamics & Early Measurement of Drug Activity

Depending on the drug and the endpoint of interest, pharmacodynamic studies and studies relating drug levels to response (PK/PD studies) may be conducted in healthy volunteer participants or in patients with the condition or disease. If there is an appropriate measure, pharmacodynamic data can provide early estimates of activity and efficacy and may guide the dosage and dose regimen in later studies.

4.3.2 Exploratory and Confirmatory Safety and Efficacy Studies

After initial clinical studies provide sufficient information on safety, clinical pharmacology and dose, exploratory and confirmatory studies (usually referred to as phases 2 and 3, respectively) are conducted to further evaluate both the safety and efficacy of the drug. Depending on the

nature of the drug and the patient population, this objective may be combined in a single or small number of studies. Exploratory and confirmatory studies may use a variety of study designs depending on the objective of the study. Exploratory studies are designed to investigate safety and efficacy in a selected population of patients for whom the drug is intended. Additionally, these studies aim to refine the effective dose(s) and regimen, refine the definition of the targeted population, provide a more robust safety profile for the drug, and include evaluation of potential study endpoints for subsequent studies. Exploratory studies may provide information on the identification and determination of factors that affect the treatment effect and, possibly combined with modelling and

simulation, serve to support the design of later confirmatory studies. Confirmatory studies are designed to confirm the preliminary evidence accumulated in earlier clinical studies that a drug is safe and effective for use for the intended indication and recipient population. These studies are often intended to provide an adequate basis for marketing approval, and to support adequate instructions for use of the drug and official product information. They aim to evaluate the drug in participants with or at risk of the condition or disease who represent those who will receive the drug once approved. This may include investigating subgroups of patients with frequently occurring or potentially relevant comorbidities (e.g., cardiovascular disease, diabetes, hepatic and renal impairment) to characterise the safe and effective use of the drug in patients with these conditions.

Confirmatory studies may evaluate the efficacy and safety of more than one dose or the use of the drug in different stages of disease or in combination with one or more other drugs. If the

intent is to administer a drug for a long period of time, then studies involving extended exposure to the drug should be conducted (ICH E1 Clinical Safety for Drugs used in Long-Term Treatment). Irrespective of the intended duration of administration, the duration of effect of the drug will also inform the duration of follow-up.

Study endpoints selected for confirmatory studies should be clinically relevant and reflect disease burden or be of adequate surrogacy for predicting disease burden or sequelae.

4.3.3 Special Populations

Some groups in the general population require additional investigation during drug development because they have unique risk/benefit considerations, or because they can be anticipated to need modification of the dose or schedule of a drug. ICH E5 and E17 provide a framework for evaluating the impact of ethnic factors on a drug's effect. Particular attention

should be paid to the ethical considerations related to informed consent in vulnerable populations (ICH E6 and E11). Studies in special populations may be conducted during any phase of development to understand the drug effects in these populations. Some considerations of special populations are the following:

4.3.3.1 Investigations in pregnant women

Investigation of drugs that may be used in pregnancy is important. Where pregnant women volunteer to be enrolled in a clinical study, or a participant becomes pregnant while participating in a clinical study, follow-up evaluation of the pregnancy and its outcome and the reporting of outcomes are necessary.

4.3.3.2 Investigations in lactating women

Excretion of the drug or its metabolites into human milk should be examined where applicable and feasible. When nursing mothers are enrolled in clinical studies their babies are usually also monitored for the effects of the drug.

4.3.3.3 Investigations in children

ICH E11 provides an outline of critical issues in paediatric drug development and approaches to the safe, efficient, and ethical study of drugs in paediatric populations.

4.3.3.4 Investigations in geriatric populations

ICH E7 provides an outline of critical issues in developing drugs for use in geriatric populations and approaches to their safe, efficient, and ethical study.

4.3.4 Post-Approval Studies

After the approval of a drug, additional studies may be conducted to further understand the safety and efficacy of the drug in its approved indication (usually referred to as phase 4). These are studies that were not considered necessary for approval but are often important for optimising the drug's use. They may be of any type but should have valid scientific objectives. Post-approval studies may be conducted to address a regulatory requirement. Post-approval studies may be performed to provide additional information on the efficacy, safety, and use of the drug in populations more diverse than included in the studies conducted prior to marketing authorisation. Studies with long-term follow-up or with comparisons to other treatment options or standards of care may provide important information on safety and efficacy. Commonly conducted studies include additional drug-drug interaction, dose-response or safety studies and studies designed to support use under the approved indication (e.g.,

mortality/morbidity studies, epidemiological studies). These studies may explore use of the drug in the real-world setting of clinical practice and may also inform health economics and

health technology assessments.

4.4 Additional Development

After initial approval, drug development may continue with studies of new or modified indications in new patient populations, new dosage regimens, or new routes of administration.

If a new dose, formulation, or combination is studied, additional non-clinical and/or human pharmacology studies may be indicated. Data from previous studies or from clinical experience with the approved drug may inform these programmes.

5. DESIGN ELEMENTS AND DATA SOURCES FOR CLINICAL STUDIES

Study objectives impact the choice of study design and data sources, which in turn impact the strength of a study to support regulatory decisions and clinical practice. As discussed in Section 4, there are a wide variety of study objectives in drug development. Similarly, there is a wide range of study designs and data sources to address these objectives. Sections 5.1 through 5.6 discuss key elements that may be used to define the study design, and Section 5.7 discusses the various data sources that may be used for the study. Clear objectives will help to specify the study design, and conversely, the process of specifying the design may help to further clarify the objectives. At the design stage, the objectives may need to be modified ifsubstantial practical considerations and limitations or other risks to critical to quality factors are identified. The study objectives are further refined through specification of estimands. Estimands, discussed in ICH E9(R1) Addendum: Statistical Principles for Clinical Trials, provide a precise description of the treatment effects reflecting the clinical questions posed by the study objectives. The estimand summarises at a population level what the outcomes would be in the same patients under the different treatment conditions

being compared.

An important distinction between studies is whether the allocation of individuals to the study drug(s) is controlled by the study procedures or allocation to the drug is not controlled but exposure to the drug(s) is observed in the study. In this document, the former case is referred to as an interventional study and the latter case is referred to as an observational study.

Interventional studies, and in particular randomised studies, play a central role in drug development, as they can better control biases. The designs of randomised studies range from simple parallel group designs to more complex variants. For example, adaptive design studies allow prospectively planned modifications to the study, such as changes in the population studied or changes in doses of the drug studied over the course of the study, based on accumulating data. Master protocol studies allow for the investigation of multiple drugs or multiple conditions under a shared framework. Platform studies allow for multiple drugs to be investigated in a continuous manner, with different drugs entering the study at different times and leaving the study based on pre-specified decision rules.

Studies without randomisation (whether interventional or observational) can play a role as well in certain settings when randomisation is not feasible. Observational studies are often conducted post-approval but can be of utility as complementary sources of evidence during development and across the life cycle of a drug.

Along with the breadth of study designs, there are multiple sources of data that studies may employ. Traditionally, studies have used study-specific data collection processes. Data such as that obtained from electronic medical records or digital health technologies may be leveraged to increase the efficiency of studies or generalisability of study results.

This section presents important elements that define the design of a clinical study including population, treatment, control group, response variable, methods to reduce bias, statistical analysis, and data sources. It is intended to assist in identifying the critical to quality factors necessary to achieve the study objectives, while also enabling flexibility in study design and promoting efficiency in study conduct. Although the focus is on interventional studies, the discussion is intended to apply to both interventional and observational studies. The elements outlined here are expected to be relevant to study types and data sources that are used in clinical studies now and that may be developed in the future.

5.1 Study Population

The population to be studied should be chosen to support the study objectives and is defined through the inclusion and exclusion criteria for the study. The degree to which a study succeeds in enrolling the desired population will impact the ability of the study to meet its objectives.

The study population may be narrowly defined to reduce the risk to study participants or to maximise the sensitivity of the study for detecting a certain effect. Conversely, it may be broadly defined to more closely represent the diverse populations for which the drug is intended. In general, studies conducted early in a development programme, when little is known about the safety of the drug, are more homogeneous in study population definitions.

Studies conducted in the later phases of drug development or post-approval are often more heterogeneous in study population definitions. Such studies should involve participants who are representative of the diverse populations which will receive the intervention in clinical practice. Available knowledge about participant characteristics that may predict disease outcomes or effects of the intervention can be used to further define the study population.

The number of participants (sample size) in a study should be large enough to provide a reliable answer to the questions addressed (see ICH E9). This number is usually determined by the primary objective of the study. If the sample size is determined on some other basis, then this should be made clear and justified. For example, a sample size determined to address safety questions or meet important secondary objectives may need larger numbers of participants than needed for addressing the primary efficacy question (see ICH E1). If study objectives include obtaining information on certain subgroups, then efforts should be made to ensure adequate representation of these subgroups.

5.2 Treatment Description

The treatment(s), including controls, under study should be described explicitly and specifically. These might be individual treatments (including different doses or regimens), combinations of treatments, or no treatments, and can include specification of background treatments. The definition of treatments should align with the objectives of the study (ICH

E9(R1)). For example, if the objective of the study is to understand the effect of the treatment in clinical practice, the study may specify that the background treatment, if any, is up to the discretion of the participants and healthcare providers. If the objectives are to understand the effect of the drug when added to a specific background treatment, the background treatment should be defined explicitly and specifically for all groups including controls.

5.3 Choice of Control Group

The major purpose of a control group is to separate the effect of the treatment(s) from the effects of other factors such as natural course of the disease, other medical care received, or

observer or patient expectations (E10 Choice of Control Group in Clinical Trials). The treatment effect of interest may be the effect relative to not receiving the drug or the effect relative to receiving other therapies. Comparisons may be made with placebo, no treatment, standard of care, other treatments, or different doses of the drug under investigation.

The source of control group data may be internal or external to the study. The intent of using an internal control group is to help ensure that the only differences between treatment groups are due to the treatment they receive and not due to differences in the selection of participants, the timing and measurement of study outcomes, or other differences. A special case of an internal control group is when each participant serves as their own internal control by receiving the drug and control at different points of time. With use of an external control group, individuals are selected from an external source, and the individuals may have been treated at an earlier time (historical control group) or during the same time but in another setting than participants in the study.

Important limitations of the use of external controls are discussed in ICH E10. Particular care is needed to minimise the likelihood of erroneous inference. The use of an external control requires that the disease course is well known and predictable. External control individuals may differ from study participants with respect to demographic and background characteristics (e.g., medical history, concurrent diseases). In addition, external control individuals may differ from participants in the study with respect to concurrent care and the measurement of study outcomes and other data elements. Because the use of internal controls generally mitigates the potential for bias better than external controls, particularly in conjunction with randomisation, the suitability of the use and choice of external control should be carefully considered and justified. Section 5.5 discusses the sources of bias which can arise in observational studies and is relevant to the use of external controls. Participant level data may not be available for some choices of external control groups. Summary measures may be available to form the basis of comparisons with treated participants to estimate drug effects and test hypotheses about those effects. There is, however, less ability to control for differences in characteristics between study individuals in the external control group and study participants in the internal treatment groups in making these comparisons or examining the quality and completeness of individual data elements. Additionally, there may not be the ability to examine subgroups or modify the response variable to be consistent with the response variable used in the study.

5.4 Response Variables

A response variable is an attribute of interest that may be affected by the drug. The response variable may relate to pharmacokinetics, pharmacodynamics, efficacy, or safety of the drug, or to the use of the drug including, for example, in adherence to risk minimisation measures post approval. Study endpoints are the response variables that are chosen to assess drug effects.

The primary endpoint should be capable of providing clinically relevant and convincing evidence related to the primary objective of the study (ICH E9). Secondary endpoints are either

supportive measurements related to the primary objective or measurements of effects related to the secondary objectives. Exploratory endpoints are used to further explain or to support study findings or to explore new hypotheses for later research. The choice of endpoints should be meaningful for the intended population and may also take into account the views of patients.

The definition of each study endpoint should be specific and include how and at what time points in a participant's treatment course of the drug and follow-up it is ascertained. Knowledge of the drug, along with the clinical context and purpose of a given study affect what response variables should be collected. For example, a proof-of-concept study of relatively short duration may employ a pharmacodynamic outcome rather than the outcome of primary interest (ICH E9). A larger study of longer duration could then be used to confirm a clinically meaningful effect on the outcome of primary interest. In other cases, such as a study where the safety profile of the drug is well characterised, the extent of safety data collection may be tailored to the objectives of the study.

5.5 Methods to Reduce Bias

The study design should address potential sources of bias that can undermine the reliability of results. Although different types of studies are subject to different sources of bias, this section addresses some common sources. ICH E9 discusses principles for controlling and reducing bias mainly in the context of interventional studies.

In studies with internal control groups, randomisation is used to ensure comparability of treatment groups, thereby minimising the possibility of bias in treatment assignment.

Randomisation at the start of the study addresses differences between the groups at the time of randomisation but does not prevent bias due to differences arising during the study. Events after randomisation (particularly intercurrent events (ICH E9(R1)) may affect the validity and interpretation of comparisons between treatment groups. Examples include treatment discontinuation or use of rescue medications. There may also be differences in the follow-up patterns between the groups due to participants in one group discontinuing the study at different rates, because of, for example, adverse events or perceived lack of efficacy. Careful consideration of the potential for intercurrent events to occur during the study and their impact will help with the identification of critical to quality factors, such as reducing study discontinuation, continuing data collection following treatment discontinuation, and retrieving data after study discontinuation, if appropriate. It is important when defining the treatment effect (estimand) to account for the occurrence of intercurrent events.

Concealing the treatment assignments (blinding) limits the occurrence of conscious or unconscious bias in the conduct and interpretation of a clinical study that may affect the course of treatment, monitoring, endpoint ascertainment, and participants' responses. In a single-blind study the investigator is aware of the treatment, but the participant is not. When the investigators who are involved in the treatment or clinical evaluation of the participants are also unaware of the treatment assignments, the study is referred to as double-blind. In an openlabel study, the consequences of the lack of blinding may be reduced through the use of prespecified decision rules for aspects of study conduct, such as recruitment, treatment assignment, participant management, safety reporting, and response variable ascertainment.

Blinding for staff at the study sites or sponsor should be implemented where feasible.

Knowledge of interim results (whether individual or treatment group level) has the potential to introduce bias or influence the conduct of the study and interpretation of study results. Specific considerations related to information flow and confidentiality are therefore necessary.

Observational studies introduce unique challenges to the assessment and control of bias. These include ensuring that the individuals have the condition under study and ensuring comparability between treatment groups, in prognostic factors associated with the choice of therapies, in the ascertainment of response variables, and in post-baseline concomitant patient care. These challenges may also exist with the use of external controls in an interventional study. Methods exist that may mitigate some of these challenges and should be considered during the design phase.

5.6 Statistical Analysis

The statistical analysis of a study encompasses important elements necessary to achieving the study objectives. The specification and documentation of the statistical analysis are important for ensuring the integrity of the study findings. The principal features of the statistical analysis should be planned during the design of the study and should be clearly specified in a protocol written before the study begins (ICH E9). Full details of the planned statistical analysis should be specified and documented before knowledge of the study results that may reveal the drug effects, which may be accomplished using a separate statistical analysis plan. The protocol should define the estimand(s) following the framework established in ICH E9(R1).

Statistical analyses of primary and secondary endpoints that address key study objectives with respect to both efficacy and safety should be described in the protocol, including any interim analyses and/or planned design adaptations. Other statistical aspects of the study that should be described in the protocol include the analytical methods for any planned estimation and tests of hypotheses about the drug effect and a justification of the sample size.

The statistical analysis should include pre-specified sensitivity analyses for assessing the impact of the assumptions made for the primary and important secondary analyses on the results of the study (E9(R1)). For example, if the analysis relies on a particular assumption about the reasons for missing data, sensitivity analyses should be planned to assess the impact of that assumption on the study results. In the case of observational studies, sensitivity analyses might, for example, consider additional potential confounders.

For double-blind studies, the statistical analysis should be finalised before treatment assignments are revealed. Therefore, if a study includes one or more interim analyses, the planned statistical analysis should not be changed after an interim analysis that involves unblinding. For open-label and single-blind studies, details pertaining to the primary and important secondary analyses would ideally be finalised before the first participant is randomised or allocated to study intervention.

Pre-specification of the analysis approach is particularly important for studies that make use of existing data sources rather than primary data collection (Section 5.7), not only for the statistical analysis planned for the study but also for any feasibility analysis to assess the applicability of the existing data. For example, for a single-arm interventional study with an external control, the specifics of the external control should be defined prior to the conduct of the interventional aspect of the study. Pre-specification of the analysis should be in place so that any review of the existing data sources prior to the design of the study does not threaten the study integrity.

The statistical analysis should be carried out in accordance with the prospectively defined analysis plan, and all deviations from the plan should be indicated in the study report (E3 Clinical Study Reports).

5.7 Study Data

Study data comprise all information generated, collected, or used in the context of the study ranging from existing source data to study-specific assessments. The study data should contain the necessary information to conduct the statistical analysis specified in the protocol and statistical analysis plan, as well as to monitor for participant safety, protocol adherence, and data integrity.

Study data can be broadly classified into two types: (1) data generated specifically for the present study (primary data collection) and (2) data obtained from sources external to the present study (secondary data use). Data generated for the study may be collected via case report forms, laboratory measurements, electronic patient reported outcomes, or mobile health tools. Examples of external sources of data include historical clinical studies, national death databases, disease and drug registries, claims data, and medical and administrative records from routine medical practice. A study may make use of both types of data.

For all data sources, procedures to ensure the protection of personal data of the individuals being studied should be implemented. The study protocol, and if applicable the informed consent, should explicitly address the protection of personal data. Regulations related to protection of individuals' data need to be followed. When considering data from external

sources, it is important to ascertain whether the regulatory authorities accept the use of such data for purposes other than the original intent.

Study data should be of sufficient quality to address the objectives of the study and, in interventional studies, to monitor participant safety. Data quality attributes include consistency (uniformity of ascertainment over time), accuracy (correctness of collection, transmission, and processing), and completeness (lack of missing information). These aspects should be proactively considered during study planning by identifying the factors, critical to the quality of the study, associated with data sourcing, collection, and processing.

The use of standards for data recording and coding (or recoding) is important to support data reliability, facilitate correct analysis and interpretation of results, and promote data sharing. Internationally accepted data standards exist for many sources of study data and should be used where applicable.

With primary data collection, the methods and standards established for use at the point of capture and the subsequent processing provide an opportunity to prospectively ensure the quality of the data.

With secondary data use, the relevance of the available data should be considered and clearly described in the study protocol. For example, when using existing electronic health record data to ascertain the study endpoint rather than through primary data collection, information in the health record about outcomes may need to be converted to the study endpoint.

In some cases, secondary data use may not be sufficient for all aspects of the study and may need to be supplemented by primary data collection. The quality of data collected for a different purpose should be evaluated when re-used in the context of the present study. Careful quality control processes may have been applied during their acquisition; where used, those processes were not necessarily designed with the objectives of the present study in mind.

There are several additional considerations with secondary data use. For example, methods to conceal the treatment should be considered when selecting and prior to analysing data from external sources. As another example, absence of affirmative information on a condition or event does not necessarily mean the condition or event is not present. There may also be a delay between the occurrence of events and their appearance in existing data sources. To the extent possible, uncertainties and potential sources of bias should be addressed at the study design stage, during data analysis, and in the interpretation of the study results.

6. CONDUCT, SAFETY MONITORING, AND REPORTING

6.1 Study Conduct

The principles and approaches set out in this guideline, including those of quality by design, should inform the approach taken to the conduct and reporting of clinical studies. Risk proportionate mitigation measures should be employed to ensure the integrity of the critical to quality factors.

6.1.1 Protocol Adherence

Adherence to the study protocol and other relevant documents is essential, and many aspects of adherence should be considered among the study's critical to quality factors. Successful application of the quality by design principles may minimise the need for modifications to the protocol and make adherence throughout the study more likely. If modification of the protocol becomes necessary, a clear description of the rationale for the modification should be provided in a protocol amendment, and the impact of the modification on study conduct should be carefully considered.

6.1.2 Training

Individuals involved in study conduct should receive training commensurate with their role in the study and this training should occur prior to their becoming involved in the study. Updated training or retraining may be needed to address issues related to critical to quality factors observed during the course of the study, and/or implement protocol modifications.

6.1.3 Data Management

The manner and timelines in which study data are collected and managed are critical contributors to overall study data quality. Operational checks, centralised data monitoring, and statistical surveillance can identify important data quality issues for corrective action. Data management procedures should account for the diversity of data sources in use for clinical studies (Section 5.7). For interventional clinical studies, further guidance on data management is available in ICH E6.

6.1.4 Access to Interim Data

Inappropriate access to data during the conduct of the study may compromise study integrity (Sections 5.5 and 5.6 and ICH E9). In studies with planned interim analyses, special attention should be given to which individuals have access to the data and results. Even in studies without planned interim analyses, special attention should be paid to any ongoing monitoring of unblinded data to avoid inappropriate access.

6.2 Participant Safety during Study Conduct

Important standards of ethical conduct and the protection of participants in clinical studies are described in Section 2.1. This section describes safety related considerations during the conduct of the study.

6.2.1 Safety Monitoring

The goals of safety monitoring are to protect study participants and to characterise the safety profile of the drug. Procedures and systems for the identification, monitoring, and reporting of safety concerns during the study should be clearly specified. The approach should reflect the type and objectives of the study, the risks to the study participants and what is known about the drug and the study population. Guidance is available on reporting of safety data to appropriate authorities and on the content and timing of safety reports (ICH E2A-E2F Pharmacovigilance, and, for interventional clinical trials in particular, ICH E6).

6.2.2 Withdrawal Criteria

Clear criteria for stopping treatment or study procedures for a study participant while remaining in the study are necessary to ensure the protection of the participants but should also minimise loss of critical data.

6.2.3 Data Monitoring Committee

An important component of safety monitoring in many clinical studies is the use of an independent data monitoring committee. This group monitors accumulating data while the study is being conducted to make recommendations on whether to continue, modify, or terminate a study.

During programme planning, the need for an independent data monitoring committee to monitor safety data across studies in a development programme should also be assessed. If a data monitoring committee is needed for either an individual study or across the development programme, procedures governing its operation and, in particular the review of unblinded data in an interventional trial, while preserving study integrity (ICH E9) should be established prior to study start.

6.3 Study Reporting

Clinical studies and their results should be adequately reported using formats appropriate for the type of study (interventional or observational studies) and information being reported. ICH E3 focuses particularly on the report format for interventional clinical trials, but the basic principles may be applied to other types of clinical studies (ICH E3 Q&A). The design of the study report should be part of the quality by design process. The report should describe the critical to quality factors in the study. The reporting of study results should be comprehensive, accurate, and timely.

Consideration should be given to providing a factual summary of the overall study results to study participants in an objective, balanced and nonpromotional manner, including relevant safety information and any limitations of the study. In addition, consideration could be given to providing individual participants with information about their study specific results (e.g., their treatment arm, test results). The information should be conveyed by someone involved in the health management of the participant (e.g., the clinical investigator). Participants should be informed about the information they will receive and when they will receive it at the time of providing informed consent.

The transparency of clinical research in drug development includes the registration of clinical studies, before they start, on publicly accessible and recognised databases, and the public posting of clinical study results. Adopting such practices for observational studies also promotes transparency. Making objective and unbiased information publicly available can benefit public health in general, as well as the indicated patient populations, through enhancing clinical research, reducing unnecessary clinical studies, and informing decisions in clinical practice.

7. CONSIDERATIONS IN IDENTIFYING CRITICAL TO QUALITY FACTORS

The identification of critical to quality factors should be supported by proactive, cross functional discussions and decision making at the time of study planning, as described in

Section 3. Different factors will stand out as critical for different types of studies, following the concepts introduced in Sections 4 through 6. In designing a study, the following aspects should be considered, where applicable, to support the identification of critical to quality factors:

- Engagement of all relevant stakeholders, including patients, is considered during study planning and design.
- The prerequisite non-clinical studies, and where applicable, clinical studies, are complete and adequate to support the study being designed.
- The study objectives address relevant scientific questions appropriate for a given study's role in the development programme, taking into account the accumulated knowledge about the product.

• The clinical study design supports a meaningful comparison of the effects of the drug when compared to the chosen control group.

• Adequate measures are used to protect participants' rights, safety, and welfare (informed consent process, Institutional Review Board/Ethics Committee review, investigator and clinical study site training, pseudonymisation).

• Information provided to the study participants should be clear and understandable.

• Competencies and training required for the study by sponsor and investigator staff, relevant to their role, should be identified.

• The feasibility of the study should be assessed to ensure the study is operationally viable.

• The number of participants included, the duration of the study, and the frequency of study visits are sufficient to support the study objective.

• The eligibility criteria should be reflective of the study objectives and be well documented in the clinical study protocol.

• The protocol specifies the collection of data needed to meet the study objectives, understand the benefit/risk of the drug, and monitor participant safety.

• The choice of response variables and the methods to assess them are well-defined and support evaluation of the effects of the drug.

• Clinical study procedures include adequate measures to minimise bias (e.g., randomisation, blinding).

• The statistical analysis plan is pre-specified and defines the analysis methods appropriate for the endpoints and the populations of interest.

• Systems and processes are in place that support the study conduct to ensure the integrity of critical study data.

• The extent and nature of study monitoring are tailored to the specific study design and objectives and the need to ensure participants' safety.

• The need for and appropriate role of a data monitoring committee is assessed.

• The reporting of the study results is planned, comprehensive, accurate, timely, and publicly accessible.

These considerations are not exhaustive and may not apply to all studies. Other aspects may need to be considered to identify the critical to quality factors for each individual study.

ICMR guidelines in conduct of Clinical trials

7.0 A clinical trial is any research/study that prospectively assigns human participants or groups of humans to one or more health-related intervention(s) to evaluate the effects on health outcomes.

The intervention could be drugs, vaccines, biosimilars, biologics, phytopharmaceuticals, radiopharmaceuticals, diagnostic agents, public health interventions, socio-behavioural interventions, technologies, devices, surgical techniques or interventions involving traditional systems of medicine, etc.

Clinical trials are usually well-controlled studies. They use a design that allows comparison of participants treated with an investigational product (IP)/any intervention to a control population (receiving placebo or an active comparator), so that the effect of the IP/intervention can be determined and differentiated from effects of other influences, such as spontaneous change, placebo effect, concomitant treatment/intervention or observer expectations.

As per the amended Schedule Y (2005) of the Drugs and Cosmetics Rules, 1945, a clinical trial refers to a systematic study of new drugs on human subjects to generate data for discovering and/or verifying the clinical, pharmacological (including pharmacodynamic and pharmacokinetic) and/or adverse effect with the objectives determining safety and/or efficacy of a new drug. The academic clinical trial as per GSR 313 (E) dated 16 March 201627 is a clinical trial intended for academic purposes in respect of approved drug formulations for any new indication or new route of administration or new dose or new dosage form. An EC has to approve such studies after due consideration of benefits and risks and all other ethical aspects and the licensing authority has to be informed as per the prescribed procedures.

7.1 General guidelines

7.1.1 All clinical trials must be planned, conducted and reported in a manner that ensures that the dignity, rights, safety and well-being of participants are protected.

7.1.2 Before a trial is initiated, foreseeable risks and inconveniences should be weighed against the anticipated benefit (direct or indirect) for the individual trial participant and/or society. A trial should be initiated and continued only if the anticipated benefits justify the risks. Clinical Trials of Drugs and other Interventions

7.1.3 All clinical trials must be conducted in accordance with the Indian GCP guidelines, the Declaration of Helsinki (2013 or later versions as applicable), National Guidelines for Biomedical and Health Research Involving Human Participants (2017), the Drugs and Cosmetics Act (1940), and Rules (1945), and applicable amendments (including Schedule Y), and other relevant regulations and guidelines, wherever applicable.

7.1.4 A participant's right to agree or decline consent to take part in a clinical trial must be respected and her/his refusal should not affect routine care.

7.1.5 At all times, the privacy of a participant must be maintained and any information gathered from the participant be kept strictly confidential.

7.1.6 Therapeutic misconception in potential participants must be avoided (for example, by having a co-investigator who is not the primary treating physician administer the consent).

7.1.7 At least one member of the research team must have the qualifications and adequate research experience in the subject on which the trial is planned.

7.1.8 All clinical trials must be approved by an EC that is constituted and functions in accordance with these guidelines and applicable regulations.

7.1.9 Applicable regulatory approvals must be taken (if required).

7.1.10 All clinical trials must be registered with the Clinical Trial Registry -India (CTRI).

7.1.11 Written informed consent must be obtained from each participant before any research related procedure is performed.

7.1.12 If the trial is planned in a vulnerable population, it should be undertaken only with due justification and with all possible participant protections in place.

7.1.13 Procedures to assure the quality of every aspect of the trial should be implemented.

7.1.14 SAEs must be reported for all trials and if applicable timelines as specified by regulators to be followed (within 24 hours to the sponsor, EC and regulator, if applicable, followed

by a due analysis report in 14 days).

7.1.15 Free medical management of AEs and SAEs, irrespective of relatedness to the clinical

trial, should be given for as long as required or till such time as it is established that theinjury is not related to the clinical trial, whichever is earlier.

7.1.16 In addition, compensation must be given if the SAE is proven to be related to the trial.

7.1.17 Ancillary care may be provided to clinical trial participants for non-study/trial related illnesses arising during the period of the trial. This could be in the form of medical care

or reference to facilities, as may be appropriate.Clinical Trials of Drugs and other Interventions

7.1.18 Institutional mechanisms must be established to allow for insurance coverage of trial related or unrelated illnesses (ancillary care) and compensation wherever deemed necessary by the EC.

7.2 Clinical drug/vaccine development

7.2.1 The broad aim of the process of clinical development of a new drug or vaccine, (referred to as an IP) is to find out whether there is a dose range and schedule at which the drug

can be shown to be simultaneously safe and effective, to the extent that the benefit–risk relationship is acceptable.

Phases of drug development

Phase 0

A Phase 0 study is an exploratory study, conducted to find out whether an investigational new

drug (IND) can modulate its intended target in human beings, and to identify its distribution in the body, or describe its metabolism. This study involves very limited human exposure, and has no therapeutic or diagnostic intent. It is conducted early in the process of drug development and allows for human use of an IND with less preclinical data and in lower doses than is required for a conventional Phase I study. This is invariably part of a regulatory study.

Phase I

Phase I starts with the initial administration of an investigational new drug/vaccine into humans. These studies usually have non-therapeutic objectives. Phase I studies are conducted on healthy participants or patients, in the case of drugs with significant potential toxicity, such as cytotoxic drugs.

Studies conducted in Phase I typically involve:

a) estimation of initial safety and tolerability;

b) pharmacokinetics;

c) assessment of pharmacodynamics (biological effects for vaccines); or early measurement of drug activity (including immunogenicity in case of vaccines).

Phase II

Phase II starts with the initiation of studies in which the primary aim is to explore therapeutic efficacy (immunogenicity in case of vaccines) in patients/participants. Phase II studies are conducted on a group of patients or participants who are selected according to relatively narrow criteria, and are closely monitored. Early studies in Phase II are designed to estimate the dose response. Later studies are planned to confirm the dose response.

Phase III

Phase III begins with the initiation of studies in which the primary objective is to demonstrate or confirm therapeutic benefit or protection rate (in case of vaccines). Such studies are:

a) designed to confirm the evidence from Phase II studies about the safety and efficacy of

a drug or vaccine for use in the intended indication and recipient population;

b) planned to provide an adequate basis for impact on clinical practice or for obtaining marketing approval, where applicable;

c) conducted to explore new uses of an already marketed drug for a new indication, dosage form, dosage regimen, or route of administration. If such studies are intended for ultimate commercial use of the drug, they require regulatory approval. Research on off label use comes under this category. See section 7.16.4 for further details; and

d) planned as bridging trials and pivotal trials.

Phase IV

Phase IV begins after product approval and is related to the use of the intervention for the approved indications. These studies are important for optimizing the use of the product.

They may include:

a) post-marketing surveillance – the practice of monitoring the safety of a product after it has been released in the market;

b) Phase IV clinical trials – a study conducted to assess safety, tolerability and effectiveness of a marketed product when prescribed in the usual manner in accordance with the terms of the marketing authorization, such as the efficacy and safety in special populations.

c) outcomes research – which aim to study the effectiveness and efficiency of the intervention after its introduction for human use; and

d) registries – which propose to maintain data about patients with certain shared characteristics and who have received a particular intervention (for example a stent) that collects ongoing and supporting data over time on well-defined outcomes of interest.

7.2.2 Ethical considerations

All clinical trials should be scientifically and ethically sound. The sponsor of the study, the researcher, institution, EC, and regulatory authority (if applicable) are responsible for ethical conduct of a study. Before any clinical trial is initiated, adequate data from preclinical investigations or previous clinical studies should be generated and be sufficient to indicate that the intervention is acceptably safe for the proposed investigation in humans.

The investigator should make an assessment to determine if a clinical trial is under the regulatory ambit and if so, to ensure that all requirements as specified by CDSCO must also be followed. If required, the EC may provide relevant guidance to the members in deciding the same.

• Phase I (for drugs and vaccines) studies

- All Phase I trials require EC approval and applicable regulatory approvals.
- A Phase I study is a non-therapeutic trial in which there is no anticipated direct clinical benefit to the participant. In general, therefore, it should be conducted in participants who can give voluntary informed consent themselves and who can sign and date the written informed consent forms themselves, unless the therapy under investigation is for diseases specific to those who cannot give consent, such as children, in which case consent of the LAR may be taken.
- As Phase I studies are most often conducted in healthy volunteers, all safeguards to protect the participants must be established, especially recruitment methods, payment for participation, evidence of non-coercion and consent procedures.
- When a Phase I study is conducted in participants with a disease such as cancer, due consideration should be given to the seriousness of the medical condition and the study procedures planned.
- The study protocol should describe measures to minimize the risks of a Phase I clinical trial in healthy volunteers and patients.

The measures to be taken to minimize risks in a Phase I clinical trial include:

• exclusion of participants who may be at increased risk from the study;

• careful review of investigational procedures posing high risk of physical harm or serious discomfort;

• evaluation of available data to decide if the IP or procedures proposed in the protocol have been associated with SAEs and steps taken to prevent or minimize such risks;

and

• careful monitoring of the condition of participants and intervention to manage adverse events.

Risks of Phase I clinical trials

- A Phase I study unit must have robust resources and tested procedures for immediate resuscitation and maintenance of life support and onward transfer to an intensive care unit, if necessary.
- A Phase I study with a high-risk IP, such as first-in-human, biologic should be carried out in a hospital where experienced personnel and facilities are immediately available to manage medical emergencies.
- Medical pharmacologist/physicians trained in clinical pharmacology should be involved in Phase I studies.

Phase II, III and IV studies

- All Phase II and III studies require EC approval and applicable regulatory approvals.
- In the case of Phase IV studies, the following are some examples of studies that require EC approval:

(i) Phase IV clinical trials
(ii) Outcome research
(iii) Registries
(iv) Data that is used to answer any research question
(v) New use/route/dose/dosage form/combination/regimen of a
marketed drug for non-commercial purpose such as academic research

- In addition to EC approval, a Phase IV clinical trial on drugs with a market authorization of less than 4 years requires regulatory approval (CDSCO).

- Routine post-marketing surveillance (PMS) may not require EC approval.

Vaccine studies

Vaccines can be prophylactic and/or therapeutic in nature. The guidelines for conducting clinical trials on investigational vaccines are similar to those governing a drug trial. However, the phases of these trials differ from drug trials as given below:

- Phase I is for the study of dose and route of administration for determining its safety and biological effects, including immunogenicity, and should involve low risk.
- Bridging studies in vaccine trials are conducted to support clinical comparability of efficacy, safety and immunogenicity of new formulations when there is a change in vaccine composition with regard to adjuvant, preservative, or a change in manufacturing process, site or scale. These are performed either before or after product licensure.

Combination vaccines –

The main goal in efficacy trial design of such vaccines is to evaluate the efficacy of each antigenic component. Non-inferiority trials should be conducted to demonstrate that the combination vaccine is not inferior in terms of immunogenicity or efficacy to vaccines with individual components.

- Vaccines administered simultaneously with combination vaccines – Immunogenicity and safety data should be obtained in Phase III (pre-licensure) studies to support the simultaneous administration of a new vaccine with already licensed vaccines that would be given to the same target population using the same (or overlapping) schedule.

Types of vaccines are listed below

- Live and attenuated vaccines (measles, mumps, rubella and chickenpox)
- Inactivated vaccine (flu vaccine)
- Toxoid vaccines (diphtheria and tetanus vaccines)
- DNA vaccines
- Recombinant vector vaccine

Some vaccines that contain active or live (attenuated) micro-organisms can possibly possess a small risk of producing that particular infection. The participant to be vaccinated should be informed of this.

- The participants in control groups, or when subjected to ineffective vaccines, run a risk of contracting the disease. In such an event, provisions be made to provide free treatment for the disease.
- For recombinant DNA vaccines and products, applicable governmental guidelines and regulations should be followed.
- Post-trial, the control group should receive the complete dose of an effective

vaccine (either one that is already available or the investigational vaccine).

7.3 Bioavailability/bioequivalence study

Bioavailability (BA) is the measurement of the proportion of the total administered dose of a therapeutically active drug that reaches the systemic circulation and is therefore available at the site of action.

Bioequivalence (BE) is a term used in pharmacokinetics when there are two or more medicinal products (proprietary preparations of a drug), containing the same active substance that need to be compared in vivo for biological equivalence. These comparative studies are used to assess if the new version (generic) produces the same concentration in the systemic circulation when given to human participants. If two products are said to be bioequivalent it means that they would be expected to be, for all intents and purposes, the same.

BE studies are used as surrogates for clinical effectiveness data for generic drugs where no clinical difference is anticipated between the two products.

7.3.1 Ethical issues

• All BA/BE studies should be scientifically sound and conducted in compliance with principles of ethical conduct described earlier for a Phase I study.

• Ethical conduct of BA/BE study requires evaluation of the benefit–risk profile of:

a. the reference (comparator) and investigational (generic) product; and

b. the study procedures such as indoor stay, fasting, screening, blood sampling.

• BA/BE studies are usually conducted in healthy volunteers. Hence, they have no direct benefit to the participant but may pose risks due to the adverse effects of the drug. Therefore, all safeguards to protect participants must be in place.

• The EC must carefully review the recruitment methods, payment for participation and consent procedures. Volunteers often regularly participate in such studies at the cost of their health and care should be taken that taking part in multiple trials is avoided by maintaining volunteer registries, biometry, follow up, etc. Care must be taken to maintain confidentiality of biometric data.

• The amount of blood drawn for a BA/BE study should be within physiological limits irrespective of study design and the EC should take specific note on the amount of blood drawn depending on whether the individual is a healthy adult or a child or a patient.

7.4 Ethical implications of study designs

Clinical trials have a wide range of methodological approaches. ECs need to look into the details of the ethical concerns involved.

7.4.1 If a SAE occurs in a blinded study, and it is imperative, in the interest of managing the event to know what the patient was receiving, unblinding mechanisms should be available to the researcher.

7.4.2 When an available therapy is effective in preventing serious harm, such as death or irreversible morbidity in the clinical trial population, it is inappropriate to use a placebo control.

7.4.3 Placebo may be used as a comparator under the conditions given below

A placebo may be used when:

• there is no established effective therapy available;

• withholding an established effective therapy would not expose participants to serious harm, but may cause temporary discomfort or delay in relief of symptoms;

• if the disease is self-limited; or

• the use of an established effective therapy as a comparator would not yield scientifically reliable results and the use of placebo would not add any additional risk of serious or irreversible harm to the participants.

7.4.4 If a placebo must be used for scientific reasons, then certain precautions must be exercised. These should be reviewed and approved by the EC.

Precautions to be taken when a placebo is used

1. The protocol must have added safeguards to protect participants from harm, such as but not restricted to having clear-cut withdrawal criteria, intensive monitoring and rescue medications.

2. Use an add-on trial design where the IP or placebo are added to standard of care.

1. Expose fewer patients to placebo groups, for example by having 2:1 randomization with 2 participants receiving IP against 1 getting placebo (unbalanced randomization).
2. An active comparator as an additional arm may also be included in such trials where randomization can be, for example, 2:2:1 (IP: active comparator: placebo)

5. Ensure transition to standard of care/active medicine for study participants after research is completed, including post-trial arrangements for implementing any positive trial results

7.5 Multicentric trials

Multicentric trials are carried out with a primary aim of providing a sound basis for the subsequent generalization of its results.

7.5.1 ECs of all sites should follow all applicable regulatory guidelines, including registration with regulating bodies.

7.5.2 The ethical review procedure for common review of multicentric research is given in section 4.10. Not applicable for clinical trials under Drugs and Cosmetic Act.

7.6 Phytopharmaceutical drugs

The Drugs and Cosmetics Rules, 8th Amendment, 2015,29 defines a new class of drugs called phytopharmaceutical drug as "purified and standardized fraction with defined minimum four bio-active or phyto-chemical compounds (qualitatively and quantitatively assessed) of an extract of a medicinal plant or its part, for internal or external use of human beings or animals for diagnosis, treatment, mitigation or prevention of any disease or disorder but does not include administration by parenteral route". All details described in 7.2 also apply to this group of drugs.

7.7 Device trials

7.7.1 A medical device is defined as a medical tool which does not achieve its primary intended action in or on the human body by pharmacological, immunological, or metabolic means but which may be assisted in its intended function by such means. It may be an instrument, apparatus, appliance, implant, material or other article, whether used alone or in combination, including a software or an accessory, intended by its manufacturer to be used specially for human beings or animals for one or more of the specific purposes of:

(i) detection, diagnosis, prevention, monitoring;

(ii) treatment or alleviation of any physiological condition or state of health, or illness;

(iii) replacement or modification or support of the anatomy or congenital deformity;

(iv) supporting or sustaining life;

(v) disinfection of medical devices; or

(vi) control of conception.

- Clinical trials should be conducted in accordance with the ethical principles described in these guidelines, Indian GCP as well as applicable regulations for medical and medicated devices, that is, GSR 78 (E) dated 31.1.2017 or as per amendments/modifications issued from time-to-time.
- Safety data of the medical device in animals should be obtained and likely risks posed by the device should be considered in the same way as for a new drug under the Drugs and Cosmetics Rules, 1945.
- Apart from safety considerations of the device, the procedures to introduce the medical device in the patient should also be evaluated for safety.
- Devices should be provided free of cost or, if expensive, at feasible reduced rates.
- Avoid therapeutic misconceptions.
- Any AE/SAE should be reported within timelines as per the schedule for a new drug. Here user error could also be the cause of AE/SAE.
- If the participant wants to withdraw from a trial, it may not be possible to remove the internal device. This must be explained to the participant before enrolling her/him. The participant, however, should be allowed to opt out of continuing in the trial without prejudice to her/his ongoing treatment.
- If feasible, post-trial obligations should be emphasized with the sponsor.
- The duration of follow-up should be long enough to detect late onset adverse reactions, especially when the device is implanted within the body.

7.7.2 Devices could be used internally or externally for diagnosis, treatment, mitigation or prevention of disease or disorder. Depending upon risks involved, devices (other than in vitro diagnostic devices) are classified as given below.

Classification of medical devices

- Class A - Low Level of risk-

  Examples: Thermometers/ bandages /tongue depressors

- Class B Low Level of risk –

  Examples: moderate Hypodermic needles /suction equipment

- Class C Moderate Level of risk –

  Examples: high Lung ventilator /bone fixation plate

- Class D High Level of risk-

  Examples: Heart valves/implantable defibrillator

7.7.3 Devices used for in vitro diagnosis could be a reagent, calibrator, control material, kit, instrument, apparatus, equipment, system, or specimen receptacle, whether used alone or in combination with any other such devices, that is intended by its manufacturer

to be used in vitro for examination of any specimen, including any blood or tissue donation derived from the human body solely or principally for the purpose of providing information. The information could be related to:

(i) a physiological or pathological state;

(ii) congenital deformity;

(iii) determining the safety and compatibility of any blood or tissue donation with a potential recipient thereof; or

(iv) monitoring of therapeutic measures.

• Diagnostics devices can be notified and non-notified. Notified are in vitro diagnostic devices for testing HIV, HBsAg, HCV and blood grouping. Non-notified are those for testing malaria, TB, dengue, chikungunya, typhoid, syphilis, cancer markers, etc.

7.8 Biologicals and biosimilars

Biologics (biopharmaceutical drug) can be composed of sugars, proteins, nucleic acids or complex combinations of these substances, or may be living cells or tissues. This section applies to products that are produced by means of biological processes with or without recombinant DNA technology. All aspects that are described in section 7.1 are also applicable to biologics.

7.8.1 As these are biologic substances, special care must be taken to review all data generated. Special expertise may be sought for such reviews so that foreseeable risks are well identified.

7.8.2 A thorough benefit-risk assessment must be carried out with available data.

7.8.3 If the study involves biosimilars, the product quality (manufacturing and characterization), preclinical data and bioassay must demonstrate similarity with a reference biologic.

7.8.4 All applicable and current regulations must be followed.

7.9 Clinical trials with stem cells in recent years, stem cell research has undergone rapid developments promising new leads in the treatment of several incurable diseases. According to the source and degree of expected risk to human participants, stem cell research is categorized into permissible (adult and cord blood), restricted (embryonic) and prohibited (reproductive cloning) areas of research. In India, only permissible and restricted areas of research are permitted with appropriate approvals. It is necessary to ensure that donors are not exploited and commodified.

To address issues related to stem cell research, ICMR and DBT published Guidelines for Stem Cell Research and Therapy in 2007, 2013 and revised as National Guidelines for Stem Cell Research in 2017.

7.9.1 Except haemopoietic stem cell transplantation for haematological disorders, any other uses of stem cells are categorized as research and must be conducted as clinical trials, needing the approval of the EC, IC-SCR (permissible research), National Apex Committee for Stem Cell Research and Therapy (NAC-SCRT) (restricted research) and CDSCO (IND products and drugs) as the case may be.Use of stem cells outside the domain of a clinical trial for any purpose is considered unethical and hence not permissible.

7.9.2 Clinical trials must be carried out with clinical grade cells processed as per applicable national Good Laboratory Practices (GLP), Good Manufacturing Practices (GMP) and GCP guidelines.

7.9.3 Each institution should maintain a registry of researchers who are conducting stem cell research. Researcher must be kept updated in accordance with changes in guidelines and regulations regarding use of these cells. It is also the responsibility of the institution to ensure that all current standards are applied.

7.9.4 All clinical trials must be approved by IC-SCR, which in turn should be registered with NAC-SCRT. All such studies should also be registered with CTRI. The EC should give final approval before initiation of the clinical trial.

7.10 Surgical interventions

Surgical interventions that are being studied systematically must be considered as research and follow all general principles described in these guidelines.

7.10.1 In any protocol where an established surgical intervention is to be studied, the researcher must provide references for the procedure and describe the most likely complications in the protocol for the EC to review and perform benefit-risk assessment. The frequency of each complication should also be mentioned.

7.10.2 In trials where a modification of the established surgical intervention is to be tested, the protocol and ICD must specify the need for this modification and the expected complications, if any. It is preferable that a comparative study be conducted where the conventional method is compared to the test surgical intervention.

7.10.3 In trials where an entirely new surgical intervention is being tested, the EC may insist on some animal data/ modeling data which establishes the efficacy and safety of the technique or case reports/case series that indicate benefits and describe risks.

7.10.4 During the conduct of a surgical interventional trial all adverse events must be reported to the EC and sponsor as applicable, within the specified timelines as described for drug trials.

7.10.5 Provision of free treatment and compensation for any study-related injury must be ensured for the trial participant. The EC must determine the compensation amount after the investigator has described the relatedness.

7.10.6 Due to inherent ethical issues, sham surgery should not be included in the design of clinical trials, except in cases where there are strong scientific reasons. Under such circumstances, certain conditions must be met.

Conditions for sham surgery

1. There has to be a clear description of the justifications to include a sham surgery group in the protocol, which must be assessed by the EC.
2. There should be no serious harm caused by the sham surgery.
3. The participant must get access to appropriate, relevant intervention at the end of the trial.

7.11 Community trials (public health interventions)

Community trials are studies involving whole communities and are conducted to evaluate preventive strategies like mass drug administration (MDA) trials, fortification of food, etc. Such studies typically involve the whole community. The study unit could be a group, area, institution, village, block, district, etc. and the whole population is expected to participate in the study. In such studies, different communities are randomized and allocated to different arms (see section 8 for further details).

7.12 Clinical trials of interventions in HIV/AIDS

Clinical trials in HIV positive patients could be for the evaluation of new drugs, vaccines, other preventive measures and diagnostic tests. Apart from the general ethical principles that apply to all clinical trials, some special issues need to be addressed when clinical trials are planned in patients with HIV/AIDS. Social stigma, culturally embedded myths about HIV, marginalization, lack of legal status or criminalization of some communities that are susceptible to HIV or the disparity in standards of care in different parts of the world are examples of special issues.

7.12.1 Global studies in HIV/AIDS in specific communities should receive approval from the relevant national authority and any other relevant authority, such as the HMSC, where applicable, in addition to approval from the EC.

7.12.2 When testing for HIV is done, consent and pre-test- and post-test counselling should be done as per National AIDS Control Organization (NACO) guidelines.

7.12.3 Issues that may arise because of discordant couples should be addressed before initiating any study in people living with HIV/AIDS.

7.12.4 As HIV is a sexually transmitted disease and is potentially life-threatening, the right to life of the sexual partner must be respected over the right to privacy of the HIV positive individual.

7.12.5 Phase I studies are permissible in patients with HIV/AIDS if the drug under study cannot be tested in healthy participants due to expected toxicity of the IP.

7.12.6 A combined Phase I/II or Phase II study can be conducted in this population when other therapeutic options have been exhausted.

7.12.7 When a trial with a preventive HIV vaccine is conducted, it can result in positive serology. This does not indicate HIV infection but can create problems for travel and employment. Under such circumstances, the project investigator should issue a certificate stating that the person in question was a participant in a vaccine trial and provide clarification on the result.

7.12.8 Research that involves sexual minorities or IV drug users should have community engagement (community leaders) throughout the life of the project, until completion and dissemination of results.

7.12.9 The EC may also consider co-opting a member from this community, if relevant for initial and continuing review of proposals.

7.12.10 Where possible, for example, if the drug is found useful, standard of care is not available or regulatory permissions are in place, the EC should ensure post-trial access of the IP for the participants.

7.12.11 For HIV positive persons, any research may be misconstrued as research on anti-HIV treatment and make them willing to participate. Therefore, the full implications in simple terms should be explained to HIV positive participants about any other research being done on them, such as research on hepatitis B.

7.13 Clinical trials on traditional systems of medicine Although traditional systems of medicine (termed complementary and alternate systems in the west) are known for their long history of safe and effective use, validation of safety and efficacy using scientific and evidence-based methodologies is needed for the purpose of universal acceptability, gaining confidence of practitioners and satisfaction of end users in the products. Government of India has recognized Ayurveda, Siddha, Unani, Yoga, Naturopathy and Homeopathy as traditional Indian systems of medicine. In 2012, Sowa Rigpa (Amchi or Tibetan medicine) was also added to the list. Ministry of AYUSH (Ayurveda, Unani, Siddha and Homeopathy) governs and regulates these systems. Drugs under these systems come under the Drugs and Cosmetics Act, 1940, as ASU and H drugs. Drugs/formulations under these systems of medicine are classified into two groups.

Classification of drugs/formulation under AYUSH

1. Classical preparations/formulations are those that are to be clinically evaluated for the same indication for which it is being used or as has been described in classical authoritative texts. These classical drugs are manufactured and named in accordance with the formulations described in the authoritative texts.

2. Patent or proprietary products are formulations containing only such ingredients mentioned in the formulae described in the authoritative books of Ayurveda (or Yoga, Naturopathy, Unani, Siddha, Homoeopathy, SOWA–RIGPA systems, as the case may be), medicine specified in the first schedule, but differ to create a new combination, or use innovation or invention to manufacture products different from the classical medicine. However, this group does not include a medicine which is administered by parenteral route.

7.13.1 Research on AYUSH and ASU interventions of traditional medicines (TM) including external medicines/ therapeutic procedures, folk medicines, and patent and proprietary medicines of TM involving human participants should be conducted in accordance with all the ethical principles described in these guidelines including SAE reporting and compensation, AYUSH GCP guidelines32, as well as other applicable regulations of the country.

7.13.2 If IPs/comparators of more than one traditional system of medicine are to be investigated, then investigator(s) from the respective systems should be included in the study as co-investigator(s).

7.13.3 The EC must co-opt a person with relevant expertise (an expert of that traditional system of medicine) to review the proposal, especially the benefits and risks of the intervention, eligibility criteria, doses of interventions, outcomes planned and traditional method of evaluation, if necessary.

7.13.4 When a folklore medicine/ethnomedicine is ready for commercialization after it has been scientifically found effective, benefit sharing should be ensured and the legitimate rights/share of the tribe or community from which the knowledge was gathered should be taken care of appropriately while applying for the IPRs and patents for the product.

7.13.5 While conducting trials using intervention(s) of traditional medicine, the investigator must ensure the quality of the interventional product.

7.14 Trials of diagnostic agents A diagnostic agent refers to any pharmaceutical product used as part of a diagnostic test, together with the equipment and procedures that are needed to assess the test result, and that is either administered into or onto the human body. Diagnostic agents must be considered as new drugs and therefore clinical trials involving diagnostic agents should be conducted in accordance with all the ethical principles described in these guidelines, Indian GCP guidelines, as well as applicable regulations of the country.

7.14.1 Benefit-risk assessment involving diagnostic agents additionally includes the assessment of benefits, such as technical performance, diagnostic performance, impact on diagnostic thinking and impact on patient management/outcome, and the risks related to the agent itself, such as immunogenicity, allergic reactions, but also risks related to incorrect handling of test procedures or incorrect diagnosis induced by its use.

7.14.2 The EC must review the pharmacology, toxicology, pharmacokinetics and safety data (preclinical and clinical data as applicable) especially for diagnostic agents which come in contact with skin or mucosal surfaces in the human body (in vivo use). Special expertise may be co-opted in the EC for review of such products.

7.14.3 These trials are usually comparative, the comparator being the reference/gold standard test to diagnose the disease. Hence, the protocol must state clearly the choice of the reference with justification. Likewise, omission of a reference standard as comparator must also be justified.

7.14.4 A placebo may be used as comparator when the response to a diagnostic test is being assessed using subjective evaluation criteria, for example, skin changes in a skin prick test or for the assessment of tolerability. There have to be clear justifications in the protocol for the use of a placebo and no irreversible harm should occur to the participant. Post-trial access to the standard of care diagnostic test must be assured.

7.14.5 Safety follow-up of patients in these trials should not be limited to the duration of the diagnostic procedure but may be extended for a longer period according to the pharmacokinetic and pharmacodynamic properties of the diagnostic agent.

7.14.6 Long-term safety (when appropriate) should be assessed especially for agents accumulating in the body, such as deposits of gadolinium in bones and skin.

7.15 Radioactive materials and X-rays

Radioactive substances contain a radioactive isotope, and may be used for therapeutic or diagnostic purposes. If the radioactive substance is to be tested as a drug then all the ethical considerations described in previous sections will apply. However, if it is to be evaluated as a diagnostic agent then section 7.15 applies. The permissible radiation limits when radioactive materials and X-rays are being evaluated must comply with regulatory authority guidelines. In India, the agency that regulates radioactive materials is the Bhabha Atomic Research Centre (BARC), Mumbai. Additionally, the following considerations must be applied:

7.15.1 The investigating site should have a license from the competent authority to store, handle and dispense the radioactive substance.

7.15.2 The investigator and clinical trial team must be competent and should have received appropriate training in handling radioactive substances and X-rays.

7.15.3 The protocol and ICD should clearly state the potential radiation exposure to which participants are likely to be exposed in quantitative terms to the whole body or per organ. This exposure must be within acceptable limits.

7.15.4 The EC may co-opt relevant expertise to review such protocols.

7.15.5 When a trial involving radioactive substances is planned in healthy participants, they should preferably have completed their family and receive radiation in a dose as low as permitted.

7.15.6 Women of childbearing age, children, radiation workers or any individual who has received more than the permissible amount of radiation in the past 12 months should be excluded from trials involving radioactive materials or X-rays.

7.15.7 In the event of death of a participant with a radiological implant, due precautions must be taken as per the prescribed radiation guidelines so as to ensure that relatives or close co-habitants are not exposed to radiation.

7.15.8 The protocol should make adequate provisions for detecting pregnancies to avoid risks of exposure to the embryo. Information must be given to the participant in the ICD about possible genetic damage to the offspring.

7.16 Investigator initiated clinical trials

Academic institutions routinely carry out investigator initiated clinical trials.

7.16.1 In such trials, the investigator has the dual responsibility of being an investigator as well as the sponsor.

7.16.2 Financial arrangements must be made by the institution/investigator for the conduct of the study as well as to pay for free management of research-related injury and compensation, if applicable. Funds should be made available or appropriate mechanisms be established.

7.16.3 The institution must have or introduce policies that establish mechanisms to ensure quality of the data generated and safety of the intervention, such as monitoring, auditing, DSMB, etc.

7.16.4 When academic clinical trials are planned for "off-label" use of a drug (when a drug that is marketed is being used for a new indication/new dose/formulation/route) for purely academic purposes and not for commercial use, then such clinical trials designed by researchers/academicians may not currently require regulatory approval.

However, an EC has to approve such studies after due consideration of benefits and risks and all other ethical aspects and the licensing authority has to be informed as per GSR 313(e) dated 16.3.2016 issued by CDSCO.

7.16.5 The trials must be registered in CTRI and there should be mechanism for appropriate methods for informed consent, conduct of trial and proper follow-up of patients.

7.16.6 For student conducting clinical trials as part of their academic thesis, the guide and the academic institution should take up the responsibilities of the sponsor.

7.17 Clinical trials on contraceptives

Several methods of contraception are available including, barrier methods, hormonal methods, emergency contraception, intra-uterine and surgical methods. Since these studies are conducted in healthy participants, all efforts to minimize risks must be in place and the proposed benefits must justify the foreseeable risks. The following issues must be addressed while undertaking research on contraceptives whether they be drugs, devices or surgeries:

7.17.1 All procedures for clinical trials will be applicable.

7.17.2 For a new contraceptive method, non-comparative studies can be accepted. However, a sufficient number of cycles should be studied to obtain the desired precision of the estimate of contraceptive efficacy.

7.17.3 The comparator should, whenever possible, be chosen from among marketed products with a similar mechanism of action and schedule of use.

7.17.4 In women where a non-biodegradable implant has been used, a proper follow-up for removal of the implant should be done after the trial is over or the participant has withdrawn from the trial.

7.17.5 The educational and socioeconomic level of women participants may be considered to judge whether they will be able to comprehend the use and risks associated with the particular contraceptive.

7.17.6 Participants should be clearly informed about the alternatives available for contraception.

7.17.7 Any pregnancies occurring during a contraceptive trial should be followed up for final outcome to mother and child.

7.17.8 Children born due to failure of contraceptives under study should be followed-up for any abnormalities if the woman does not opt for medical termination of pregnancy (MTP).

7.17.9 A compensation policy must be established at the beginning of the trial to provide a cover for this contingency or issues related to trial.

7.18 Pregnancy and clinical trials

Any clinical trial conducted in women of childbearing age raises ethical issues that need to be addressed. Similarly, studies conducted in women who are pregnant need to be evaluated with care and ethical issues addressed.

7.18.1 When clinical trials are conducted in women of childbearing age, they must be counselled to use effective contraceptive methods. These must be stated in the ICD and it should be ensured that these methods are understood and followed by the woman participant.

7.18.2 In clinical trials that include women of reproductive age, there may be occasional inadvertent pregnancy. In such an instance the woman should be withdrawn from the study and efforts should be made to collect data on the drug effects as well as the outcome for both mother and foetus. This follow-up plan of pregnancy and care of foetus must be stated in the protocol and ICD.

7.18.3 EC to review the need if, during research participation, the female sexual partner of a male participant gets pregnant, the protocol and ICD must state a plan to document this and both pregnant partner and foetus must be followed for outcome and reported.

7.18.4 Pregnant women have the right to participate in clinical research relevant to their healthcare needs such as gestational diabetes, pregnancy induced hypertension and HIV.

7.18.5 Benefit–risk assessment must be done at all stages for both the mother and the foetus.

7.18.6 Research involving pregnant women and foetuses must only take place when the object of the research is to obtain new knowledge directly relevant to the foetus, the pregnancy or lactation. The criteria described in Box 7.8 must be fulfilled.

Criteria for research involving pregnant women and foetuses

1. Appropriate studies on animals and non-pregnant individuals should have been completed (if applicable).
2. The risk to the foetus must be the least possible risk for achieving the objectives of the trials, including when the purpose of the trial is to meet the health needs of the mother or the foetus, or the risk to the foetus is minimal.
3. Researchers should not participate in decision making regarding any termination of a pregnancy.
4. No procedural changes, which will cause greater than minimal risk to the woman or foetus, will be introduced into the procedure for terminating the pregnancy solely in the interest of the trial.

7.18.7 Women should not be encouraged to discontinue nursing for the sake of participation in research except in those studies where breast-feeding is harmful to the infant. In case a woman decides to cease breastfeeding, harm of cessation to the nursing child should be properly assessed. Supplementary food, such as milk formula should be considered in such instances.

7.18.8 For the conduct of research related to termination of pregnancy only pregnant women who undergo MTP as per the Medical Termination of Pregnancy Act, 1971 can be included.

7.19 Clinical trials in oncology

There are several ethical issues when research is conducted in terminally ill patients for whom this may be a last hope for cure, or a way to get free treatment for their disease which may be otherwise beyond their reach. These need to be addressed during planning, conduct, oversight and publication of such trials. Three primary factors motivate participation in oncology clinical trials: hope for a cure; altruism that even if the patient does not benefit, it may ultimately help others; and trust that the physician would not recommend a treatment (the investigational drug) unless she/he thought it might be helpful.

All criteria described in section 7.1 and stated in drug trials, biologics and radioactive substances, apply to oncology clinical trials. In addition, while reviewing oncology studies, the following should be kept in mind:

7.19.1 Phase I studies with oncology drugs are conducted in patients. However, there may or may not be any benefit and there may be a high degree of therapeutic misconception. Further, there will be foreseeable and unforeseeable risks that need to be considered before a protocol is approved.

7.19.2 The patient population may be vulnerable as they are often terminally ill. Economically disadvantaged populations may participate in the research to gain free access to an intervention. It is important to ensure that the participant has understood that this is research and the benefits expected may be small or they may not occur at all.

7.19.3 Participants must be made to understand that they may be randomized to a placebo group and therefore receive an inert drug, in case of a placebo-controlled study.

7.19.4 If the trial is a placebo- or active-controlled trial, all the groups must be given the current standard of care to which the IP, placebo or active control is added.

7.19.5 Perceptions of benefits and risks may be different for patients, healthcare workers and EC members. All these perspectives must be taken into consideration while reviewing the protocol.

7.19.6 Undue inducement must be avoided.

7.19.7 Patients should not be charged for any intervention including standard of care in the control arm. If the trial is an add-on design, the background standard of care may not be given free. The EC should review this carefully.

7.19.8 A post-trial access plan must be in place for patients who show benefit from an IP. In case it is a placebo controlled trial, those participants who have been in the placebo group may be offered post-trial access to the IP if found effective in other patients.

7.20 Clinical trials of products using any new technology

If any product using new technologies (such as nanotechnology) is developed for human use and is to be evaluated in human beings, the following ethical issues have to be taken into consideration in addition to all the general ethical guidelines for clinical trials as elaborated in the guidelines.

7.20.1 Compliance with GLP, GMP, and GCP norms should be observed in research using new technology products.

7.20.2 Before the use of a new technology product in a human being, preclinical studies should be carried out and all applicable regulatory requirements fulfilled.

7.20.3 The new technology-based products should be contained and released into the environment in a step-wise manner after clearance from the appropriate authority regarding environmental safety.

7.20.4 Differing process based technologies can result in similarly functioning biological products which can give rise to IPR issues.

7.20.5 The research on new technologies should have a well-established mechanism or system for assessing the risk, both in terms of severity and temporality. The unpredictable metabolic behaviour in a human system during clinical trial cannot exclude long-term side effects which may manifest later, leading to compensation issues.

7.20.6 Training of all stakeholders should address issues regarding safe research, handling of products, environmental safety and community misconceptions.

7.21 Synthetic biology

Synthetic biology is the application of science, technology and engineering to "facilitate and accelerate the design, manufacture and/or modification of genetic material of living organisms".The ethical, legal and social issues pertain to the impact of this science on society, biosafety, biosecurity, IPRs, governance of such research, and socioeconomics. Creation of organisms, molecular compounds and biological systems by manipulating biology through standardized engineering techniques has led to the rise of the biotechnology industry which includes genetically modified organisms, stem cells, cloning, artificial life forms like biofuels, bioweapons, vaccines, diagnostics, etc. Software and bioinformatics as design tools, along with constructional and diagnostic tools, play a major role in the synthesis. EC review, pre-market approval and registration should be aimed at protection of human beings and the environment.

7.21.1 Special considerations

- Precautionary principle: This applies to the prevention of harm to humans, environment and ecosystem because development of a new technology may emit hazardous elements like X-ray radiation, electro-magnetic currents and non-ionizing magnetic waves in the environment, which may manifest only later. Safety measures should be followed as per the Environmental Protection Act, 1986, Atomic Energy Act34, Biomedical Waste Management Rules35, and other relevant laws.
- Biosecurity: Sometimes, the product can have dual use, that is, one beneficial use for a particular purpose and the other for harmful use which could be unintentional or intentional, for example, use as a biological weapon. Therefore, to maintain security, the ICMR code of conduct for researchers involved in life sciences should be followed along with creation of a system for reporting and maintaining vigilance to prevent misuse. There should be effective partnership between researchers and policy makers to create a secure system.

- GLP, GMP and GCP should be observed when conducting clinical trials.
- Products should be contained and released into the environment in a step-wise manner after clearance from the appropriate authority regarding its safety. Training should be given for safe handling ofthe product and conduct of research and should address community misconceptions.
- Testing of biomaterials and biocompatibility should be as per relevant Indian regulatory standards or American Society for Testing and Materials (ASTM)international standards until Indian standards for biomaterials are in place. The testing of such standards shall be done in a laboratory certified by the National Accreditation Board for Testing and Calibration Laboratories (NABL).
- Appropriate training for safety of healthcare workers should be given and they should be provided periodic health check-ups due to exposure to occupational risks.

Drug Safety Reporting

IND application sponsors are required to notify FDA in a written safety report of:

any adverse experience associated with the use of the drug that is both serious and unexpected or any findings from tests in laboratory animals that suggest a significant risk for human subjects including reports of mutagenicity, teratogenicity, and carcinogenicity.

Adverse event means any untoward medical occurrence associated with the use of a drug in humans, whether or not considered drug related.

Suspected adverse reaction means any adverse event for which there is a reasonable possibility that the drug caused the adverse event. For the purposes of IND safety reporting, 'reasonable possibility' means there is evidence to suggest a causal relationship between the drug and the adverse event. A suspected adverse reaction implies a lesser degree of certainty about causality than an adverse reaction.

Adverse reaction means any adverse event caused by a drug. Adverse reactions are a subset of all suspected adverse reactions where there is reason to conclude that the drug caused the event.

Unexpected adverse event or suspected adverse reaction refers to an event or reaction that is not listed in the investigator's brochure or is not listed at the specificity or severity that has been observed; or, if an investigator's brochure is not required or available, is not consistent with the risk information described in the general investigational plan or elsewhere in the current IND application.

Serious adverse event or suspected adverse reaction refers to an event or reaction that, in the view of either the investigator or sponsor, results in any of the following outcomes: death, a life-threatening adverse event, in-patient hospitalization or prolongation of existing hospitalization, a persistent or significant incapacity or substantial disruption of the ability to conduct normal life functions, or a congenital anomaly or birth defect.

Life-threatening adverse event or suspected adverse reaction is considered "life-threatening" if, in the view of the investigator or sponsor, its occurrence places the patient or subject at immediate risk of death. It does not include an adverse event or suspected adverse reaction that, had it occurred in a more severe form, might have caused death.

Important medical events that may not result in death, be life-threatening, or require hospitalization may be considered serious when, based upon appropriate medical judgment, they may jeopardize the patient or research subject and may require medical or surgical intervention to prevent one of the outcomes listed as serious.

Mandatory Safety Reporting

Initial reporting: IND application sponsor must report any suspected adverse reaction or adverse reaction to study treatment that is both serious and unexpected.

Unexpected serious suspected adverse reactions and observations from animal studies suggesting significant risk to human subjects must be reported to FDA as soon as possible but no later than within 15 calendar days following the sponsor's initial receipt of the information.

Unexpected fatal or life-threatening suspected adverse reactions represent especially important safety information and must be reported to FDA as soon as possible but no later than 7 calendar days following the sponsor's initial receipt of the information.

Follow-up reporting: Any relevant additional information obtained by the sponsor that pertains to a previously submitted IND safety report must be submitted as a Follow-up IND Safety Report. Such report should be submitted without delay, as soon as the information is available but no later than 15 calendar days after the sponsor receives the information.

All IND safety reports must be submitted on Form 3500A (if from clinical trials) or in a narrative format (if from animal or epidemiological studies) and be accompanied by Form 1571 (PDF - 830KB). The type of report (initial or follow-up) should be checked in the respective boxes on Forms 3500A and 1571. See Instructions for Completing Form 3500A.

The submission must be identified as:

"IND safety report" for 15-day reports, or

"7-day IND safety report" for unexpected fatal or life-threatening suspected adverse reaction reports, or

"Follow-up IND safety report" for follow-up information.

The report must be submitted to an appropriate Review division that has the responsibility to review the IND application under which the safety report is submitted. FDA recommends that sponsors submit safety reports electronically. Other means of rapid communication to the respective review division's Regulatory Project Manager (e.g., telephone, facsimile transmission, email) may also be used.

For detailed explanation of the above definitions, requirements, and procedures related to IND application safety reports and the responsibilities of IND applications sponsors with regard to such reporting, refer to Guidance for Industry and Investigators: Safety Reporting Requirements for INDs and BA/BE Studies.

For additional information on safety reporting refer to the Final Rule: Investigational New Drug Safety Reporting Requirements for Human Drug and Biological Products and Safety Reporting Requirements for Bioavailability and Bioequivalence Studies in Humans.

Sponsor Responsibilities—Safety Reporting Requirements and Safety Assessment for IND and Bioavailability/ Bioequivalence Studies Guidance for Industry

Investigator Responsibilities – Safety Reporting for Investigational Drugs and Devices.

Questions

1.Elist the steps of drug development process?

2.Define clinical research?

3.Wha is FDA Post marketing drug safety monitorin?

4.Define active surveillance?

5.Explain in detail about drug development process?

6.What is mean by investigator New Drug Applicatin (IND)?

7.Name 3 types of IND?

8.Enlist different categories of IND?

9.Role of CDER (center for drug evaluation and research)?

10.What are guidence documents for IND?

11.What is CFR(Code of federal regulations) in clinical research?

12.Give any two examples for IND forms?

13.Explain in detail about instructions for filling out form FDA 3926?

14.What is mean by pre IND consultation program?

15. Explain in detail about ethics in biomedical research?

16.What is mean by declaration of Helsinki?

17.What are the Principles of ethics in biomedical research?

18.What are the rationale for biomedical research?

19.Explain the statement of general principles in biomedical research involving human participants?

20.Role and responsibilities of Ethical Committe in clinical trial?

21.IRE/IEC Responsibilities?
22.Compositions, Functions and operations of IRB/IEC?
23.Procedure of IRB?
24.Ethical issues in biomedical Research?
25.What are the challenges in implimentation in ethical guidelines?
26.What are ICH-GCP guidelines to conduct clinical trial?
27.Explain ICMR guidelines to conducting clinical trial?
28.Explain about Drug safety reporting?
29.Define Adverse event, suspected adverse reaction, unexpected adverse event, serious adverse event.

CHAPTER TWO

Types and Designs used in Clinical Research

Planning and execution of clinical trials

A clinical trial is an experiment aimed at testing a hypothesis regarding the efficacy of a given intervention on an event, symptom or impaired quality of life in patients with a defined condition and a particular profile.

Steps of the planning phase:

Step 0. Idea
Step 1. Literature overview
Step 2. Problem formulation
Step 3. Synopsis
Step 4. Call for investigators
Step 5. Draft protocol
Step 6. Fund seeking
Step 7. Patient consent
Step 8. Ethical boards
Step 9. Study organization
Step 10. Operating manual and procedures
Step 11. Quality assurance
Step 12. Selection of investigators
Step 13. Finalized protocol
Step 14. Operating manual and procedures
Step 15. Programming
Step 16. Investigator training
Step 17. Site supply
Step 18. First patient recruitment

Various Phases of clinical trials

Phase refers to the stage of a clinical trial studying a drug or biological product, based on definitions developed by the U.S. Food and Drug Administration (FDA). The phase is based on the study's objective, the number of participants, and other characteristics.

There are five phases: Early phase 1 (formerly listed as Phase 0), Phase 1, Phase 2, Phase 3, and Phase 4. Not Applicable is used to describe trials without FDA-defined phases, including trials of devices or behavioural interventions.

There are three phases to complete in the clinical trial process before a sponsor can submit their treatments* to the FDA for consideration to be sold on the market. Each stage of a clinical trial has its own purpose in ensuring that a treatment is safe and effective for use by the public.

Phase 0 trials

Phase 1 trials are usually the earliest trials of drugs in people. These studies aim to find out if a drug behaves in the way researchers expect it to from their laboratory studies.

Phase 0 studies usually only involve a small number of people and they only have a very small dose of a drug. The dose of the drug is too small to treat target disease, less likely to have side effects.

Phase 0 trials aim to find out things such as:

- whether the drug reaches the target cells
- what happens to the drug in the body
- how target cells in the body respond to the drug

Phase 1 trial

Phase 1 is sometimes written as phase I. They are usually small trials, recruiting only a few patients. The trial may be open to people with targeted disease, usually those who have already had all other available treatments.

Phase 1 trials aim to find out:

- how much of the drug is safe to give
- what the side effects are
- what happens to the drug in the body
- if the treatment helps to cure disease

Patients are recruited very slowly onto phase 1 trials. So even though they don't recruit many people, they can take a long time to complete.

They are often dose escalation studies. This means that the first few patients that take part have a very small dose of the drug. If all goes well, the next few people have a slightly higher dose. And so on until they find the best dose to give. The researchers monitor the side effects people have and how they feel.

In a phase 1 trial may have lots of blood tests because the researchers look at how body copes with and gets rid of the drug. They carefully record any side effects.

The main aim of phase 1 trials is to find out about doses and side effects. They need to do this first, before testing the potential new treatment to see if it works. Some people taking part may benefit from the new treatment, but many won't.

Phase 2 trials

Phase 2 is sometimes written as phase II. Not all treatments tested in a phase 1 trial make it to a phase 2 trial.

Phase 2 trials aim to find out:

- if the new treatment works well enough to be tested in a larger phase 3 trial
- which types of cancer the treatment works for
- more about side effects and how to manage them
- more about the best dose to give

These treatments have been tested in phase 1 trials, but you may still have side effects that the doctors don't know about. Treatments can affect people in different ways. Some people taking part may benefit from the new treatment, but some won't.

Phase 2 trials are usually larger than phase 1. There may be up to 100 or so people taking part. Sometimes in a phase 2 trial, a new treatment is compared with another treatment already in use, or with a dummy drug (placebo).Some phase 2 trials are randomised. This means the researchers put the people taking part into treatment groups at random.

Phase 3 trials

Phase 3 is sometimes written as phase III. These trials compare new treatments with the best currently available treatment (the standard treatment).

Phase 3 trials aim to find out:

- which treatment works better for a particular type of disease
- more about the side effects
- how the treatment affects people's quality of life

They may compare standard treatment with:

- a completely new treatment
- different doses of the same treatment
- having the same treatment more, or less, often
- a new way of giving a standard treatment (radiotherapy for example)

Phase 3 trials usually involve many more patients than phase 1 or 2. This is because differences in success rates may be small. So, the trial needs many patients to be able to show the difference.

Sometimes phase 3 trials involve thousands of people in many different hospitals and even different countries. Most phase 3 trials are randomised. This means the people taking part are put into treatment groups at random.

Phase 4 trials

Phase 4 is sometimes written as phase IV. These trials are done after a drug has been shown to work and has been licenced.

Phase 4 trials aim to find out:

- more about the side effects including the rarer side effects and safety of the drug
- what the long-term risks and benefits are
- how well the drug works when it's used more widely for people not included in the phase 3 trial

Bioavailability and Bioequivalence studies

Bioavailability

Bioavailability means the rate and extent to which the active ingredient or active moiety is absorbed from a drug product and becomes available at the site of action (21 CFR 320.1(a)). BA data provide an estimate of the fraction of the drug absorbed, as well as provide information related to the pharmacokinetics of the drug.

Bioequivalence

Bioequivalence means the absence of a significant difference in the rate and extent to which the active ingredient or active moiety in pharmaceutical equivalents or pharmaceutical alternatives become available at the site of drug action when administered at the same molar dose under similar conditions in an appropriately designed study (21 CFR 320.1(e)).

Studies to establish BE between two products are important for certain formulation or manufacturing changes occurring during the drug development and post approval stages.

In BE studies, the exposure profile of a test drug product is compared to that of a reference drug product.

BA for a given formulation provides an estimate of the relative fraction of the orally administered dose that is absorbed into the systemic circulation. BA for orally administered drug products can be documented by comparing a systemic exposure profile to that of a suitable

reference product. A profile can be generated by measuring the concentration of active ingredients and/or active moieties over time and, when appropriate, active metabolites over time in samples collected from the systemic circulation. Systemic exposure profiles reflect both release of the drug substance from the drug product and a series of possible pre systemic/systemic actions on the drug substance after its release from the drug product.

FDA's regulations at 21 CFR 320.25 set forth guidelines for in vivo BA studies. As provided in this regulation, the reference product for BA studies should be a solution, suspension, or intravenous (IV) dosage form (21 CFR 320.25(d)(2) and (3)). The purpose of conducting a BA study with an oral solution as a reference is to assess the impact of formulation on BA.

Conducting a BA study with an IV reference enables assessment of the impact of route of administration on BA and defines the absolute BA of the drug released from the drug product.

Demonstrating BE involves a more formal comparative test that uses specific references with specified criteria for comparisons and predetermined BE limits for such criteria.

Preapproval Changes

BE documentation can be useful during the IND period to compare (1) early and late clinical trial formulations; (2) formulations used in clinical trials and stability studies, if different; (3) clinical trial formulations and to-be-marketed drug products, if different; and (4) product strength equivalence, as appropriate.

Post approval Changes

In the presence of certain major changes in components, composition, manufacturing site, and/or method of manufacture after approval, FDA recommends that in vivo BE be demonstrated for the drug product after the change in comparison to the drug product before the change.

BE Considerations

BE studies are usually conducted using a crossover design. For such studies, intrasubject variability should be considered when determining the study sample size. In cases when a parallel design is necessary to evaluate BE, consideration should be given to total variability, including inter subject variability instead of just intrasubject variability.

A test product might fail to demonstrate bioequivalence because it has measures of rate and/or extent of absorption compared to the reference product outside acceptable higher or lower limits.

For example,

when the test product results in a systemic exposure that is significantly higher than that of the reference product, the concern is the typically limited experience from a safety standpoint for higher systemic concentrations.

When the test product has a systemic exposure that is significantly lower than that of the reference product, the concern is potentially a lack of therapeutic efficacy of the test product.

When the variability of the test product is greater than the reference product, the concern relates to both safety and efficacy, because it may suggest that the performance of the test product is not comparable to the reference product, and the test product may be too variable to be clinically useful.

When BE is not demonstrated, the sponsor should demonstrate that the differences in rate and extent of absorption do not significantly affect the safety and efficacy based on available dose-response or concentration-response data. In the absence of this evidence, failure to demonstrate BE may suggest that the test product should be reformulated, or the method of manufacture for the test product should be changed, or additional safety or efficacy data may be needed for the test product.

In some cases, conclusions of BE based on the peak drug concentration (Cmax) and area under the plasma concentration time curve (AUC) between the test product and the reference product may be insufficient to demonstrate that there is no difference in safety or efficacy if the systemic concentration181 time profiles of the test product and the reference product are different (e.g., time to reach peak drug concentration (Tmax) is different). For example, differences in the shape of the systemic concentration profile between the test and reference products could imply that the test product may not produce the same clinical response as the reference product. In such cases, additional data analysis (e.g., partial AUCs), exposure-response evaluation, or clinical studies may be recommended to evaluate the BE of the two products.

METHODS TO DOCUMENT BA AND BE

Under FDA's regulations, applicants must use the most accurate, sensitive, and reproducible method available to demonstrate BA or BE of a product (21 CFR 320.24(a)). As noted in 21 CFR 320.24, several in vivo and in vitro methods can be used to measure BA and to establish BE. These include, in general order of preference, pharmacokinetic (PK) studies, in vitro tests predictive of human in vivo BA (in vitro-in vivo correlation), pharmacodynamic (PD) studies, studies with clinical benefit endpoints, and other in vitro studies. In addition, where in vivo data are appropriate to demonstrate BA, our regulations provide guidelines on specific types of in vivo BA studies (see 21 CFR 320.25 through 320.29). This guidance predominantly focuses on the use of PK studies to document BA or BE.

A. Pharmacokinetic Studies

1. General Considerations

FDA's regulations generally define BA and BE in terms of rate and extent of absorption of the active ingredient or moiety to the site of action. For in vivo studies, the regulations also provide for use of PK measures in an accessible biological matrix such as blood, plasma, and/or serum to indicate release of the drug substance from the drug product into the systemic circulation.10 BA and BE frequently rely on PK measures such as AUC to assess extent of systemic exposure and Cmax and Tmax to assess rate of systemic absorption.

PK-based comparisons to describe relative BA or make BE determinations are predicated on an understanding that measuring the active moiety or ingredient at the site of action is generally not possible and on an assumption that some relationship exists between the efficacy/safety and concentration of the active moiety and/or its important metabolite(s) in the systemic circulation. A typical study is conducted as a crossover study. The crossover design reduces variability caused by patient-specific factors, thereby increasing the ability to discern differences because of formulation.

2. Pilot Study

If the sponsor chooses, a pilot study in a small number of subjects can be carried out before proceeding with a full-scale BA or BE study. The pilot study can be used to validate analytical methodology, assess PK variability, determine sample size to achieve adequate power, optimize sample collection time intervals, and determine the length of the washout period needed between treatments. For example, for conventional immediate-release products, careful timing of initial samples may avoid a subsequent finding in a full-scale study that the first sample collection occurs after the Cmax.

For modified-release products, a pilot study can help determine the sampling schedule needed to assess lag time and dose dumping. The results of a pilot study can be used as the sole basis to document BA or BE provided the study's design and execution are suitable and a sufficient number of subjects have completed the study.

3. Full-Scale Study

General recommendations for a standard BA or BE study based on PK measurements are provided in Appendix A. Nonreplicated crossover study designs are recommended for BA and BE studies of immediate-release and modified-release dosage forms. However, sponsors and/or applicants have the option of using replicate designs for BE studies.

Replicate crossover designs are used to allow estimation of (1) within-subject variance for the reference product, or for both the test and reference products, and (2) the subject

by formulation interaction variance component. This design accounts for the inter241 occasion variability that may confound the interpretation of a BE study as compared to a non-replicate crossover approach. The recommended method of analysis for nonreplicated or replicate studies to evaluate BE is average BE, as discussed in section IV. Recommendations for conducting and evaluating replicate study designs can be found in the FDA guidance for industry Statistical Approaches to Establishing Bioequivalence.

4. Study Population

Subjects recruited for BA or BE studies should be 18 years of age or older and capable of giving informed consent. In general, BA and BE studies should be conducted in healthy volunteers if the product can be safely administered to this population. A study in healthy volunteers is likely to produce less PK variability compared with that in patients with potentially confounding factors such as underlying and/or concomitant disease and concomitant medications. Male and female subjects should be enrolled in BA and BE studies unless there is a specific reason to exclude one sex. Such exclusions could be related to the drug product being indicated in only one sex or a greater potential for adverse reactions in one sex compared to the other.

For example, oral contraceptives are evaluated in female subjects because the indication is specific to females. If a drug has the potential to be a teratogen, the drug product should be evaluated in male subjects.

Female subjects enrolled in the study should not be pregnant at the beginning of the study and should not become pregnant during the study. In some instances (e.g., when safety considerations preclude use of healthy subjects), it may be necessary to evaluate BA and BE in patients for whom the drug product is intended. In this situation, sponsors and/or applicants should attempt to enrol patients whose disease process is expected to be stable for the duration of the study.

5. Single-Dose and Multiple-Dose (Steady State) Testing

This guidance generally recommends single-dose PK studies to assess BA and BE because they are generally more sensitive than steady-state studies in assessing rate and extent of release of the drug substance from the drug product into the systemic circulation.

FDA's regulations at 21 CFR 320.27 provide guidelines on the design of a multiple-dose in vivo BA study. This regulation also identifies instances in which multiple-dose BA studies may be required:

i. There is a difference in the rate of absorption but not in the extent of absorption.

ii. There is excessive variability in bioavailability from subject to subject.

iii. The concentration of the active drug ingredient or therapeutic moiety, or its metabolite(s), in the blood resulting from a single dose is too low for accurate determination by the analytical method.

iv. The drug product is an extended-release dosage form.11

FDA recommend that if a multiple-dose study design is performed, appropriate dosage administration and sampling be carried out to document attainment of steady state.

6. Bioanalytical Methodology

FDA recommend that sponsors ensure that bioanalytical methods for BA and BE studies be accurate, precise, specific, sensitive, and reproducible. A separate FDA guidance, Bioanalytical Method Validation, is available to assist sponsors in validating bioanalytical methods.

7. Administration Under Fasted/Fed Conditions

The BA or BE study should be conducted under fasting conditions (after an overnight fast of at least 10 hours) except when tolerability issues are anticipated with fasting. In these cases, we recommend that applicants conduct only a fed study. A separate FDA guidance, Food-Effect Bioavailability and Fed Bioequivalence Studies is available to assist sponsors.

8. Moieties to Be Measured

The active ingredient that is released from the dosage form or its active moiety and, when appropriate, its active metabolites13 should be measured in biological fluids collected in BA studies.

- Measurement of the active ingredient or the active moiety, rather than metabolites, is generally recommended for BE studies because the concentration-time profile of the active ingredient or the active moiety is more sensitive to changes in formulation performance than that of the metabolite, which is more reflective of metabolite formation, distribution, and elimination. The following are instances when an active metabolite(s) should be measured.
- Measurement of a metabolite(s) is necessary when the active ingredient or the active moiety concentrations are too low to allow reliable analytical measurement in blood, plasma, or serum. In this case, the metabolite should be measured in lieu of the active ingredient or active moiety.FDA recommend that the confidence interval approach be applied to the metabolite data obtained from these studies.
- Measurement of a metabolite(s) is necessary in addition to the active ingredient or active moiety if the metabolite is formed by pre systemic metabolism and contributes meaningfully to efficacy and/or safety. The confidence interval approach should be used for all moieties measured. However, the BE criteria are only generally applied to the active ingredient or active moiety. Sponsors should contact the appropriate review division to determine

which moieties should be measured.

9. Pharmacokinetic Measures of Systemic Exposure

This guidance recommends that systemic exposure measures be used to evaluate BA and BE. Exposure measures are defined relative to peak, partial, and total portions of the plasma, serum, or blood concentration-time profile, as describe here:

- **Peak Exposure**

We recommend that peak exposure be assessed by measuring the Cmax obtained directly from the systemic drug concentration data without interpolation. The Tmax can provide important information about the rate of absorption. The first point of a concentration340 time curve based on blood and/or plasma measurements is sometimes the highest concentration, which raises a question about the measurement of true Cmax because of

insufficient early sampling times. A carefully conducted pilot study may help to avoid this problem. Collection of an early time point between 5 and 15 minutes after dosing

followed by additional sample collections (e.g., two to five) in the first hour after dosing may be sufficient to assess early peak concentrations. If this sampling approach is followed, we consider the data to be adequate, even when the highest observed concentration occurs at the first time point.

- **Total Exposure (Extent of Absorption)**

For single-dose studies, we recommend that the measurement of total exposure be:

- Area under the plasma, serum, or blood concentration time curve from time zero to time t (AUC0-t), where t is the last time point with a measurable concentration.

- Area under the plasma, serum, or blood concentration time curve from time zero to time infinity (AUC0-), where AUC0-? = AUC0-t + Ct/?z. Ct is the last measurable drug concentration and ?z is the terminal or elimination rate constant calculated according to an appropriate method.

For steady-state studies, we recommend that the measurement of total exposure be the area under the plasma, serum, or blood concentration time curve from time zero to time tau over a dosing interval at steady state (AUC0-tau), where tau is the length of the dosing interval.

- **Partial Exposure**

For orally administered drug products, BA and BE can generally be demonstrated by measurements of peak and total exposure. For certain classes of drugs and under certain circumstances (e.g., to assess onset of an analgesic effect), an evaluation of the partial exposure could be used to support the performance of different formulations by providing further evidence of therapeutic effect. This guidance recommends the use of partial AUC as a partial exposure measure. The time to truncate the partial area should be related to a clinically relevant PD measure. We also recommend that sufficient quantifiable samples be collected to allow adequate estimation of the partial area.

For questions on the suitability of the PD measure or use of partial exposure in general, we recommend that sponsors and/or applicants consult the appropriate review division.

10. Comparison of PK measures in BE studies

An equivalence approach is recommended for BE comparisons. The recommended approach relies on (1) a criterion to allow the comparison, (2) a confidence interval for the criterion, and (3) a BE limit. Log-transformation of exposure measures before statistical analysis is recommended. This guidance recommends use of an average BE criterion to compare systemic exposure measures for replicate and nonreplicated BE studies of both immediate- and modified-release products. For additional information on data analysis, refer to Appendix A and to the FDA guidance for industry on Statistical

Approaches to Establishing Bioequivalence.

B. Other Approaches to Support BA/BE

In certain circumstances, other approaches are recommended to support a demonstration of BA/BE. Below are some general considerations regarding these other approaches. Sponsors should consult FDA's guidance for industry for additional information on these methods as well.

1. **In Vitro Tests Predictive of Human In Vivo BA**

In vitro-in vivo correlation (IVIVC) is an approach to describe the relationship between an in vitro attribute of a dosage form (e.g., the rate or extent of drug release) and a relevant in vivo response (e.g., plasma drug concentration or amount of drug absorbed). This model relationship facilitates the rational development and evaluation of extended-release dosage forms. Once an IVIVC is validated, the in vitro test serves as a surrogate for BA and/or BE testing, as well as a tool for formulation screening and setting of the dissolution/drug-release acceptance criteria.

Specifically, in vitro dissolution/drug-release characterization is encouraged for all extended-release product formulations investigated (including prototype formulations), particularly if in vivo absorption characteristics are being defined for the different product formulations. Such efforts may enable the establishment

of an IVIVC. When an IVIVC or association is established (21 CFR 320.24(b)(1)(ii)), the in vitro test can serve not only as a quality control specification for the manufacturing process, but also as an indicator of how the product will perform in vivo.

Additional information on the development and validation of an IVIVC can be found in the FDA guidance for industry Extended-Release Oral Dosage Forms:

Development, Evaluation, and Application of In Vitro/In Vivo Correlations.

2. Pharmacodynamic Studies

PD studies are not recommended for orally administered drug products when the drug is absorbed into systemic circulation and a PK approach can be used to assess systemic exposure and evaluate BA or BE. PK endpoints are preferred because they are generally the most accurate, sensitive, and reproducible approach. However, in instances where a PK endpoint is not possible, a well431 justified PD endpoint can be used to demonstrate BA or BE.

3. Comparative Clinical Studies

Clinical endpoints can be used in limited circumstances for example, for orally administered drug products when the measurement of the active ingredients or active moieties in an accessible biological fluid (PK approach) or PD approach is not possible. Because these circumstances do not occur very often, use of this approach is expected to be rare.

4. In Vitro Studies

Under certain circumstances, BA and BE can be evaluated using in vitro approaches (e.g., dissolution/drug-release testing) during the preapproval and post approval phases (see 21 CFR 320.24(b)(5) and (6)).

For example, orally administered drugs that are highly soluble and highly permeable, and for which the drug product is rapidly dissolving, documentation of BE using an in vitro approach (dissolution/drug-release studies) may be appropriate based on the Biopharmaceutics Classification System.

The following FDA guidance provide recommendations on the development of dissolution methodology, setting specifications, and the regulatory applications of dissolution testing:

- Dissolution Testing of Immediate-Release Solid Oral Dosage Forms
- Extended-Release Oral Dosage Forms: Development, Evaluation, and Application of In Vitro/In Vivo Correlations

In addition, we recommend that sponsors consult other FDA guidance for additional information on when in vitro data may be appropriate to demonstrate BA or BE of a product.

Randomization techniques

Randomization is the process of assigning participants to treatment and control groups, assuming that each participant has an equal chance of being assigned to any group.

Many procedures have been proposed for the random assignment of participants to treatment groups in clinical trials. Common randomization techniques, including simple randomization, block randomization, stratified randomization, and covariate adaptive randomization.

Researchers demand randomization for several reasons. First, participants in various groups should not differ in any systematic way. In a clinical trial, if treatment groups are systematically different, trial results will be biased. Suppose that participants are assigned to control and treatment groups in a study examining the efficacy of a walking intervention. If a greater proportion of older adults is assigned to the treatment group, then the outcome of the walking intervention may be influenced by this imbalance. The effects of the treatment would be indistinguishable from the influence of the imbalance of covariates, thereby requiring the researcher to control for the covariates in the analysis to obtain an unbiased result.

Second, proper randomization ensures no a priori knowledge of group assignment (ie, allocation concealment). That is, researchers, participants, and others should not know to which group the participant will be assigned. Knowledge of group assignment creates a layer of potential selection bias that may taint the data. Schulz and Grimes stated that trials with inadequate or unclear randomization tended to overestimate treatment effects up to 40% compared with those that used proper randomization. The outcome of the trial can be negatively influenced by this inadequate randomization. Statistical techniques such as analysis of covariance (ANCOVA), multivariate ANCOVA, or both, are often used to adjust for covariate imbalance in the analysis stage of the clinical trial. However, the interpretation of this post adjustment approach is often difficult because imbalance of covariates frequently leads to unanticipated interaction effects, such as unequal slopes among subgroups of covariates.

One of the critical assumptions in ANCOVA is that the slopes of regression lines are the same for each group of covariates (ie, homogeneity of regression slopes). The adjustment needed for each covariate group may vary, which is problematic because ANCOVA uses the average slope across the groups to adjust the outcome variable. Thus, the ideal way of balancing covariates among groups is to apply sound randomization in the design stage of a clinical trial (before the adjustment procedure) instead of after data collection. In such instances, random assignment is necessary and guarantees validity for statistical tests of significance that are used to compare treatments.

Simple Randomization

Randomization based on a single sequence of random assignments is known as simple randomization.10 This technique maintains complete randomness of the assignment of a person to a particular group. The most common and basic method of simple randomization is flipping a coin. For example, with 2 treatment groups (control versus treatment), the side of the coin (ie, heads 5 control, tails 5 treatment) determines the assignment of each participant. Other methods include using a shuffled deck of cards (eg, even 5 control, odd 5 treatment) or throwing a die (eg, below and equal to 3 5 controls, over 3 5 treatment). A random number table found in a statistics book or computer-generated random numbers can also be used for simple randomization of participants.

This randomization approach is simple and easy to implement in a clinical trial. In large trials (n . 200), simple randomization can be trusted to generate similar numbers of participants among groups. However, randomization results could be problematic in relatively small sample size clinical trials (n , 100), resulting in an unequal number of participants among groups. For example, using a coin toss with a small sample size (n 5 10) may result in an imbalance such that 7 participants are assigned to the control group and 3 to the treatment group.

Block Randomization

The block randomization method is designed to randomize participants into groups that result in equal sample sizes. This method is used to ensure a balance in sample size across groups over time. Blocks are small and balanced with predetermined group assignments, which keeps the numbers of participants in each group similar at all times. According to Altman and Bland,10 the block size is determined by the researcher and should be a multiple of the number of groups (ie, with 2 treatment groups, block size of either 4 or 6). Blocks are best used in smaller increments as researchers can more easily control balance. After block size has been determined, all possible balanced combinations of assignment within the block (ie, equal number for all groups within the block) must be calculated. Blocks are then randomly chosen to determine the participants' assignment into the groups. For a clinical trial with control and treatment groups involving 40 participants, a randomized block procedure would be as follows: (1) a block size of 4 is chosen, (2) possible balanced combinations with 2 C (control) and 2 T (treatment) subjects are calculated as 6 (TTCC, TCTC, TCCT, CTTC, CTCT, CCTT), and (3) blocks are randomly chosen to determine the assignment of all 40 participants (eg, one random sequence would be [TTCC / TCCT / CTTC / CTTC / TCCT / CCTT / TTCC / TCTC / CTCT / TCTC]). This procedure results in 20 participants in both the control and treatment groups (Figure 2). Although balance in sample size may be achieved with this method, groups may be generated that are rarely comparable in terms of certain covariates.

For example, one group may have more participants with secondary diseases (eg, diabetes, multiple sclerosis, cancer) that could confound the data and may negatively influence the results of the clinical trial. Pocock and Simon stressed the importance of controlling for these covariates because of serious consequences to the interpretation of the results. Such an imbalance could introduce bias in the statistical analysis and reduce the power of the study. Hence, sample size and covariates must be balanced in small clinical trials.

Stratified Randomization

The stratified randomization method addresses the need to control and balance the influence of covariates. This method can be used to achieve balance among groups in terms of participants' baseline characteristics (covariates). Specific covariates must be identified by the researcher who understands the potential influence each covariate has on the dependent variable. Stratified randomization is achieved by generating a separate block for each combination of covariates, and participants are assigned to the appropriate block of covariates. After all participants have been identified and assigned into blocks, simple randomization occurs within each block to assign participants to one of the groups. The stratified randomization method controls for the possible influence of covariates that would jeopardize the conclusions of the clinical trial. For example, a clinical trial of different rehabilitation techniques after a surgical procedure will have a number of covariates. It is well known that the age of the patient affects the rate of healing. Thus, age could be a confounding variable and influence the outcome of the clinical trial. Stratified randomization can balance the control and treatment groups for age or other identified covariates

For example, with 2 groups involving 40 participants, the stratified randomization method might be used to control the covariates of sex (2 levels: male, female) and body mass index (3 levels: underweight, normal, overweight) between study arms. With these 2 covariates, possible block combinations total 6 (eg, male, underweight). A simple randomization procedure, such as flipping a coin, is used to assign the participants within each block to one of the treatment groups (Figure 3). Although stratified randomization is a relatively simple and useful technique, especially for smaller clinical trials, it becomes complicated to implement if many covariates must be controlled.

For example, too many block combinations may lead to imbalances in overall treatment allocations because a large number of blocks can generate small participant numbers within the block. Therneau21 purported that a balance in covariates begins to fail when the number of blocks approaches half the sample size. If another 4-level covariate was added to the example, the number of block combinations would increase from 6 to 24 (2 3 3 3 4), for an average of fewer than 2 (40 / 24 5 1.7) participants per block, reducing the usefulness of the procedure to balance the covariates and jeopardizing the validity of the clinical trial. In small studies, it may not be feasible to stratify more than 1 or 2 covariates because the number of blocks can quickly approach the number of participants.10 Stratified randomization has another limitation: it works only when all participants have been identified before group assignment. This method is rarely applicable, however, because clinical trial participants are often enrolled one at a time on a continuous basis. When baseline characteristics of all participants are not available before assignment, using stratified randomization is difficult.

Covariate Adaptive Randomization

Covariate adaptive randomization has been recommended by many researchers as a valid alternative randomization method for clinical trials. In covariate adaptive randomization, a new participant is sequentially assigned to a particular treatment group by taking into account the specific covariates and previous assignments of participants. Covariate adaptive randomization uses the method of minimization by assessing the imbalance of sample size among several covariates. This covariate adaptive approach was first described by Taves. The Taves covariate adaptive randomization method allows for the examination of previous participant group assignments to make a case-by-case decision on group assignment for each individual who enrols in the study. Consider again the example of 2 groups involving 40

participants, with sex (2 levels: male, female) and body mass index (3 levels: underweight, normal, overweight) as covariates. Assume the first 9 participants have already been randomly assigned to groups by flipping a coin. The 9 participants' group assignments are broken down by covariate level in Figure 4. Now the 10th participant, who is male and underweight, needs to be assigned to a group (ie, control versus treatment). Based on the characteristics of the 10th participant, the Taves method adds marginal totals of the corresponding covariate categories for each group and compares the totals. The participant is assigned to the group with the lower covariate total to minimize imbalance. In this example, the appropriate categories are male and underweight, which results in the total of 3 (2 for male category + 1 for underweight category) for the control group and a total of 5 (3 for male category + 2 for underweight category) for the treatment group. Because the sum of marginal totals is lower for the control group (3 , 5), the 10th participant is assigned to the control group (Figure 5). The Pocock and Simon method11 of covariate adaptive randomization is similar to the method Taves23 described. The difference in this approach is the temporary assignment of participants to both groups. This method uses the absolute difference between groups to determine group assignment. To minimize imbalance, the participant is assigned to the group determined by the lowest sum of the absolute differences among the covariates between the groups. For example, using the previous situation in assigning the 10th participant to a group, the Pocock and Simon method would (1) assign the 10th participant temporarily to the control group, resulting in marginal totals of 3 for male category and 2 for underweight category; (2) calculate the absolute difference between control and treatment group (males: 3 control – 3 treatment 5 0; underweight: 2 control – 2 treatment 5 0) and sum (0 + 0 5 0); (3) temporarily assign the 10th participant to the treatment group, resulting in marginal totals of 4 for male category and 3 for underweight category; (4) calculate the absolute difference between control and treatment group (males: 2 control – 4 treatment 5 2; underweight: 1 control – 3 treatment 5 2) and sum (2 + 2 5 4); and (5) assign the 10th participant to the control group because of the lowest sum of absolute differences (0 , 4). Pocock and Simon11 also suggested using a variance approach. Instead of calculating absolute difference among groups, this approach calculates the variance among treatment groups. Although the variance method performs similarly to the absolute difference method, both approaches suffer from the limitation of handling only categorical covariates.25 Frane18 introduced a covariate adaptive randomization for both continuous and categorical types. Frane used P values to identify imbalance among treatment groups: a smaller P value represents more imbalance among treatment groups. The Frane method for assigning participants to either the control or treatment group would include (1) temporarily assigning the participant to both the control and treatment groups; (2) calculating P values for each of the covariates using a t test and analysis of variance (ANOVA) for continuous variables and goodness-of-fit x2 test for categorical variables; (3) determining the minimum P value for each control or treatment group, which indicates more imbalance among treatment groups; and (4) assigning the participant to the group with the larger minimum P value (ie, try to avoid more imbalance in groups). Going back to the previous example of assigning the 10th participant (male and underweight) to a group, the Frane method would result in the assignment to the control group. The steps used to make this decision were calculating P values for each of the covariates using the x2 goodness-of-fit test represented in the Table. The t tests and ANOVAs were not used because the covariates in this example were categorical. Based on the Table, the lowest minimum P values were 1.0 for the control group and 0.317 for the treatment group. The 10th participant was assigned to the control group because of the higher minimum P value, which indicates better balance in the control group (1.0 . 0.317). Covariate adaptive randomization produces less imbalance than other conventional randomization methods and can be used successfully to balance important covariates among control and treatment groups.6 Although the balance of covariates among groups using the stratified randomization method begins to fail when the number of blocks approaches half the sample size, covariate adaptive randomization can better handle the problem of increasing numbers of covariates (ie, increased block combinations).9 One concern of these covariate adaptive randomization methods is that treatment assignments sometimes become highly predictable. Investigators using covariate adaptive randomization sometimes come to believe that group assignment for the next participant can be readily predicted, going against the basic concept of randomization.

Restricted randomization

Restricted randomization occurs in the design of experiments and in particular in the context of randomized experiments and randomized controlled trials. Restricted randomization allows intuitively poor allocations of treatments to experimental units to be avoided, while retaining the theoretical benefits of randomization.

For example, in a clinical trial of a new proposed treatment of obesity compared to a control, an experimenter would want to avoid outcomes of the randomization in which the new treatment was allocated only to the heaviest patients.

Types of research designs based on Controlling Method

Research designs can be classified into three major types, in descending order of ability to determine causal relationships: experimental designs, quasi-experimental designs, and non-experimental designs.

Experimental designs

Experimental designs must have the following characteristic elements: one or more comparison groups, and the use of random assignment to these groups. In addition, the researcher controls the participants' exposure to the experimental condition, such as an intervention. Experimental designs control for most threats to internal validity. Two examples of experimental designs are the pretest-posttest control group design, and the posttest-only control group design.

Quasi-experimental designs

Quasi-experimental designs may or may not use comparison groups. When they do, participants are not randomly assigned to these groups. Thus the groups are considered to be non-equivalent. They are still able to control for several threats to internal validity, and they might allow for determination of causal relationships. Two examples are the non-equivalent control group design, and time series designs. The non-equivalent control group design is the same as the experimental pretest-posttest control group design, except that participants are not randomly assigned to the two groups.

Non-experimental designs

Non-experimental designs control for very few, if any, threats to internal validity, and they are appropriately used only when the purpose of the study is exploratory or descriptive. They do not allow for the determination of causal relationships. Three examples of non-experimental designs are the one group pretest-posttest design, the static group comparison, and the cross-sectional survey design.

If we begin with the Pretest-Posttest Design with Nonequivalent Groups and then take away the comparison group, we are left with the One Group Pretest-Posttest Design.

Time Sequences

(Prospective and Retrospective)

Prospective study

A prospective study is a scientific investigation that researchers perform in order to learn more about a particular medical topic. This research involves a specific group of participants, or cohorts, who are prone or predisposed to the outcome of interest. This means that researchers collect and analyze data with the goal of developing medical treatments or tracking the progression of a disease. Researchers may also design studies, recruit participants and collect baseline exposure data before the research subjects develop the medical condition.

For example, researchers would carry out a prospective study to learn about how people that are susceptible to a particular virus might react to exposure, without them actually developing the virus. Prospective studies are often longitudinal, meaning that researchers then follow up with participants or track their health over time to monitor whether they develop the medical condition in question.

Advantages

Three advantages of a prospective study are:

- **Tracking participant changes:** Prospective cohort studies may track changes in the participant's health or behavior because of exposure or development of the outcome of interest. This offers researchers more information about the development and progression of the condition or disease.
- **Minimizes the likelihood of bias:** Considering the outcome of the patient's interaction with and exposure to the subject of interest, there's less likelihood of bias during data analysis. Since researchers may not have a list of preexisting data sources to choose from, as with retrospective studies, they may create new data through observation and interviews.
- **Collects specific data exposure:** Because researchers carry out their study in the present and in the future, they can collect specific data exposure information and can have more control over the procedures than in a retrospective study.

Disadvantages

Three disadvantages of a prospective study are:

- **Relies on participant contact:** A prospective study monitors the participant over time and through various potential exposures to the outcome or subject of study. This means that the research is reliant on the participant reporting back to the research team, and being fully honest and transparent about their experiences for the research to be valid.
- **Doesn't account for latency:** Because the researchers are interested in tracking the participant's encounters with a disease, virus or other medical condition, this can be a challenging method to use if the outcome of interest takes a long time to produce results. However, this method can still yield valuable results.
- **Less effective for rare diseases:** If you're interested in developing a treatment for or tracking the progression of a rare disease, a prospective study may not be the ideal model. In a prospective study, you're required to assemble a significant amount of participants with the same condition in order to produce reliable analyses and conclusions.

Retrospective study

A retrospective study is a research project that involves reviewing the results of exposure to and developments of medical incidents that have already occurred. Similar to a prospective study, researchers conducting this study are also interested in learning about participants' development of a particular medical condition. They use this data to identify and create a cohort of people that were prone to the condition in question and study the subject's exposure status and medical outcome. Researchers typically use pre-existing data to make new analyses and conclusions about the outcome of interest.

Advantages

Three advantages to a retrospective study are:

- **Minimizes cost and use of resources:** Retrospective studies don't require researchers to spend resources on contacting and locating participants for a study, meaning that they're able to minimize costs compared to other study techniques.
- **Increases speed of data analysis:** Because researchers are reviewing existing documents to collect data rather than gathering a group of participants to interview, the data analysis process in a retrospective study may be faster. Researchers may also gather results directly related to the incident or outcome they're studying, resulting in more

efficient data collection methods.

- **Focus on the use of prior information:** Retrospective studies often focus on preexisting data and may not follow up or depend on a participant's willingness to take part in the research.

Disadvantages

Three disadvantages of a retrospective study are:

- **Risk of bias from resources:** Because researchers aren't collecting participant's information themselves, they're relying on others' information which may lead to misclassification or recall bias. However, researchers may try to account for this by checking to ensure that their resources are from reputable scientists and studies.
- **Data set requirements:** If the outcomes of interest are rare, for example, a rare reaction to treatment, researchers may require large amounts of data to produce conclusive results. While this might mean that researchers spend more time gathering data, it can also show that their research is valuable to the field.
- **Comparison group limitations:** Since you're collecting data retrospectively, you're limited to the information available to you. This means that identifying and creating a comparison group to relate to the participants that contracted the medical condition may be a challenge.

Prospective vs. Retrospective study

While they're both types of cohort studies, there are several differences between the two which include:

Data collection

The primary difference between retrospective and prospective studies is data collection. In a retrospective study, researchers investigate existing information regarding exposure factors and their impact. Researchers may also use resources that are already documented or published, including medical reports and magazine or newspaper articles.

Data collection for a prospective study includes researchers performing the interviews and observation themselves. This allows the researchers to be present at the time of exposure and observe the impact of exposure firsthand. In a prospective study, there are likely no records of the incident of interest because it involves events that have not yet occurred.

Data analysis

Considering that the data collection techniques for prospective and retrospective studies differ, the processes for data analysis are different as well. A researcher may analyze the data in a retrospective study immediately if there's enough information readily available in documents and medical reports to lead to a conclusion. For a prospective study, the time frame for conducting a data analysis or making a conclusion may depend on the amount of data the researcher can collect and the execution of the research.

Use and purpose

The purpose of a retrospective study is typically to add to existing research and information or elaborate on a recent discovery. Researchers use retrospective studies to analyze why something happened and to explain a recent event or discovery. Prospective studies differ because they're future-oriented, meaning researchers use them to discover if an event will happen.

Scientists can use either kind of study to learn about a particular subject. The key difference between the two study types is their approach. If researchers are interested in learning about what caused the outbreak of an illness, they may use a retrospective study to investigate. Alternatively, if they're interested in learning about the impact of treatments on patients who have the illness, they may use a prospective study.

Time and cost

Typically, a retrospective study costs less and takes less time than a prospective study. This is because a retrospective study doesn't involve observing and interviewing participants, so there's less time and cost spent on data collection. In a retrospective study, data is readily available for collection and analysis, requiring a smaller research team and fewer resources.

Prospective studies can often be longitudinal, meaning that they take a set amount of time in order to measure and analyze the effect of exposure on the participants. In a prospective study, researchers may contact and gather participants and collect background data besides typical data collection and analysis.

Sampling methods

(Cohort study, Case Control study and Cross-Sectional Study)

Sampling method or sampling technique is the process of studying the population by gathering information and analysing that data.In Statistics, there are different sampling techniques available to get relevant results from the population.

The two different types of sampling methods are:

- Probability Sampling
- Non-probability Sampling

Probability sampling methods

- Simple random sampling

Every member of the population has the same probability of being randomly selected into the sample.

- Systematic sampling

One selects every nth (ie, 10th) subject in the population to be in the sample

- Stratified sampling

The population is divided into non-overlapping groups, or strata; a random sample of population members is then collected from within each stratum

- Clustered sampling

The researcher divides the population into separate groups, called clusters. Then, a simple random sample of clusters is selected from the population. Note that the clusters are used as the sampling unit, rather than individuals

Nonprobability sampling methods

- Convenience sampling

Participants are selected based on availability and willingness to take part

- Quota sampling

A tailored sample that is in proportion to some characteristic or trait of a population

- Purposive sampling

Also known as judgmental or subjective sampling. It relies on the judgment of the researcher when choosing members of the population to participate in a study

- Snowball sampling

Existing study subjects recruit future subjects from among their acquaintances

Cohort Study

The term "cohort" in modern epidemiology refers to "a group of people with defined characteristics who are followed up to determine the incidence of, or mortality from, some specific disease, all causes of death, or some other outcome."

Advantages

- Can investigate multiple outcomes that may be associated with multiple exposures
- Able to study the change in exposure and outcome over time
- Good for examining rare exposures
- Can measure incidence of outcome
- May be able to infer causality

Prospective Study

- Able to control design, sampling, data collection, and follow-up methods
- Can measure all variables of interest

Retrospective Study

- Time-efficient and inexpensive
- Easy to obtain large sample

Disadvantages

- Susceptible to loss to follow-up compared with cross-sectional studies
- Confounding variables are the major problem in analyzing the data compared with RCTs

Prospective Study

- May be expensive to conduct
- Time-consuming

Retrospective Study

- Less control over variables
- Susceptible to information bias and recall bias

A cohort study observes people as two or more groups, from exposure to outcome.

A key feature of the cohort study design is that subjects are followed up over time. It begins with subjects who are exposed and not exposed to a factor and then evaluates the subsequent occurrence of an outcome.

Unlike cross-sectional studies, which are often used to determine prevalence, cohort studies are used to study incidence, causes, and prognosis. In clinical research, cohort studies are appropriate when there is evidence to suggest an association between an exposure and an outcome, and the time interval between exposure and the development of outcome is reasonable. Cohort studies are the design of choice for determining the incidence and natural history of a condition.

Due to their longitudinal design feature, one can look at disease progression and natural history. Cohort studies allow us to calculate the incidence rate, cumulative incidence, relative risk, and hazard ratio. Causality cannot be established definitively through a cohort study. Nevertheless, cohort studies are useful to provide evidence that suggests causality and information regarding the strength of the association between the risk factors and the outcome

Description of Subtypes of Cohort Studies

Cohort studies can be either prospective or retrospective. The type of cohort study is determined by the outcome status. If the outcome has not occurred at the start of the study, then it is a prospective study; if the outcome has already occurred, then it is a retrospective study. Figure 1 presents a graphical representation of the designs of prospective and retrospective cohort studies. The distinguishing feature of a prospective cohort study is that at the time that the investigators begin enrolling subjects, none of the subjects has developed the outcome of interest. In contrast, a retrospective study is conceived after subjects have already developed the outcome. The investigators jump back in time to identify a cohort of subjects at a point in time when they did not have the outcome. A prospective cohort study design is ranked higher in the hierarchy of evidence than a retrospective design because the outcome, predictor, and confounding variables can be better measured and controlled.5 Information gained from a retrospective study can be helpful in planning a future prospective study.

A study combining two study designs, the case-cohort design, is a combination of a case-control and cohort design that can be either prospective or retrospective. The case-cohort design can be viewed as a variant of the nested case-control design. In a nested case-control study, one starts with identifying cases that have already occurred (retrospective) or as they occur (prospective) in a defined cohort. A specific number of control subjects are then selected from among those in the cohort.

Limitations in this type of design include:

(1) inefficiency due to the need to align each selected case subject to its matched control subject; and

(2) when there is more than one outcome considered, strict implementation of the design requires the selection of a new set of control subjects for each distinct disease outcome. The case cohort design was proposed by Prentice8 as a cost-effective alternative to the nested case-control design. In a case-cohort design, a sub cohort is randomly drawn from the full cohort, and the case-cohort sample consists of the sub cohort plus those subjects from the entire cohort whose outcome occurred during the study period. Figure 2 illustrates the subject selection process of a case cohort sample. The case-cohort study design is efficient when only a very small fraction of the full cohort develops the outcome in the given study time frame and the exposure measurement of interest is expensive to obtain.

Example

Nijkeuter et al conducted a prospective cohort study to understand the natural course of hemodynamically stable pulmonary embolism (PE). The study aimed to evaluate the incidence of recurrent VTE, haemorrhagic complications, and mortality in patients with PE, and to identify risk factors and the time course of these events. Between November 2002 and September 2004, a total of 3,503 patients with clinically suspected PE were screened, and PE was diagnosed in 674 patients. Three-month follow-up was completed in 673 of the 674 patients with PE. The authors found that recurrent VTE occurred in a small percentage of patients treated for an acute PE, and the majority of recurrent VTEs were fatal. Immobilization, hospitalization, age, COPD, and malignancies were risk factors for recurrent VTE, bleeding, and mortality.

Case Control Study

A case-control study is a type of observational study commonly used to look at factors associated with diseases or outcomes. The case-control study starts with a group of cases, which are the individuals who have the outcome of interest. The researcher then tries to construct a second group of individuals called the controls, who are similar to the case individuals but do **not** have the outcome of interest. The researcher then looks at historical factors to identify if some exposure(s) is/are found more commonly in the cases than the controls. If the exposure is found more commonly in the cases than in the controls, the researcher can hypothesize that the exposure may be linked to the outcome of interest.

For example, a researcher may want to look at the rare cancer Kaposi's sarcoma. The researcher would find a group of individuals with Kaposi's sarcoma (the cases) and compare them to a group of patients who are similar to the cases in most ways but do not have Kaposi's sarcoma (controls). The researcher could then ask about various exposures to see if any exposure is more common in those with Kaposi's sarcoma (the cases) than those without Kaposi's sarcoma (the controls). The researcher might find that those with Kaposi's sarcoma are more likely to have HIV, and thus conclude that HIV may be a risk factor for the development of Kaposi's sarcoma.

Advantages

- Case-control approach allows for the study of rare diseases. If a disease occurs very infrequently, one would have to follow a large group of people for a long period of time to accrue enough incident cases to study. Such use of resources may be impractical, so a case-control study can be useful for identifying current cases and evaluating historical associated factors.

For example,

if a disease developed in 1 in 1000 people per year (0.001/year) then in ten years one would expect about 10 cases of a disease to exist in a group of 1000 people. If the disease is much rarer, say 1 in 1,000,0000 per year (0.0000001/year) this would require either having to follow 1,000,0000 people for ten years or 1000 people for 1000 years to accrue ten total cases. As it may be impractical to follow 1,000,000 for ten years or to wait 1000 years for recruitment, a case-control study allows for a more feasible approach.

- Case-control study design makes it possible to look at multiple risk factors at once.

In the example above about Kaposi's sarcoma, the researcher could ask both the cases and controls about exposures to HIV, asbestos, smoking, lead, sunburns, aniline dye, alcohol, herpes, human papillomavirus, or any number of possible exposures to identify those most likely associated with Kaposi's sarcoma.

- Case-control studies can also be very helpful when disease outbreaks occur, and potential links and exposures need to be identified. This study mechanism can be commonly seen in food-related disease outbreaks associated with contaminated products, or when rare diseases start to increase in frequency, as has been seen with measles in recent years.

Because of these advantages, case-control studies are commonly used as one of the first studies to build evidence of an association between exposure and an event or disease.

In a case-control study, the investigator can include unequal numbers of cases with controls such as 2:1 or 4:1 to increase the power of the study.

Disadvantages and Limitations

- The potential for recall bias.

Recall bias in a case-control study is the increased likelihood that those with the outcome will recall and report exposures compared to those without the outcome. In other words, even if both groups had exactly the same exposures, the participants in the cases group may report the exposure more often than the controls do. Recall bias may lead to concluding that there are associations between exposure and disease that do not, in fact, exist. It is due to subjects' imperfect memories of past exposures. If people with Kaposi's sarcoma are asked about exposure and history (e.g., HIV, asbestos, smoking, lead, sunburn, aniline dye, alcohol, herpes, human papillomavirus), the individuals with the disease are more likely to think harder about these exposures and recall having some of the exposures that the healthy controls.

Case-control studies, due to their typically retrospective nature, can be used to establish a **correlation** between exposures and outcomes, but cannot establish **causation.** These studies simply attempt to find correlations between past events and the current state.

When designing a case-control study, the researcher must find an appropriate control group. Ideally, the case group (those with the outcome) and the control group (those without the outcome) will have almost the same characteristics, such as age, gender, overall health status, and other factors. The two groups should have similar histories and live in similar environments.

If, for example, our cases of Kaposi's sarcoma came from across the country but our controls were only chosen from a small community in northern latitudes where people rarely go outside or get sunburns, asking about sunburn may not be a valid exposure to investigate.

Similarly, if all of the cases of Kaposi's sarcoma were found to come from a small community outside a battery factory with high levels of lead in the environment, then controls from across the country with minimal lead exposure would not provide an appropriate control group. The investigator must put a great deal of effort into creating a proper control group to bolster the strength of the case-control study as well as enhance their ability to find true and valid potential correlations between exposures and disease states.

Similarly, the researcher must recognize the potential for failing to identify confounding variables or exposures, introducing the possibility of confounding bias, which occurs when a variable that is not being accounted for that has a relationship with both the exposure and outcome.

The major method for analyzing results in case-control studies is the odds ratio (OR). The odds ratio is the odds of having a disease (or outcome) with the exposure versus the odds of having the disease without the exposure. The most straightforward way to calculate the odds ratio is with a 2 by 2 table divided by exposure and disease status (see below). Mathematically we can write the odds ratio as follows.

Odds ratio = [(Number exposed with disease)/(Number exposed without disease)]/[(Number not exposed to disease)/(Number not exposed without disease)]

This can be rewritten as:

Function

Odds ratio = [(Number exposed with disease) x (Number not exposed without disease)] / [(Number exposed without disease) x (Number not exposed with disease)]

The odds ratio tells us how strongly the exposure is related to the disease state. An odds ratio of greater than one implies the disease is more likely with exposure. An odds ratio of less than one implies the disease is less likely with exposure and thus the exposure may be protective. For example, a patient with a prior heart attack taking a daily aspirin has a decreased odds of having another heart attack (odds ratio less than one). An odds ratio of one implies there is no relation between the exposure and the disease process.

Odds ratios are often confused with Relative Risk (RR), which is a measure of the probability of the disease or outcome in the exposed vs unexposed groups. For very rare conditions, the OR and RR may be very similar, but they are measuring different aspects of the association between outcome and exposure. The OR is used in case-control studies because RR cannot be estimated; whereas in randomized clinical trials, a direct measurement of the development of events in the exposed and unexposed groups can be seen. RR is also used to compare risk in other prospective study designs.

Cross-Sectional Study

A cross-sectional study is a type of observational study design that involves looking at data from a population at one specific point in time. In a cross-sectional study, investigators measure outcomes and exposures of the study subjects at the same time. It is described as taking a "snapshot" of a group of individuals.

Unlike in case-control studies (subjects selected based on the outcome status) or cohort studies (subjects selected based on the exposure status), the subjects in a cross-sectional study are simply chosen from an available population of potential relevance to the study question. There is no prospective or retrospective follow-up. Once the subjects are selected, the investigators will collect the data and assess the associations between outcomes and exposures.

Cross-sectional studies have been mainly used to understand the prevalence of a disease in clinical research. Prevalence refers to the proportion of persons in a population who have a particular disease or attribute at a given time, regardless of when they first developed the disease. It is important to distinguish prevalence from incidence. Incidence refers to the number of new cases that develop in a given period of time. In a cross-sectional study, researchers typically describe the distribution of variables in a population. They may assess the prevalence of a disease or association of an exposure to an outcome in a population.

In a simple hypothetical example of a cross-sectional study, we record the prevalence of COPD and investigate the association between COPD and smoking status in adult patients. The outcome variable is the presence or absence of COPD, and the exposure is the smoking status. This study can be conducted by interviewing participants about their smoking history and, at the same time, assessing COPD status clinically.

Because the outcome and exposure variables are measured at the same time, it is relatively difficult to establish causal relationships from a cross-sectional study. Cross-sectional studies are usually fast and inexpensive to conduct. They are suitable for generating hypotheses and may provide information about the prevalence of outcomes and exposures that informs other study designs. In this paper, we review the essential characteristics, describe strengths and weaknesses, discuss methodological issues, and give our recommendations on design and statistical analysis for cross-sectional studies.

Description of Subtypes of Cross-Sectional Studies

Cross-sectional studies can be classified as descriptive or analytical, depending on whether the outcome variable is assessed for potential associations with exposures or risk factors. Descriptive cross-sectional studies simply characterize the prevalence of one or multiple health outcomes in a specified population. In analytical cross-sectional studies, investigators collect data for both exposures and outcomes at one specific point in time for the purpose of comparing outcome differences between exposed and unexposed subjects. The exposures and outcomes are measured simultaneously; therefore, it is difficult to determine whether the exposures preceded or followed the outcomes in an analytical cross-sectional study.

In a subtype of cross-sectional study, known as the repeated (or serial) cross-sectional study, data collection is conducted on the same target population at different time points. At each time point, investigators take a different sample (different subjects) of the target population. Thus, repeated cross-sectional studies can be used for analyzing population changes over time (also known as aggregate change over time). They cannot be used to look at individual change (as in a cohort study).

Example 1

Thomas et al conducted a descriptive cross-sectional survey on the prevalence of dysfunctional breathing in patients treated for asthma in primary care. Of the 4,381 patients aged 17 to 65 years registered with a diagnosis of asthma from the medical records of a semirural general practice, 307 (7%) met the entry criteria and were sent the Nijmegen Questionnaire for self-completion. A total of 227 questionnaires were returned after one mailing (response rate, 74%), of which 219 were suitable for analysis. The main outcome was a score ≥ 23 on the Nijmegen Questionnaire. In this study, the investigator found that about one-third of women and one-fifth of men had scores suggestive of dysfunctional breathing.

Example 2

Janson et al performed an analytical cross-sectional study to investigate the association between passive smoking and respiratory symptoms in the European Community Respiratory Health Survey. The analysis included data from 7,882 adults who had never smoked, from 36 centers in 16 countries. Information was gathered through a structured interview. Spirometry and methacholine challenge were performed, and total and specific IgE were measured. Regression analysis was conducted on the variables of interest to study the association between passive smoking on respiratory symptoms and lung function. The prevalence of passive smoking in the workplace varied from 2.5% to 53.8%. The study found that passive smoking was significantly associated with nocturnal chest tightness, nocturnal breathlessness, breathlessness after activity, and increased bronchial responsiveness.

Strengths and Weaknesses of Cross-Sectional Studies

Strengths

- Relatively quick and inexpensive to conduct
- No ethical difficulties
- Data on all variables are only collected at one time point
- Multiple outcomes and exposures can be studied
- Easy for generating hypotheses
- Many findings can be used to create an in-depth research study

Weaknesses

- Unable to measure the incidence
- Difficult to make a causal inference
- Associations identified might be difficult to interpret
- Unable to investigate the temporal relation between
- outcomes and risk factors
- Not good for studying rare diseases
- Susceptible to biases such as nonresponse bias and recall bias

Health outcome measures

Clinical outcome measures/ Assessment

A clinical outcome assessment is a measure that describes or reflects how a patient feels, functions, or survives. Types of COAs include:

- Patient-reported outcome (PRO) measures
- Observer-reported outcome (ObsRO) measures
- Clinician-reported outcome (ClinRO) measures
- Performance outcome (PerfO) measures

Patient-reported outcome (PRO) measures

A type of clinical outcome assessment. A measurement based on a report that comes directly from the patient (i.e., study subject) about the status of a patient's health condition without amendment or interpretation of the patient's response by a clinician or anyone else. A PRO can be measured by self-report or by interview provided that the interviewer records only the patient's response. Symptoms or other unobservable concepts known only to the patient can only be measured by PRO measures. PROs can also assess the patient perspective on functioning or activities that may also be observable by others. PRO measures include:

- Rating scales (e.g., numeric rating scale of pain intensity or Minnesota Living with Heart Failure Questionnaire for assessing heart failure)
- Counts of events (e.g., patient-completed log of emesis episodes or micturition episodes)

Observer-reported outcome (ObsRO) measures

A type of clinical outcome assessment. A measurement based on a report of observable signs, events or behaviors related to a patient's health condition by someone other than the patient or a health professional. Generally, ObsROs are reported by a parent, caregiver, or someone who observes the patient in daily life and are particularly useful for patients who cannot report for themselves (e.g., infants or individuals who are cognitively impaired). An ObsRO measure does not include medical judgment or interpretation. ObsRO measures include:

Rating scales, such as:

- Acute Otitis Media Severity of Symptoms scale (AOM-SOS), a measure used to assess signs and behaviors related to acute otitis media in infants
- Face, Legs, Activity, Cry, Consolability scale (FLACC), a measure used to assess signs and behaviors related to pain
- Counts of events (e.g., observer-completed log of seizure episodes)

Clinician-reported outcome (ClinRO) measures

A type of clinical outcome assessment. A measurement based on a report that comes from a trained health-care professional after observation of a patient's health condition. Most ClinRO measures involve a clinical judgment or interpretation of the observable signs, behaviors, or other manifestations related to a disease or condition. ClinRO measures cannot directly assess symptoms that are known only to the patient. ClinRO measures include:

Reports of particular clinical findings (e.g., presence of a skin lesion or swollen lymph nodes) or clinical events (stroke, heart attack, death, hospitalization for a particular cause), which can be based on clinical observations together with biomarker data, such as electrocardiogram (ECG) and creatine phosphokinase (CPK) results supporting a myocardial infarction

Rating scales, such as:

- Psoriasis Area and Severity Index (PASI) for measurement of severity and extent of a patient's psoriasis
- Hamilton Depression Rating Scale (HAM-D) for assessment of depression

Performance outcome (PerfO) measures

A type of clinical outcome assessment. A measurement based on standardized task(s) actively undertaken by a patient according to a set of instructions. A PerfO assessment may be administered by an appropriately trained individual or completed by the patient independently.

PerfO assessments include:

- Measures of gait speed (e.g., timed 25 foot walk test using a stopwatch or using sensors on ankles)
- Measures of memory (e.g., word recall test)

Roles and responsibilities of Investigator

Investigator's Qualifications and Agreements

- The investigator(s) should be qualified by education, training, and experience to assume responsibility for the proper conduct of the trial, should meet all the qualifications specified by the applicable regulatory requirement(s), and should provide evidence of such qualifications through up-to-date curriculum vitae and/or other relevant documentation requested by the sponsor, the IRB/IEC, and/or the regulatory authority(ies).
- The investigator should be thoroughly familiar with the appropriate use of the investigational product(s), as described in the protocol, in the current Investigator's brochure, in the product information and in other information sources provided by the sponsor.

- The investigator should be aware of, and should comply with, GCP and the applicable regulatory requirements
- The investigator/institution should permit monitoring and auditing by the sponsor, and inspection by the appropriate regulatory authority(ies).
- The investigator should maintain a list of appropriately qualified persons to whom the investigator has delegated significant trial-related duties

Adequate Resources

- The investigator should be able to demonstrate a potential for recruiting the required number of suitable subjects within the agreed recruitment period.
- The investigator should have sufficient time to properly conduct and complete the trial within the agreed trial period.
- The investigator should have available an adequate number of qualified staff and adequate facilities for the foreseen duration of the trial to conduct the trial properly and safely.

Medical Care of Trial Subjects

- A qualified physician (or dentist, when appropriate), who is an investigator or a sub-investigator for the trial, should be responsible for all trial-related medical (or dental) decisions.
- During and following a subject's participation in a trial, the investigator/institution should ensure that adequate medical care is provided to a subject for any adverse events, including clinically significant laboratory values, related to the trial.
- Although a subject is not obligated to give his/her reason(s) for withdrawing prematurely from a trial, the investigator should make a reasonable effort to ascertain the reason(s), while fully respecting the subject's rights.

Communication with IRB/IEC

- Before initating a trial, the investigator/institution should have written and dated approval/favorable opinion from the IRB/IEC for the trial protocol, written informed consent form, consent form updates, subject recruitment procedures(e.g., advertisements), and any other written information to be provided to subjects.
- During the trial the investigator/institution should provide to the IRB/IEC all documents subject to review

Compliance with Protocol

- The investigator/institution should conduct the trial in compliance with the protocol agreed to by the sponsor and, if required, by the regulatory authority(ies) and which was given approval/favorable opinion by the IRB/IEC.
- The investigator may implement a deviation from, or a change of, the protocol to eliminate an immediate hazard(s) to trial subjects without prior IRB/IEC approval/favorable opinion.

Investigational Product(s)

- Responsibility for investigational product(s) accountability at the trial site(s) rests with the investigator/institution. The investigator/institution and/or a pharmacist or other appropriate individual, who is designated by the investigator/institution, should maintain records of the product's delivery to the trial site, the inventory at the site, the use by each subject, and the return to the sponsor or alternative disposition of unused product(s).

Randomization Procedures and Un-blinding

- The investigator should follow the trial's randomization procedures, if any, and should ensure that the code is broken only in accordance with the protocol. If the trial is blinded, the investigator should promptly document and explain to the sponsor any premature un-blinding

Informed Consent of Trial Subjects

- Prior to the beginning of the trial, the investigator should have the IRB/IEC's written approval/favourable opinion of the written informed consent form and any other written information to be provided to subjects.
- Neither the investigator, nor the trial staff, should coerce or unduly influence a subject to participate or to continue to participate in a trial.
- All questions about the trial should be answered to the satisfaction of the subject or the subject's legally acceptable representative.

Records and Reports

- The investigator should ensure the accuracy, completeness, legibility, and timeliness of the data reported to the sponsor in the CRFs and in all required reports.
- Data reported on the CRF, that are derived from source documents, should be consistent with the source documents or the discrepancies should be explained.

Progress Reports

- The investigator should submit written summaries of the trial status to the IRB/IEC annually, or more frequently, if requested by the IRB/IEC.

Safety Reporting

- All serious adverse events (SAEs) should be reported immediately to the sponsor except for those SAEs that the protocol or other document (e.g., Investigator's Brochure) identifies as not needing immediate reporting. The immediate reports should be followed promptly by detailed, written reports.

Premature Termination or Suspension of a Trial

- If the trial is prematurely terminated or suspended for any reason, the investigator/institution should promptly inform the trial subjects, should assure appropriate therapy and follow-up for the subjects, and, where required by the applicable regulatory requirement(s), should inform the regulatory authority(ies).

Final Report(s)

- Upon completion of the trial, the investigator, where applicable, should inform the institution; the investigator/ institution should provide the IRB/IEC with a summary of the trials outcome, and the regulatory authority(ies) with any reports required.

Roles and responsibilities of Sponsor

Quality Assurance and Quality Control

- The sponsor is responsible for implementing and maintaining quality assurance and quality control systems with written SOPs to ensure that trials are conducted and data are generated, documented (recorded), and reported in compliance with the protocol, GCP, and the applicable regulatory requirements.
- The sponsor is responsible for securing agreement from all involved parties to ensure direct access to all trial related sites, source data/documents , and reports for the purpose of monitoring and auditing by the sponsor, and inspection by domestic and foreign regulatory authorities.
- Quality control should be applied to each stage of data handling to ensure that all data are relicable and have been processed correctly.
- Agreements, made by the sponsor with the investigator/institution and any other parties involved with the clinical trial, should be in writing, as part of the protocol or in a separate agreement.

Contract Research Organization (CRO)

A sponsor may transfer any or all of the sponsor's trial-related duties and functions to a CRO, but the ultimate responsibility for the quality and intergrity of the trial data always resides with sponsor. The CRO should implement quality assurance and quality control.

- Any trial-related duty and function that is transferred to and assumed by a CRO should be specified in writing
- All references to a sponsor in this guideline also apply to a CRO to the extent that a CRO has assumed the trial related duties and funtions of a sponsor.

Medical Expertise

- The sponsor should designate appropriately qualified medical personnel who will be readily available to advise on trial related medical questions or problems. If necessary, outside consultant(s) may be appointed for this purpose.

Trial Design

- The sponsor should ultilize qualified individuals (e.g. biostatisticians, clinical pharmacologists, and physicians) as appropriate, throughout all stages of the trial process, from designing the protocol and CRF's and planning the analyses to analyzing and preparing interim and final clinical trial reports.
- For further guidance: Clinical Trial protocol and protocol amendment(s), the ICH Guideline for structure and Content of Clinical Study Reports, and other appropriate ICH guidance on trial design, protocol and conduct.

Trial Management, Data Handling, and Record Keeping

- The sponsor should utilize appropriately qualified individuals to supervise the overall conduct of the trial, to handle the data, to verify the data , to conduct the statistical analyses, and to prepare the trial reports.
- The sponsor may consider establishing an independent data-monitoring committee (IDMC) to assess the progress of a clinical trial, including the safety data and the critical efficacy endpoints at intervals, and to recommend to the sponsor whether to continue, modify, or stop a trial. The IDMC should have written operating procedures and maintain written records of all its meetings.

When using electronic trial data handling and/or remote electronic trial data systems, the sponsor should:

a. Ensure and document that the electronic data processing system(s) conforms to the sponsor's established requirements for completeness, accuracy, reliability, and consistent intended performance (i.e. validation).
b. Maintains SOP's for using these systems.
c. Maintain a security system that prevents unauthorized access to the data.

d. Maintain a list of the individuals who are authorized to make data changes
e. Maintain adequate backup of the data.
f. Safeguard the blinding, if any (e.g. maintain the blinding during data entry and processing).

Investigator Selection

- The sponsor is responsible for selecting the investigator(s)/institution(s). Each investigator should be qualified by training and experience and should have adequate resources to properly conduct the trial for which the investigator is selected. If organization of a coordinating committee and/or selection of coordinating investigator(s) are to be utilized in multicentre trials, their organization and/or selection is the sponsor's responsibility.

Allocation of Responsibilities

- Prior to intiating a trial, the sponsor should define, establish, and allocate all trial-related duties and functions.

Compensation to Subjects and investigators

- If required by the applicable regulatory requirement(s), the sponsor should provide insurance or should indemnity (legal and financial coverage) the investigator/the institution against claims arising from the trial, except for claims that arise from malpractice and/or negligance.

Financing

- The financial aspects of the trial should be documented in an agreement between the sponsor and the investigator/institution.

Notification/submission to Regulatory Authority(ies)

- Before initiating the clinical trial(s), the sponsor (or the sponsor and the investigator, if required by the applicable regulatory requirement(s)) should submit any required application(s) to the appropriate authority(ies) for review, acceptance, and/or permission (as required by the applicable regulatory requirement(s)) to begin the trial(s).

Manufaturing packaging, Labelling, and coding Investigational product(s)

- The sponsor should ensure that the investigational product(s) (including active comparable(s) and placebo, if applicable) is charaterized as appropriate to the stage of development of the product(s), is manufactured in accordance with any applicable GMP, and is coded and labelled in a manner that protects the blinding, if applicable regulatory requirement(s).
- The sponsor should determine, for the investigational product(s), acceptable storage temperatures, storage conditions (e.g. protection from light), storage times, reconstitution fluids and procedures, and devices for product infusion, if any.

i. In blinded trials, the coding system for the investigational product(s) should include a mechanism that permits rapid identification of the product(s) in case of a medical emergency, but does not permit undetectable breaks of the blinding.

v. If significant formulation changes are made in the investigational or comparator product(s) during the course of clinical development, the results of any additional studies of the formulated product(s) (e.g. stability, dissolution rate, bioavailability) needed to assess whether these changes would significantly alter the pharmaokinetic profile of the product should be available prior to the use of the new formulation in clinical trials.

Record Access

- The sponsor should ensure that it is specified in the protocol or other written agreement that the investigator(s)/documents for trial-related monitoring, audits, IRB/IEC review, and regulatory inspection.

Safety Information

- The sponsor is responsible for the ongoing safety evaluation of the investigational product(s).

Adverse Drug Reaction Reporting

- The sponsor should expedite the reporting to all concerned investigator(s)/institutions(s), to the IRB(s)/IEC(s), where required, and to the regulatory authority(ies) of all adverse drug reactions (ADRs) that are both serious and unexpected.

Monitoring

a. Selection of qualified monitors
b. The sponsor should ensure that the trials are adequately monitored.
c. Assign Monitor's Responsibilities
d. Verifying for the investigational product(s)
e. Establish SOP's as well as procedures that are specified for monitoring a specific trial
f. Monitoring Reports should be evaluated on timely basis.

Roles And Responsibilities of Clinical Research Coordinator

The CRC is a vital link between the research subjects and their family, the investigator, and other site team members. They are also the liaison between the Sponsor, CRO, SMO, Central laboratory, Courier, the institutional Review Board (IRB), and other players involved in the trial.

Because of an increase in the number of clinical trials and the need for complicated and data intensive research, many sponsors today are reluctant to place a trial at a site that does not have a trained CRC to work along with the investigator.

Responsibilities of CRC's

CRCs work in a team under the direct supervision of the Pls. CRCs usually have to handle multiple responsibilities. The responsibilities of a CRC can be broadly categorized as:

v. **General responsibilities**
v. **Trial specific responsibilities**

General Responsibilities

- **Capacity Building**

The CRC ensures that the potentical pool of potential investigators and sites keep increasing. The CRC is always on the lookout for new trial sites with Investigators who are research native.

They conduct an in-depth survey of the new sites to assess:

- Manpower presence and competence
- Support staff and constant support
- Infrastructure
- Presence of a functional Ethics Committee
- Compatible management
- Major diseases – incidence and prevalence rates

Training new CRCs

Experienced CRCs are an asset and often are the best persons to hand-hold and train the newcomes in the field of clinical research. The training may include conducting feasibility studies, designing trial documents, setting up of sites, conduct of the trial and trial closeout

<u>Trial – related Responsibilities</u>

- **Site Identification**

A key responsibility of the CRC is to identify the right site for the trial- one that fulfills all the criteria set forth by the clinical trial guidelines and trial protocol. A CRC who has worked at a particular site earlier is often the best judge to identify the site for another trial. Having worked at a site for over a period of time, the CRC understands the needs, expectations, and the potential of the site. He/she knows how the site can function to its optimum.

- **Pretrial Documentation**

A CRC has to collect the updated and signed resume of each member of the site team. He/She must ensure that the following pretrial documents are completed within the specified timeline:

- Form 1572
- Financial Disclosure Form
- Undertaking from the PI
- Confidentiality Non-Disclosure Agreement

Coordinating with the IRB

You can actively follow up through the site team with the IRB for a faster approval of the trial. You will also look into the timely submission of all the safety reports and the amendments of the trial documents to the IRB.

- **Financial Responsibilities**

Sometimes a senior CRC may be empowered to negotiate the trial budgets at the site. This includes the investigator fees, the IRB fees, the site administration fees, laboratory costs, study subject travel and other reimbursements.

Track the trial on a routine basis. Inform the concerned personnel on reaching specific milestones. All milestone –related payments will be followed up by you.

- **Training the site staff**

The CRC must be ready to train the site staff on a regular basis throughout the trial. He/she can highlight on:

- Inclusion criteria
- Exclusion criteria
- Schedule of visits
- Window period
- Visit specific activities
- Safety guidelines and reporting timelines as per the protocol

Investigator's Meeting and Site initiation visits

The CRC may be in charge of conducting the entire investigators' meeting for the trial. They also have to ensure that all the requirements are in place for the site initiation visit.

- **Informed Consent Forms**

The CRC ensures that the informed consent form sent by the sponsor is translated and back-translated into the local language as advised by the investigator.

- **Patient recruitment and follow up**

During the subject enrollment, he/she ensures that all queries are clarified up to the subjects' satisfaction and that the ICF is administered by the investigator as per the ICH GCP guidelines.

- **Research Pharmacy, Drug Accountability, and Laboratory Responsibilities**

The CRC also have to manage the storage of the study drug –account for study drug received from sponsor, distributed to the patient, returned from the patient and finally back to the sponsor.

They ensure that all laboratory specimens such as blood, urine, tissue etc are properly labeled, packaged and stored before shipment to the central lab. They even coordinate with the central lab on a regular basis for the timely receipt of the reports.

- **Amendments**

They follow up with the sponsor for any amendments in the study protocol or the ICF and ensure that the amended versions are implemented at the site only after the favorable written approval by the IRB.

- **Post –trial activities**

Once the hospital phase of the trial is over, completing the study documentation will become the key focus3. They do a final check of the case report forms (CRFs), maintain an archival inventory of records and CRFs in a secure place and coordinate the close out visits.

Roles and responsibilities of Monitor

Monitoring Purpose

The purposes of trial monitoring are to verify that:

(a) The rights and well-being of human subjects are protected.

(b) The reported trial data are accurate, complete, and verifiable from source documents.

(c) The conduct of the trial is in compliance with the currently approved protocol/amendment(s), with GCP, and with the applicable regulatory requirement(s)

Selection and Qualifications of Monitors

(a) Monitors should be appointed by the sponsor.

(b) Monitors should be appropriately trained, and should have the scientific and/or clinical knowledge needed to monitor the trial adequately. A monitor's qualifications should be documented.

(c) Monitors should be thoroughly familiar with the investigational product(s), the protocol, written informed consent form and any other written information to be provided to subjects, the sponsor's SOPs, GCP, and the applicable regulatory requirement(s).

Extent and Nature of Monitoring

The sponsor should ensure that the trials are adequately monitored. The sponsor should determine the appropriate extent and nature of monitoring. The determination of the extent and nature of monitoring should be based on considerations such as the objective, purpose, design, complexity, blinding, size, and endpoints of the trial. In general, there is a need for on-site monitoring, before, during, and after the trial; however, in exceptional circumstances the sponsor may determine that central monitoring in conjunction with procedures such as investigators' training and meetings, and extensive written guidance can assure appropriate conduct of the trial in accordance with GCP. Statistically controlled sampling may be an acceptable method for selecting the data to be verified.

Monitor's Responsibilities

The monitor(s) in accordance with the sponsor's requirements should ensure that the trial is conducted and documented properly by carrying out the following activities when relevant and necessary to the trial and the trial site:

(a) Acting as the main line of communication between the sponsor and the investigator.

(b) Verifying that the investigator has adequate qualifications and resources and remain adequate throughout the trial period, that facilities, including laboratories, equipment, and staff, are adequate to safely and properly conduct the trial and remain adequate throughout the trial period.

(c) Verifying, for the investigational product(s):

(i) That storage times and conditions are acceptable, and that supplies are sufficient throughout the trial.

(ii) That the investigational product(s) are supplied only to subjects who are eligible to receive it and at the protocol specified dose(s).

(iii) That subjects are provided with necessary instruction on properly using, handling, storing, and returning the investigational product(s).

(iv) That the receipt, use, and return of the investigational product(s) at the trial sites are controlled and documented adequately.

(v) That the disposition of unused investigational product(s) at the trial sites complies with applicable regulatory requirement(s) and is in accordance with the sponsor.

(d) Verifying that the investigator follows the approved protocol and all approved amendment(s), if any.

(e) Verifying that written informed consent was obtained before each subject's participation in the trial.

(f) Ensuring that the investigator receives the current Investigator's Brochure, all documents, and all trial supplies needed to conduct the trial properly and to comply with the applicable regulatory requirement(s).

(g) Ensuring that the investigator and the investigator's trial staff are adequately informed about the trial.

(h) Verifying that the investigator and the investigator's trial staff are performing the specified trial functions, in accordance with the protocol and any other written agreement between the sponsor and the investigator/institution, and have not delegated these functions to unauthorized individuals.

(i) Verifying that the investigator is enrolling only eligible subjects.

(j) Reporting the subject recruitment rate.

(k) Verifying that source documents and other trial records are accurate, complete, kept up-to-date and maintained.

(l) Verifying that the investigator provides all the required reports, notifications, applications, and submissions, and that these documents are accurate, complete, timely, legible, dated, and identify the trial.

(m) Checking the accuracy and completeness of the CRF entries, source documents and other trial-related records against each other. The monitor specifically should verify that:

(i) The data required by the protocol are reported accurately on the CRFs and are consistent with the source documents.

(ii) Any dose and/or therapy modifications are well documented for each of the trial subjects.

(iii) Adverse events, concomitant medications and intercurrent illnesses are reported in accordance with the protocol on the CRFs.

(iv) Visits that the subjects fail to make, tests that are not conducted, and examinations that are not performed are clearly reported as such on the CRFs.

(v) All withdrawals and dropouts of enrolled subjects from the trial are reported and explained on the CRFs.

(n) Informing the investigator of any CRF entry error, omission, or illegibility. The monitor should ensure that appropriate corrections, additions, or deletions are made, dated, explained (if necessary), and initialled by the investigator or by a member of the investigator's trial staff who is authorized to initial CRF changes for the investigator. This authorization should be documented.

(o) Determining whether all adverse events (AEs) are appropriately reported within the time periods required by GCP, the protocol, the IRB/IEC, the sponsor, and the applicable regulatory requirement(s).

(p) Determining whether the investigator is maintaining the essential documents (see 8. Essential Documents for the Conduct of a Clinical Trial).

(q) Communicating deviations from the protocol, SOPs, GCP, and the applicable regulatory requirements to the investigator and taking appropriate action designed to prevent recurrence of the detected deviations.

Roles and responsibilities of Contract Research Organization (CRO)

- A sponsor may transfer any or all of the sponsor's trial-related duties and functions to a CRO, but the ultimate responsibility for the quality and integrity of the trial data always resides with the sponsor. The CRO should implement quality assurance and quality control.
- Any trial-related duty and function that is transferred to and assumed by a CRO should be specified in writing Any trial-related duties and functions not specifically transferred to and assumed by a CRO are retained by the sponsor.
- All references to a sponsor in this guideline also apply to a CRO to the extent that a CRO has assumed the trial related duties and functions of a sponsor.

ADDENDUM

The sponsor should ensure oversight of any trial-related duties and functions carried out on its behalf, including trial-related duties and functions that are subcontracted to another party by the sponsor's contracted CRO(s)

Questions

1.Explain in detail about planning and execution of clinical trial?

2.Enlist the steps involved in planning phase of clinical trial?

3.What are he various phases of clinical trial?

4.Shor note on Phase 1 trial?

5.Shor note on Phase 2 trial?

6.Shor note on phase 3 trial?

7.Shor note on phase 4 trial?

8.Explain in detail about Bioavailability and bioequivalence study?
9.Explain the methods to document BA & BE studies?
10.Short note on Pilot study?
11.Short note on full scale study?
12.Short note on single dose and multiple dose testing?
13.What are the randomization technique in clinical research?
14.Short note on Simple randomization?
15.Short note on Block Randomization?
16.Short note on Covariate adaptive randomization?
17.Short note on Restricted randomization ?
18.Write the difference between experimental designs and quasiexperimental designs?
19.What is mean by prospective study? advantages and disadvantages?
20.Enlist the differences between prospective and retrospective study?
21.Explain in detail about the sampling methods in clinical research?
22.Write note on cohort study with examples?
23.Write note on case control study wih examples?
24.Write note on cross sectional study with examples?
25.Explain in detail about health outcome measures in clinical research?
26.Role and responsibilities of Investigator in clinical trial?
27.Role and responsibilities of Sponser in clinical trial?
28.Role and responsibilities of Clinical Research coordinator in clinical trial?
29.Role and responsibilities of Monitor in clinical trial?
30.Role and responsibilities of Contract research organization in clinical trial?

CHAPTER THREE

Clinical trial Documents

Guidelines to the preparation of Protocols Clinical Research Protocol

The term "protocol" is defined as a complete written description of, and scientific rationale for, a research activity involving human subjects.Clinical research is conducted according to a plan (a protocol) or an action plan. The protocol demonstrates the guidelines for conducting the trial. It illustrates what will be made in the study by explaining each essential part of it and how it is carried out. It also describes the eligibility of the participants, the length of the study, the medications and the related tests.

Purpose of a Research Proposal

1) To raise the question to be researched and clarify its importance.

2) To collect existing knowledge and discuss the efforts of other researchers who have worked on the related questions (Literature review).

3) To formulate a hypothesis and objectives.

4) To clarify ethical considerations.

5) To suggest the methodology required for solving the question and achieving the objectives.

6) To discuss the requirements and limitations in achieving the objectives.

Protocol Review

Clinical trials must be approved and monitored by an Institutional Review Board that ensures that the risks are negligible and are worth any potential benefits. It is an independent committee that consists of physicians, dentists, statisticians, and members of the community. The committee ensures that clinical trials are ethical and that the rights of all participants are protected. The board must initially approve and periodically review the research.

Writing the Protocol

Protocol writing allows the researcher to review and critically evaluate the published literature on the interested topic, plan and review the project steps and serves as a guide throughout the investigation.

Components of a Research Protocol

1) Title of the study

2) Administrative details

3) Project summary

4) Introduction to the research topic, background (Literature review)

5) Preliminary studies

6) Study objectives and/or questions. Statement of the problem.

7) Methodology: Study design, study population and methods of recruitment, variables list, sample size, methods of data collection, data collection tools, plan of analysis (analysis of data)

8) Project management: Work plan (Timeline - proposed schedule)

9) Strengths and limitations of the study

10) Issues for ethical review and approvals

11) Operational Planning and Budgeting (Budget Summary)

12) Reference System

1) Title of the study

Title should be accurate, short, concise. It should make the main objective clear, convey the main purpose of the research and mention the target population. Carry maximum information about the topic in a few words; it is a good practice to keep the title to within 12-15 words. It should convey the idea about the area of research and what methods are going to be used in a compact, relevant, accurate, attractive, easy to understand, and informative way.

It should Identify

- What is the study about
- Who are the targets
- Where is the setting of the study
- When it is launched, if applicable

2) Administrative Details

The following administrative details and a protocol content summary should follow the title page:

- Contents page list of relevant sections and sub-sections with corresponding page number.
- Signature page is signed by senior members of the research team and dated to confirm that the version concerned has been approved by them.
- Contact details for the research team members listing postal, e-mail addresses and telephone numbers.

3) Project Summary

The summary should be distinctive, concise and should sum up all the essentials of the protocol.

4) Introduction (Background)

- The background should be concise and refer to the subject straight forwardly. In writing the review, attention should be drawn to the positives, negatives and limitations of the studies quoted.
- Introduction is concluded by explaining how the present study will benefit the community.
- The literature review should logically lead to the statement of the aims of the proposed project and end with the aims and objectives of the study.
- The review should include the most recent publications in the field and the topic of the research is selected only after completing the literature review and finding some gaps in it.
- Introduction should briefly answer the importance of the topic, the gaps/lacunae in the literature, the purpose of the study and benefits for the society, from the study.
- The research question should be described precisely and concisely. It is going to be the basis of designing the project.
- The definition of the problem should be clear so that a reader can straight forwardly recognize the real meaning of it.

5) Study Objectives (Aims):

- Aims should be logical and coherent, feasible, concise, realistic, considering local conditions, phrased to clearly meet the purpose of the study and related to what the specific research is intended to accomplish.
- For example, to evaluate knowledge level regarding dental caries in primary school children in KSA (this is not detailed). The following should be added: Causes, treatment, preventive measures, etc.
- The objectives should be (SMART objective): Specific, Measurable, Achievable, Relevant and Time based. Specific Aims: Details of each objective that will finally lead to the achievement of the goal should be stated. Specific aims one by one should be listed concisely.

- It is good practice not to include too many aims in the study (2-5 best); too many objectives often lead to inaccurate and poorly defined results. Furthermore, aims should be achievable, realistic and specific with no general and ambiguous statements. They should be stated in action verbs that illustrate their purpose: i.e., "to determine, to compare, to verify, to calculate, to reduce, to describe, etc."

Secondary Objectives (Optional):

These are referred to as ancillary and minor objectives that could be studied during the course of the study.

The formulation of objectives helps to focus the study and to avoid the collection of any unnecessary data and hence organize the study in clear and distinct stages. Hypothesis: It is a statement based on sound scientific theory that recognizes the predicted correlation between two or additional assessable variables . It is always developed in response to the purpose statement or to answer the research questions posed. Furthermore, hypothesis transforms research questions into a format amendable to testing or into a statement that predicts an expected outcome.

Types of hypothesis statements:

- **Null hypothesis:**

A null hypothesis is a statement that there is no actual relationship between variables (H0 or HN). It may be read as there is no difference between the groups to be compared and no relationship between the exposure and outcome under investigation. H0 states the contradictory of what the researchers expect. The final conclusion of the investigators will either keep a null hypothesis or reject it in support of an alternative hypothesis. It does not essentially mean that H0 is accurate when not rejecting it as there might not be an adequate proof against it.

- **Alternative hypothesis**:

An alternative hypothesis is a statement that suggests a potential outcome that the researcher may expect (H1 or HA). This hypothesis is derived from previous studies where an evident difference between the groups to be compared is present. It is recognized only when a null hypothesis is rejected. Practically, hypotheses are stated in the null form, because they have their inferential statistics. Such hypotheses of no difference will be challenged by researchers and the result of the statistical testing gives the probability that the hypothesis of no difference is true or false.

Aims should be logically linked and arranged according to the tested hypothesis statement.

Example:

- Research question: Is there a difference in fluoride release between the Compomer and Glass- ionomer cement?
- Null Hypothesis: There is no difference in fluoride release between the Compomer and Glass- ionomer cement.
- Alternate Hypothesis: There is a difference in fluoride release between the Compomer and Glass-ionomer cement.

The statement of the problem should provide a summary of exactly what the project is trying to achieve.

- What exactly do you want to study?
- Why is it worth studying?
- Does the proposed study have theoretical and/or practical significance?
- Does it contribute to a new understanding of a phenomenon? (i.e., Does it address new or little-known material or does it treat familiar material in a new way or does it challenge an existing understanding or extend existing knowledge?)

The justification of the research should be a convincing statement for the need to do it:

- How does the research relate to the priorities of the region and the country?
- What knowledge and information will be obtained?
- What is the ultimate purpose that the knowledge obtained from the study will serve?
- How will the results be disseminated?
- How will the results be used, and who will be the beneficiaries

1. **Methods and Materials**

It should describe in detail the 'Where', 'Who', 'How' the research will be conducted. It explains the study design and procedures and techniques used to achieve the proposed objectives. It defines the variables and demonstrates in detail how the variables will be measured. It details the proposed methodology for data gathering and processing. Methodology composes an important part of the protocol. It assures that the hypothesis will be confirmed or rejected. It also refers to a thorough strategy to attain the objectives.

The methods and materials are divided into various subheadings:

a. **Study design (cross-sectional, case-control, intervention study, RCT, etc.):**

Proper explanation should be given as to why a particular design was chosen (on the basis of proposed objectives and availability of resources). A study design is in fact the researcher's general plan to acquire the answer (s) to the hypothesis being tested. Here, strategies will be applied to develop balanced, correct, objective and meaningful information. It explains the methods that will be used to collect and analyze data. Proper selection of the study design is important to attain reliable and valid scientific results. Ethics, logistic concerns, economic features and scientific thoroughness will determine the design of the study. Here, a chief concern is given to the legality of the results including potential bias mystifying issues. Randomized controlled clinical trial is the best to document a causal relationship between an exposure and its outcome.

b) Study population (Study subjects):

Where are you going to do the research and who is the study population (why doing research in this place and why selecting this population?). It describes in detail about the study subjects, all aspects of the selection procedure and sample size calculation. Proper definition of eligibility, inclusion, exclusion and discontinuation criteria of the study subjects should be stated. Allocation of subjects to study arms should be explained and described in details bearing in mind the concealment and randomization process.

c)Sample size:

Sample size calculation is recommended for economical and ethical reasons. The calculation of the sample size must be explained including the power of the sample. The sampling technique should be mentioned, e.g., randomization that will be used in order to obtain a representative sample for your target population. Each step involved in the recruitment of the study subjects should be described according to the selection criteria (inclusion and exclusion criteria). "Informed consent" should be mentioned (Permission granted in full knowledge of the possible consequences).

a. **Proposed intervention:**

Full description of proposed intervention should be given. Here, all the activities and actions should be recorded and thoroughly explained in their order of occurrence.

- When using drugs, both scientific and brand name should be mentioned followed by the name of the manufacturing company, city, and country. Drug route, dosage, frequency of administration, and total duration of treatment with the drug should be mentioned.
- When using apparatus its name should be given followed by the name of the manufacturer, city and country.

Involved personnel should precisely define:

- Who will be responsible for the interventions?
- What activities each personnel will perform and with what frequency and intensity?

a. **Data collection methods, instruments used:**

Data collection tools are:

- Retrospective data (medical records)
- Questionnaires

• Interviews (Structured, Semi-Structured)

• Laboratory test (literature or personal knowledge should be referenced, if established test, or description should be provided in details, if not established)

• Clinical examinations

• Description of instruments, tools used for data collection, as well as the methods used to test the validity and reliability of the instrument should be provided.

2. **Data Management and Analysis Plan:**

This section should be written following statistical advice from a statistician. The analysis plan and which statistical tests will be used to check the significance to the research question/hypothesis with appropriate references should be described. Names of variables that will be used in the analyses and the name of statistical analysis that will be performed to assess the outcome should be listed. If computer programs are to be applied, it is important to mention the software used and its version.

3. **Project Management: Work plan**

A work plan is an outline of activities of all the phases of the research to be carried out according to an anticipated time schedule. Proper time table for accomplishing each major step of the study should be defined. Assigning time frame to each step in the trial will be helpful in organizing the structure of the research trial. The personnel (investigators, assistants, laboratory technicians etc.) involved in the study or data collection should be properly trained.

4. **Strengths and Limitations:**

It is important to mention the strengths or limitations of the study, i.e., what study can achieve or cannot achieve is important, so as to prevent wasteful allocation of resources. 10) Ethical Considerations (Issues for Ethical Review and Approvals): It should indicate whether the procedures to be followed are in accord with the Declaration of Helsinki. In any case, study should not start unless approval from ethics committee is received.

The following points should be explained:

• The benefits and risks for the subjects involved. The physical, social and psychological implications of the research.

• Details of the information to be given to the study patients including alternative treatments/approaches.

• Information should be provided on the free informed consent of the participants.

Information form should contain: Justification for research, outline of study, risks, confidentiality, and voluntary participation should be told patients about the freedom to withdraw from the study whenever they wish to. Confidentiality indicates how the personal information obtained from the patient will be kept secret (Data safety).

5. **Operational Planning and Budgeting (Budget Summary):**

Outline the budget requirement showing head wise expenditure for the study-manpower, transportation, instruments, laboratory tests, and cost of the drug. Budget estimate is to be attached in the annexure. All costs including personnel, consumables, equipment, supplies, communication, and funds for patients and data processing are all included in the budget. Each item should be justified.

6. **Reference System:**

Referencing is the regular method of recognizing information taken from other researchers' work. A proper citation will enable the readers to follow-up any reference of interest. Plagiarism refers to claiming and acquiring someone else's ideas, an action that is considered a criminal action. Failure to reference an idea that you have found in your research, or to acknowledge the work of other team members in a team assignment falls under the category of plagiarism. Therefore referencing is an extremely important aspect of the research protocol. The two most commonly used citation systems in clinical writing are the Vancouver system and the Harvard system . The choice of referencing system is dependent upon the funding organizations where the research protocol is being submitted. These frequently identify their preferred system of referencing and this should be strictly adhered to. The most common style used in the dental literature is Vancouver style.

7. **Annexure:**

The following annexes are to be attached at the end of the protocol:
1. Informed consent form.
2. Letters from ethics committees.
3. Study questionnaire (copies of any questionnaires or draft questionnaires).
4. Case Record Forms (CRFs).
5. Budget details.
6. Curriculum Vitae (CV) of the chief investigator and coinvestigator and their role in the study. It will ensure that the role of each investigator is well defined.

Guidelines to the preparation of Investigator's Brochure

The Investigator's Brochure (IB) is a compilation of the clinical and nonclinical data on the investigational product(s) that are relevant to the study of the product(s) in human subjects. Its purpose is to provide the investigators and others involved in the trial with the information to facilitate their understanding of the rationale for, and their compliance with, many key features of the protocol, such as the dose, dose frequency/interval, methods of administration: and safety monitoring procedures. The IB also provides insight to support the clinical management of the study subjects during the course of the clinical trial. The information should be presented in a concise, simple, objective, balanced, and non-promotional form that enables a clinician, or potential investigator, to understand it and make his/her own unbiased risk-benefit assessment of the appropriateness of the proposed trial. For this reason, a medically qualified person should generally participate in the editing of an IB, but the contents of the IB should be approved by the disciplines that generated the described data.

This guideline delineates the minimum information that should be included in an IB and provides suggestions for its layout. It is expected that the type and extent of information available will vary with the stage of development of the investigational product. If the investigational product is marketed and its pharmacology is widely understood by medical practitioners, an extensive IB may not be necessary. Where permitted by regulatory authorities, a basic product information brochure, package leaflet, or labelling may be an appropriate alternative, provided that it includes current, comprehensive, and detailed information on all aspects of the investigational product that might be of importance to the investigator. If a marketed product is being studied for a new use (i.e., a new indication), an IB specific to that new use should be prepared. The IB should be reviewed at least annually and revised as necessary in compliance with a sponsor's written procedures. More frequent revision may be appropriate depending on the stage of development and the generation of relevant new information. However, in accordance with Good Clinical Practice, relevant new information may be so important that it should be communicated to the investigators, and possibly to the Institutional Review Boards (IRBs)/Independent Ethics Committees (IECs) and/or regulatory authorities before it is included in a revised IB.

Generally, the sponsor is responsible for ensuring that an up-to-date IB is made available to the investigator(s) and the investigators are responsible for providing the up-to-date IB to the responsible IRBs/IECs. In the case of an investigator sponsored trial, the sponsor-investigator should determine whether a brochure is available from the commercial manufacturer. If the investigational product is provided by the sponsor-investigator, then he or she should provide the necessary information to the trial personnel. In cases where preparation of a formal IB is impractical, the sponsor-investigator should provide, as a substitute, an expanded background information section in the trial protocol that contains the minimum current information described in this guideline.

General Considerations the IB should include:

1.Title Page

This should provide the sponsor's name, the identity of each investigational product (i.e., research number, chemical or approved generic name, and trade name(s) where legally permissible and desired by the sponsor), and the release date. It is also suggested that an edition number, and a reference to the number and date of the edition it supersedes, be provided. An example is given in Appendix 1.

2 Confidentiality Statement

The sponsor may wish to include a statement instructing the investigator/recipients to treat the IB as a confidential document for the sole information and use of the investigator's team and the IRB/IEC.

3 Contents of the Investigator's Brochure

The IB should contain the following sections, each with literature references where appropriate:

a) Table of Contents

An example of the Table of Contents is given in Appendix 2

b) Summary

A brief summary (preferably not exceeding two pages) should be given, highlighting the significant physical, chemical, pharmaceutical, pharmacological, toxicological, pharmacokinetic, metabolic, and clinical information available that is relevant to the stage of clinical development of the investigational product.

c) Introduction

A brief introductory statement should be provided that contains the chemical name (and generic and trade name(s) when approved) of the investigational product(s), all active ingredients, the investigational product (s) pharmacological class and its expected position within this class (e.g., advantages), the rationale for performing research with the investigational product(s), and the anticipated prophylactic, therapeutic, or diagnostic indication(s). Finally, the introductory statement should provide the general approach to be followed in evaluating the investigational product.

d)Physical, Chemical, and Pharmaceutical Properties and Formulation

A description should be provided of the investigational product substance(s) (including the chemical and/or structural formula(e)), and a brief summary should be given of the relevant physical, chemical, and pharmaceutical properties. To permit appropriate safety measures to be taken in the course of the trial, a description of the formulation(s) to be used, including excipients, should be provided and justified if clinically relevant. Instructions for the storage and handling of the dosage form(s) should also be given. Any structural similarities to other known compounds should be mentioned.

e)Nonclinical Studies

Introduction:

The results of all relevant nonclinical pharmacology, toxicology, pharmacokinetic, and investigational product metabolism studies should be provided in summary form. This summary should address the methodology used, the results, and a discussion of the relevance of the findings to the investigated therapeutic and the possible unfavourable and unintended effects in humans.

The information provided may include the following, as appropriate, if known/available:

- Nature and frequency of pharmacological or toxic effects
- Severity or intensity of pharmacological or toxic effects
- Time to onset of effects
- Reversibility of effects
- Duration of effects

- Dose response

- Species tested
- Number and sex of animals in each group
- Unit dose (e.g., milligram/kilogram (mg/kg))
- Dose interval
- Route of administration
- Duration of dosing
- Information on systemic distribution
- Duration of post-exposure follow-up
- Results, including the following aspects:

Tabular format/listings should be used whenever possible to enhance the clarity of the presentation.

The following sections should discuss the most important findings from the studies, including the dose response of observed effects, the relevance to humans, and any aspects to be studied in humans. If applicable, the effective and nontoxic dose findings in the same animal species should be compared (i.e., the therapeutic index should be discussed). The relevance of this information to the proposed human dosing should be addressed. Whenever possible, comparisons should be made in terms of blood/tissue levels rather than on a mg/kg basis.

(a) Nonclinical Pharmacology

A summary of the pharmacological aspects of the investigational product and, where appropriate, its significant metabolites studied in animals, should be included. Such a summary should incorporate studies that assess potential therapeutic activity (e.g. efficacy models, receptor binding, and specificity) as well as those that assess safety (e.g., special studies to assess pharmacological actions other than the intended therapeutic effect(s)).

a. ***Pharmacokinetics and Product Metabolism in Animals***

A summary of the pharmacokinetics and biological transformation and disposition of the investigational product in all species studied should be given. The discussion of the findings should address the absorption and the local and systemic bioavailability of the investigational product and its metabolites, and their relationship to the pharmacological and toxicological findings in animal species.

(c) Toxicology

A summary of the toxicological effects found in relevant studies conducted in different animal species should be described under the following headings where appropriate:

f) Effects in Humans

Introduction:

A thorough discussion of the known effects of the investigational product(s) in humans should be provided, including information on pharmacokinetics, metabolism, pharmacodynamics, dose response, safety, efficacy, and other pharmacological activities. Where possible, a summary of each completed clinical trial should be provided. Information should also be provided regarding results of any use of the investigational product(s) other than from in clinical trials, such as from experience during marketing.

(a) Pharmacokinetics and Product Metabolism in Humans.

(b) Safety and Efficacy

A summary of information should be provided about the investigational product's/products' (including metabolites, where appropriate) safety, pharmacodynamics, efficacy, and dose response that were obtained from preceding trials in humans (healthy volunteers and/or patients). The implications of this information should be discussed. In cases where a number of clinical trials have been completed, the use of summaries of safety and efficacy across multiple trials by indications in subgroups may provide a clear presentation of the data. Tabular summaries of adverse drug reactions for all the clinical trials (including those for all the studied indications) would be useful. Important differences in adverse drug reaction patterns/incidences across indications or subgroups should be discussed.

The IB should provide a description of the possible risks and adverse drug reactions to be anticipated on the basis of prior experiences with the product under investigation and with related product.

A description should also be provided of the precautions or special monitoring to be done as part of the investigational use of the product(s).

a. ***Marketing Experience***

The IB should identify countries where the investigational product has been marketed or approved. Any significant information arising from the marketed use should be summarised (e.g., formulations, dosages, routes of administration, and adverse product reactions). The IB should also identify all the countries where the investigational product did not receive approval/registration for marketing or was withdrawn from marketing/registration.

g) Summary of Data and Guidance for the Investigator

This section should provide an overall discussion of the nonclinical and clinical data, and should summarise the information from various sources on different aspects of the investigational product(s), wherever possible. In this way, the investigator can be provided with the most informative interpretation of the available data and with an assessment of the implications of the information for future clinical trials. Where appropriate, the published reports on related products should be discussed. This could help the investigator to anticipate adverse drug reactions or other problems in clinical trials.

The overall aim of this section is to provide the investigator with a clear understanding of the possible risks and adverse reactions, and of the specific tests, observations, and precautions that may be needed for a clinical trial. This understanding should be based on the available physical, chemical, pharmaceutical, pharmacological, toxicological, and clinical information on the investigational product(s). Guidance should also be provided to the clinical investigator on the recognition and treatment of possible overdose and adverse drug reactions that is based on previous human experience and on the pharmacology of the investigational product

TITLE PAGE (Example)

SPONSOR'S NAME
Product:
Research Number:
Name(s): Chemical, Generic (if approved)
Trade Name(s) (if legally permissible and desired by the sponsor)
INVESTIGATOR'S BROCHURE
Edition Number:
Release Date:
Replaces Previous Edition Number:
Date:

TABLE OF CONTENTS OF INVESTIGATOR'S BROCHURE (Example)

- Confidentiality Statement (optional)
- Signature Page (optional)

1 Table of Contents
2 Summary
3 Introduction
4 Physical, Chemical, and Pharmaceutical Properties and Formulation
5 Nonclinical Studies
5.1 Nonclinical Pharmacology
5.2 Pharmacokinetics and Product Metabolism in Animals
5.3 Toxicology

6 Effects in Humans
6.1 Pharmacokinetics and Product Metabolism in Humans
6.2 Safety and Efficacy
6.3 Marketing Experience
7 Summary of Data and Guidance for the Investigator
NB: References on
1. Publications
2. Reports
These references should be found at the end of each chapter
Appendices (if any)

- Single dose
- Repeated dose
- Carcinogenicity
- Special studies (e.g. irritancy and sensitisation)
- Reproductive toxicity
- Genotoxicity (mutagenicity)

  - A summary of information on the pharmacokinetics of the investigational product(s) should be presented, including the following, if available:
  - Pharmacokinetics (including metabolism, as appropriate, and absorption, plasma protein binding, distribution, and elimination).
  - Bioavailability of the investigational product (absolute, where possible, and/or relative) using a reference dosage form.
  - Population subgroups (e.g., gender, age, and impaired organ function).
  - Interactions (e.g., product-product interactions and effects of food).
  - Other pharmacokinetic data (e.g., results of population studies performed within clinical trial(s).

Guidelines to the preparation of Informed Consent Form

The term *informed consent* is mistakenly viewed as synonymous with obtaining a subject's signature on the consent form. FDA believes that obtaining a subject's oral or written informed consent is only part of the consent process. Informed consent involves providing a potential subject with adequate information to allow for an informed decision about participation in the clinical investigation, facilitating the potential subject's comprehension of the information, providing adequate opportunity for the potential subject to ask questions and to consider whether to participate, obtaining the potential subject's voluntary agreement to participate, and continuing to provide information as the clinical investigation progresses or as the subject or situation requires. To be effective, the process must provide sufficient opportunity for the subject to consider whether to participate. (21 CFR 50.20.) FDA considers this to include allowing sufficient time for subjects to consider the information and providing time and opportunity for the subjects to ask questions and have those questions answered. The investigator (or other study staff who are conducting the informed consent interview) and the subject should exchange information and discuss the contents of the informed consent document. This process must occur under circumstances that minimize the possibility of coercion or undue influence. (21 CFR 50.20.)

The consent process begins with subject recruitment, and it includes advertising used to recruit subjects into the clinical trial. Once a potential subject is identified, a person knowledgeable about the clinical investigation and capable of answering questions raised by the potential subject should conduct a consent interview.

The consent form must contain information to allow the subject to make an informed decision about participation in a clinical investigation (see section III, FDA Informed Consent Requirements and Discussion). (21 CFR 50.20 and 21 CFR 50.25.) The consent form serves several purposes, including helping to ensure that the subject receives the required information, providing a "take home" reminder of the elements of the clinical investigation, providing contact information in case additional questions or concerns arise, and documenting the subject's voluntary agreement to participate.

The informed consent process often continues after the consent form is signed. Depending on the clinical investigation, additional information may need to be given to the subject, and the subject may need additional opportunities to ask questions and receive answers throughout the clinical investigation. (See section III.C.5, Providing Significant New Findings to Subjects, for a discussion of when findings developed during the clinical investigation must be communicated to subjects.)

General Requirements for Informed Consent

1. Exceptions to Informed Consent

Informed consent is required for participation in FDA-regulated clinical investigations except under limited circumstances as described in 21 CFR 50.23 (involving certain life-threatening situations, military operations, or public health emergencies) and 21 CFR 50.24 (involving emergency research)

2. Coercion and Undue Influence

The conditions under which informed consent is sought and the relationship between the subject and the person obtaining consent must be carefully considered to minimize the possibility of coercion or undue influence (21 CFR 50.20). According to the Belmont Report, "Coercion occurs when an overt threat of harm is intentionally presented by one person to another in order to obtain compliance. Undue influence, by contrast, occurs through an offer of an excessive, unwarranted, inappropriate or improper reward or other overture in order to obtain compliance."

For example, when an employing party seeks to enroll employees in a clinical investigation sponsored or conducted by the employing party, the protocol should contain safeguards to ensure that participation is voluntary and that there is no undue influence by supervisors, peers, or others. Similarly, because of a potential conflict of interest and the nature of the physician-patient relationship, when the investigator is also the prospective subject's physician, the physician should be careful to ensure that the prospective subject understands that enrollment in the clinical investigation is voluntary and that a decision to forego enrollment will not adversely affect his/her medical care. The consent form should emphasize that an individual's participation is truly voluntary.

Note that coercion and undue influence may be situational. For example, in a clinical investigation involving the surgical insertion of an investigational device, waiting to obtain informed consent until the potential subject is in the preoperative area may fail to minimize the possibility of undue influence.

In addition, statements that claim investigational test articles are safe or effective for the purposes for which they are being investigated are prohibited. (21 CFR 312.7(a) and 21 CFR 812.7(d).) Likewise, statements that inappropriately overstate the possibility of benefit should be avoided because they may unduly influence potential subjects. Careful wording is needed in order to avoid overstating potential benefits that may contribute to a subject's therapeutic misconception.

Furthermore, statements such as "FDA has given permission for the clinical investigation to proceed" or "FDA has approved the clinical investigation" should be avoided, because such statements may contribute to the misimpression that the investigation has FDA's endorsement.

3. Language Understandable to the Subject or the Legally Authorized Representative

The information given to the subject, which could include information provided orally during the consent interview or written information in the consent form, must be in language understandable to the potential subject or legally authorized representative (21 CFR 50.20). "Understandable" means the information presented to potential subjects is in a language and at a level the subjects can comprehend (including an explanation of scientific and medical terms). In ensuring that information is understandable, it should be noted that more than one-third of U.S. adults, 77 million people, have basic or below basic health literacy. Limited health literacy affects adults in all racial and ethnic groups. In addition, more than one-half of U.S. adults have basic or below basic quantitative literacy and are challenged by numerical presentations of health, risk, and benefit data.

4. Exculpatory Language

The consent process may not include exculpatory language through which a subject is made to waive or appear to waive any of his or her legal rights, or release or appear to release the investigator, the sponsor, the institution, or its agents from liability for negligence (21 CFR 50.20). FDA considers *exculpatory language* to be language that has the general effect of freeing or appearing to free an individual or an entity from malpractice, negligence, blame, fault, or guilt.

The following are examples of exculpatory language that would violate 21 CFR 50.20, and therefore cannot appear in consent forms:

- I waive any possibility of compensation, including any right to sue, for injuries that I may receive as a result of participation in this research.
- If you suffer a research-related injury, neither the institution nor the investigator can assume financial responsibility or liability for the expenses of treatment for such injury.
- In the event that you suffer a research-related injury, your medical expenses will be your responsibility or that of your third party payer.

An example of one potential way to explain that a subject's legal right to seek to collect compensation for research-related injuries in certain situations is not being waived is included below. Other language that similarly conveys this concept would also be acceptable (see section III.B.6, Compensation and Medical Treatment in Event of Injury, for additional examples):

- In the event that you suffer a research-related injury, your medical expenses will be your responsibility or that of your third-party payer, although you are not precluded from seeking to collect compensation for injury related to malpractice, fault, or blame on the part of those involved in the research.

B. Basic Elements of Informed Consent

(a) Basic elements of informed consent. In seeking informed consent, the following information shall be provided to each subject: (21 CFR 50.25(a).)

1. Description of Clinical Investigation

A statement that the study involves research, an explanation of the purposes of the research and the expected duration of the subject's participation, a description of the procedures to be followed, and identification of any procedures which are experimental. (21 CFR 50.25(a)(1).)

A clear statement that the clinical investigation involves research is important so prospective subjects are aware that, although preliminary data (bench, animal, pilot studies, literature) may exist, the purpose of their participation is primarily to contribute to research (for example, to evaluate the safety and effectiveness of the test article, to evaluate a different dose or route of administration of an approved drug, etc.) rather than to their own medical treatment.

FDA recommends that potential subjects first be informed of the care a patient would likely receive if not part of the research and then be provided with information about the research. This sequence allows potential subjects to understand how the research differs from the care they might otherwise receive. The description should identify tests or procedures that would be part of usual care that will not be performed as well as those required by the protocol that would not be part of their care outside of the research, for example, drawing blood samples for a pharmacokinetic study. The information provided should also inform prospective subjects about the potential consequences of these differences in care. Note that all experimental procedures must be identified as such. (21 CFR 50.25(a)(1).) Procedures related solely to research (for example, protocol-driven versus individualized dosing, randomized assignment to treatment, blinding of subject and investigator, and receipt of placebo if the study is placebo-controlled) must be explained.

The description of the clinical investigation must describe the test article and the control. The description should include relevant information of what is known about both the test article and the control. For example, the description should indicate whether the test article is approved/cleared for marketing and describe that use. Clarification may be provided that a marketed product may be prescribed by a health care practitioner for the labeled indication as well as other conditions/diseases he/she determines are reasonable. The description should also provide relevant information about any control used in the study. For example, whether the control is a medically recognized standard of care [14] or is a placebo (including an explanation of what a placebo is). The information provided about the test article and control should include appropriate and reliable information about the benefits and risks of each, to the extent such information is available.

The consent process should outline what the subject's participation will involve in order to comply with the protocol, for example, the number of clinic visits, maintenance of diaries, and medical or dietary restrictions (including the need to avoid specific medications or activities, such as participation in other clinical investigations (see section v.g. Subject Participation in More Than One Clinical Investigation)). If describing every procedure would make the consent form too lengthy or detailed, FDA recommends providing the general procedures in the consent form with an addendum describing all study procedures. It may be helpful to provide a chart outlining what happens at each visit to simplify the consent form and assist the subject in understanding what participation in the clinical investigation will involve. FDA believes that removing procedural details from the consent form will reduce its length, enhance its readability, and allow its focus to be on more important content, such as the risks and anticipated benefits, if any.

The informed consent process must clearly describe the expected duration of the subject's participation in the clinical investigation (see 21 CFR 50.25(a)(1)), which includes their active participation as well as long-term follow-up, if appropriate. The subject must be informed of the procedures that will occur during such follow-up, which may be provided in a chart as described above. (21 CFR 50.25(a)(1).)

2. Risks and Discomforts

A description of any reasonably foreseeable risks or discomforts to the subject. (21 CFR 50.25(a)(2).)

The informed consent process must describe the reasonably foreseeable risks or discomforts to the subject. This includes risks or discomforts of tests, interventions and procedures required by the protocol (including standard medical procedures, exams and tests), especially those that carry significant risk of morbidity or mortality. Possible risks or discomforts due to changes to a subject's medical care (e.g., by changing the subject's stable medication regimen or by randomizing to placebo) should also be addressed. The explanation of potential risks of the test article and control, if any, and an assessment of the likelihood of these risks occurring should be based on information presented in the protocol, investigator's brochure, package labeling, and previous research reports.

Reasonably foreseeable discomforts to the subject must also be described. (21 CFR 50.25(a)(2).) For example, the consent form should disclose the severity and duration of pain from a surgical procedure or the discomfort of prolonged immobilization for MRI.

All possible risks do not need to be described in detail in the informed consent form, especially if it could be overwhelming for subjects to read. Information on risks that are more likely to occur and those that are serious should be included. The discussion may include information on whether a risk is reversible and the probability of the risk based on existing data. Information on what may be done to mitigate the most likely to occur and serious risks and discomforts should also be considered for inclusion.

The description should not understate the probability and magnitude of the reasonably foreseeable risks and discomforts. If applicable, the consent document should include a description of the reasonably foreseeable risks not only to the subject, but also to "others" (for example, radiation therapy where close proximity to subjects post procedure may be of some risk to others). When appropriate, a statement must be included that the clinical investigation may involve currently unforeseeable risks to the subject (or to the subject's embryo or fetus, if the subject is or may become pregnant). (21 CFR 50.25(b)(1).) (See section III.C.1. Unforeseeable Risks.)

3. Benefits

A description of any benefits to the subject or to others which may reasonably be expected from the research. (21 CFR 50.25(a)(3).)

The description of potential benefits should be clear, balanced, and based on reliable information to the extent such information is available. This element requires a description of the potential benefits not only to the subject (for example, "This product is intended to decrease XXX; however, we cannot guarantee that you will benefit"), but also to "others" (for example, "your participation in this research may not benefit you but may benefit future patients with your disease or condition"). Overly optimistic representations of the clinical investigation may be misleading and may violate FDA regulations that prohibit promotion of investigational drugs and devices (see 21 CFR 312.7 and 21 CFR 812.7). Because the purpose of the study is to determine the safety and/or effectiveness of the test article compared to the control, it is not yet known whether the test article may or may not provide a benefit.

FDA considers payment to subjects for participation in clinical investigations to be compensation for expenses and inconveniences, not a benefit of participation in research. If payments are provided, the consent process should not identify them as benefits.

4. Alternative Procedures or Treatments

A disclosure of appropriate alternative procedures or courses of treatment, if any, that might be advantageous to the subject. (21 CFR 50.25(a)(4).)

To enable an informed decision about taking part in a clinical investigation, consent forms must disclose appropriate alternatives to entering the clinical investigation, if any, that might be advantageous to the subject. (21 CFR 50.25(a)(4).) Prospective subjects must be informed of the care they would likely receive if they choose not to participate in the research. This includes alternatives such as approved therapies for the patient's condition, other forms of therapy (e.g., surgical), and when appropriate, supportive care with no disease-directed therapy. This disclosure must include a description of the current medically recognized standard of care, particularly in studies of serious illness. Standard of care may include uses or treatment regimens that are not included in a product's approved labeling (or, in the case of a medical device cleared under the 510(k) process, in the product's statement of intended uses). FDA believes that treatment options lacking evidence of therapeutic value do not need to be discussed.

When disclosing appropriate alternative procedures or courses of treatment, FDA believes a description of any reasonably foreseeable risks or discomforts and potential benefits associated with these alternatives must be disclosed. Where such descriptions or disclosures can contain quantified comparative estimates of risks and benefits (e.g., from the clinical literature), they should do so. The agency does not believe that imposing such a strict requirement for every case would be realistic or appropriate. Where such well-defined estimates are not possible, the agency believes that a description of the risks and benefits will be sufficient.

It may be appropriate to refer the subject to a healthcare professional who can more fully discuss the alternatives, for example, when alternatives include various combinations of treatments such as radiation, surgery and chemotherapy for some cancers. This referral should be completed prior to the subject signing and dating the consent form.

FDA recognizes that, while an individual subject may be eligible for more than one clinical investigation, that determination and the decision as to which trial would be most appropriate for a particular subject would need to be made on a case-by-case basis. FDA believes that the discussion of other trials for which the subject may be eligible is best left to the informed consent discussion rather than the informed consent document and may need to include the subject's primary care provider.

As applicable, the informed consent process should advise that participation in one clinical investigation may preclude an individual's eligibility to participate in other clinical investigations for the same or other indications. When there are multiple clinical investigations for evaluating the treatment of a particular disease, the sequence in which a subject may participate in the protocols may be important and should be discussed with the subject and the subject's primary care provider, if appropriate.

5. Confidentiality

A statement describing the extent, if any, to which confidentiality of records identifying the subject will be maintained and that notes the possibility that the Food and Drug Administration may inspect the records. (21 CFR 50.25(a)(5).)

The consent process must describe the extent to which confidentiality of records identifying subjects will be maintained (21 CFR 50.25(a)(5)) and should identify all entities, for example, the study sponsor, who may gain access to the records relating to the clinical investigation. The consent process must also note the possibility that FDA may inspect records (21 CFR 50.25(a)(5)), and should not state or imply that FDA needs permission from the subject for access to the records. Please note that under the Health Insurance Portability and Accountability Act (HIPAA) Privacy Rule, FDA does not need permission to inspect records containing health information (45 CFR 164.512). FDA may inspect study records, for example, to assess investigator compliance with the study protocol and the validity of the data reported by the sponsor.

Under the Federal Food, Drug, and Cosmetic Act (FD&C Act), FDA may inspect and copy all records relating to the clinical investigation. 21 U.S.C. § 374(a)(1). See also 21 CFR 312.58(a), 312.68, and 812.145(b). FDA generally will not copy records that include the subject's name unless there is reason to believe the records do not represent the actual cases studied or results obtained. When FDA requires subject names, FDA will generally treat such information as confidential, but on rare occasions, FDA may be required to disclose this information to third parties, for example, to a court of law. See 21 CFR 20.63(a) and 20.83(a)-(b). Therefore, the consent process should not promise or imply absolute confidentiality by FDA.

6. Compensation and Medical Treatment in Event of Injury

For research involving more than minimal risk, an explanation as to whether any compensation and an explanation as to whether any medical treatments are available if injury occurs and, if so, what they consist of, or where further information may be obtained. (21 CFR 50.25(a)(6).)

For clinical investigations involving more than minimal risk, the informed consent process must describe any compensation and medical treatments available to subjects if injury occurs. (21 CFR 50.25(a)(6).) Because available compensation and medical treatments may vary depending on the medical circumstances of the individual subject or the policies of the institution, the consent process should include an explanation to subjects of where they may obtain further information. An example of an adequate statement is, "the sponsor has made plans to pay for medical costs related to research-related injuries" followed by an explanation of how to obtain further information. If no compensation is available, the consent process should include statements such as:

- Because of hospital policy, the hospital is not able to offer financial compensation should you be injured as a result of participating in this research. However, you are not precluded from seeking to collect compensation for injury related to malpractice, fault, or blame on the part of those involved in the research, including the hospital.
- Because of hospital policy, the hospital makes no commitment to provide free medical care or payment for any unfavorable outcomes resulting from participation in this research. Medical services will be offered at the usual charge. However, you are not precluded from seeking to collect compensation for injury related to malpractice, fault, or blame on the part of those involved in the research, including the hospital.

Also, see section III.A.4, Exculpatory Language.

7. Contacts

An explanation of whom to contact for answers to pertinent questions about the research and research subjects' rights, and whom to contact in the event of a research-related injury to the subject. (21 CFR 50.25(a)(7).)

The consent process must provide information on how to contact an appropriate individual for pertinent questions about the clinical investigation and the subjects' rights, and whom to contact in the event that a research-related injury to the subject occurs. (21 CFR 50.25(a)(7).) This information should include contact names (or offices) and their telephone numbers. FDA recommends that the individual or office named for questions about subjects' rights not be part of the investigational team. Subjects may be hesitant to report specific concerns or identify possible problems to someone who is part of the investigational team. In addition, the consent process should include information on whom to contact and what to do in the event of an emergency, including 24-hour contact information, if appropriate.

If contact information changes during the clinical investigation, then the new contact information must be provided to the subject. (21 CFR 50.25(a)(7).) This may be done through a variety of ways, for example, a card providing the relevant contact information for the clinical investigation.

8. Voluntary Participation

A statement that participation is voluntary, that refusal to participate will involve no penalty or loss of benefits to which the subject is otherwise entitled, and that the subject may discontinue participation at any time without penalty or loss of benefits to which the subject is otherwise entitled. (21 CFR 50.25(a)(8).)

This element requires that subjects be informed that they may decline to take part in the clinical investigation or may stop participation at any time without penalty or loss of benefits to which subjects are entitled. (21 CFR 50.25(a)(8).) Language that limits the subject's right to decline to participate or withdraw from the clinical investigation must not be used. If special procedures should be followed for the subject to withdraw from the clinical investigation, the consent process must outline and explain the procedures (21 CFR 50.25(b)(4), see section III.C.4, Consequences of Subject's Decision to Withdraw). Also note that subjects may not withdraw data that was collected about them prior to their withdrawal, as discussed in Section V.I, Data Retention upon the Withdrawal of Subjects.

C. Additional Elements of Informed Consent

The regulations identify additional elements of informed consent to be included, when appropriate. (21 CFR 50.25(b).)

(b) Additional elements of informed consent. When appropriate, one or more of the following elements of information shall also be provided to each subject:

The following elements are appropriate to provide to prospective subjects when the IRB determines the information is material to prospective subjects' decisions to participate:

1. Unforeseeable Risks

A statement that the particular treatment or procedure may involve risks to the subject (or to the embryo or fetus, if the subject is or may become pregnant) which are currently unforeseeable. (21 CFR 50.25(b)(1).)

When appropriate, the consent process must contain a statement that the particular test article or procedure may involve risks to subjects (or to the embryo or fetus, if the subject is or may become pregnant) that are currently unforeseeable. (21 CFR 50.25(b)(1).) If long-term safety studies (such as bench and animal testing) are not completed, the informed consent process should explain that researchers have not completed studies that may identify potential risks, for example, carcinogenicity or teratogenicity.

2. Involuntary Termination of Subject's Participation

Anticipated circumstances under which the subject's participation may be terminated by the investigator without regard to the subject's consent. (21 CFR 50.25(b)(2).)

When appropriate, the consent process must inform the subject of anticipated circumstances under which the investigator may end the subject's participation without the subject's consent. (21 CFR 50.25(b)(2).) Such circumstances may arise if, for example, the subject is unable to comply with procedures required by the clinical investigation, if the subject no longer meets the eligibility criteria for continuing in the study, or if the site withdraws from the study. A simple statement that the investigator or sponsor may withdraw the subject from participation at any time is inadequate and does not inform the subject of anticipated circumstances that may trigger his/her withdrawal from the clinical investigation. For example, the consent process may inform the subject that the investigator may withdraw the subject's participation in the clinical investigation if the subject does not follow the instructions given to him/her by the investigator, such as repeatedly failing to return for protocol-required clinic visits or repeatedly failing to follow dosing or device instructions. If a subject is withdrawn from the study, the clinical investigator should explain to the subject the reasons for withdrawal, discuss other available treatment or research options, and, if appropriate, discuss plans to follow the subject after withdrawal for side effects.

3. Additional Costs to Subject

Any additional costs to the subject that may result from participation in the research. (21 CFR 50.25(b)(3).)

If subjects may incur additional expense because they are taking part in the clinical investigation, the consent process must explain the added costs. (21 CFR 50.25(b)(3).) FDA recommends that the cost of any tests, procedures and/or products that may be charged to the subject, the subject's insurance or other reimbursement mechanism be explained as part of the informed consent process. Subjects should be made aware that insurance or other reimbursement mechanisms might not fund the medical care they receive because they are participating in a clinical investigation even when the care is the standard care they would otherwise receive if not participating in a clinical investigation.

Additionally, insurance or other forms of reimbursement might not pay for care related to complications or injuries arising from participation in a clinical investigation. (See also section III.B.6, Compensation and Medical Treatments in Event of Injury.) If the subject's insurance is charged and there are deductibles or copayments, the subject should be informed of whether he/she will be responsible for these costs. If funds will be available to cover costs not covered by insurance or other forms of reimbursement, the consent form should describe how these funds will be made available to subjects or direct subjects on how to obtain further information. Because these issues may be complex, it may be appropriate to refer the subject to a knowledgeable financial counselor or reimbursement specialist to explain the costs and the insurance and reimbursement issues prior to signing the consent form.

Beyond the costs directly related to participation in the research, it may be appropriate to identify additional costs that the subject may incur, such as loss of income when the subject takes time off from work to participate in the clinical investigation and transportation costs.

In some cases, the cost of an investigational product may be charged to the subject. In clinical investigations involving investigational devices, the sponsor is permitted to recover the costs of research, development, manufacture, and handling of investigational devices (see 21 CFR 812.7(b)). FDA may authorize sponsors in certain clinical investigations of drugs to recover the direct costs of making the investigational drug available, such as costs to manufacture, ship, and handle (e.g., store) the drug (see 21 CFR 312.8). When these costs are passed to the subject, the consent process must identify these costs.

4. Consequences of Subject's Decision to Withdraw

The consequences of a subject's decision to withdraw from the research and procedures for orderly termination of participation by the subject. (21 CFR 50.25(b)(4).)

When appropriate, the consent process must describe the consequences of a subject's decision to withdraw from the clinical investigation and the procedures for orderly termination of participation by the subject. (21 CFR 50.25(b)(4).) For example, when withdrawal from a clinical investigation may adversely affect the subject, the informed consent process must explain the withdrawal procedures that are recommended in order to ensure the subject's safety, and should specifically state why they are important to the subject's welfare. For some clinical investigations, an intervention should be withdrawn gradually or the investigator may recommend follow-up to ensure the subject's safety when an investigational intervention is prematurely terminated due to a subject's withdrawal. In these cases, the consent process must explicitly inform the subject of the potential adverse effects of premature termination of the investigational intervention. If applicable, the consent process must explain whether a subject who withdraws early will receive future payments.

5. Providing Significant New Findings to Subjects

A statement that significant new findings developed during the course of the research which may relate to the subject's willingness to continue participation will be provided to the subject. (21 CFR 50.25(b)(5).)

The consent process must, when appropriate, include a statement that significant new findings that may relate to the subject's willingness to continue participation, such as new risk information, will be provided to the subject. (21 CFR 50.25(b)(5).) Significant new findings may include an unexpected adverse event or an adverse event occurring at greater frequency or severity than previously stated in the consent process. FDA encourages the inclusion of this statement in the consent form for clinical investigations where knowledge of risk is limited, for example, clinical investigations of the first use in humans, novel therapies, and new molecular entities, or complex clinical investigations that involve significant risk.

6. Number of Subjects

The approximate number of subjects involved in the study. (21 CFR 50.25(b)(6).)

The informed consent process must state the approximate number of subjects who will be involved in the clinical investigation, when appropriate. (21 CFR 50.25(b)(6).) For example, a subject's decision may be influenced by knowledge that the clinical investigation is a small initial trial of the product (such as a phase 1 or 2 drug clinical investigation or a device feasibility clinical investigation where only a small number of subjects participate).

Guidelines to the preparation of Case report forms

Case report form (CRF) is a specialized document in clinical research. Guidelines for Good Clinical Practice define the CRF as: A printed optical or electronic document designed to record all of the protocol – required information to be reported to the sponsor on each trial subject.

Case report form designing requires enormous planning and attention to minute detail. Designing a CRF is crucial in a clinical trial as it will aid in assessing the safety and efficacy of the medicinal product accurately. CRF should be designed for optimal collection of data in accordance with the study protocol compliance, regulatory requirements and shall enable the researcher test the hypothesis or answer the trial related questions.

Paper Case Report Form Versus Electronic Case Report Form.

There are two types of CRFs used in clinical research, that is, traditional paper CRF and improvised electronic CRF (eCRF). Paper CRF is the traditional way of data capture and a better option if studies are small or vary in design, whereas eCRFs are considered if studies are large with similar designs.

In the current global scenario, eCRFs are preferred over paper CRFs as they are less time-consuming, and also encourage the sponsor/pharmaceutical company to carry out large multicentric studies at the same time due to the ease of administration. It is designed in such a way that data entry can be done with zero/minimal errors. Moreover, the regulatory authorities are readily accepting submissions in which validated electronic data capture (EDC) systems are used.

While designing an eCRF, repetitive data such as protocol ID, site code, subject ID, and patient initials will be generated by the system automatically from the first page to all others, thus ensuring no duplication of CRF pages. In eCRF, linking the data between two related pages of CRFs becomes easy and quick. They have built-in edit checks tagged to each data fi eld as well as to the CRF as a whole. Therefore, majority of data cleaning activities will take place during the completion of the eCRFs, thus reducing the time and effort required by data management personnel. Instant query resolution reduces the time spent on obtaining the clarification from the site/investigator and hence, clean data is obtained much quickly, resulting in timely database lock, faster regulatory submission, and subsequent approval. Designing a paper CRF is a tedious job that could result in data errors and wrong conclusions, requiring meticulous attention to minimize duplication of CRF pages. Chances of error during data transfer from the source document to paper CRF are common. Moreover, for studies with large sample size if traditional method of data collection through paper CRFs is opted, then manual data cleaning may be a major concern. However, this method may not require user training and system validation as in the case of EDC systems, where such things are essential before implementing it. Despite their many advantages, eCRFs have not been accepted widely. Main reasons behind this are lack of available on-site technology, investigators' lack of motivation, complexity of installation, and maintenance of the software and high investment cost.

STANDARD CASE REPORT FORM DESIGN

Designing a CRF is an art that should to be based on scientific practices and the design should be implemented keeping the end-user (the one who enters data in the CRF) in mind. While designing, all important sections of the CRF should be included with care; always it is worth to remember that insufficient/inaccurate data collection would prove expensive during analysis. Hence, it is advisable to have a standard operating procedure for CRF preparation and to follow best practices of CRF designing. Primary objective of CRF designing is to gather complete and accurate data by avoiding duplication and facilitating transcription of data from source documents onto the CRF. CRF should be designed with the primary safety and efficacy endpoints as the main goal of data collection.[6] Ideally, it should be well-structured, easy to complete without much assistance and should collect data of the highest quality. Always minimum amount of data needed to answer the study hypotheses should be collected avoiding collection of elaborate, unimportant information. For ordinal data, to ensure uniformity and clarity among raters, adequate explanation should be provided adjacent to the CRF fi elds. Capturing the same piece of data in more than one place (duplication) on the CRF should also be avoided. In other words, CRF should collect data in sufficient detail without ambiguity and at the same time, should avoid redundancy and avoid capture of unwanted details. Hence, striking the perfect chords to ensure balance between effective data collection and structuring the CRF to support accurate data entry is essential. Collecting the data in the coded form whenever possible is ideal as it facilitates data entry (at CRF and at the database levels) and helps the statistician in data interpretation and analysis. Important part of the CRF is an informative header and footer, which can be customized. In general, the header includes protocol ID, site code, subject ID, and patient initials. Whereas, the footer includes investigator's signature, date of signature, version number, and page number. In order to enhance easy reading/understanding and accurate data entry, an uncrowded CRF layout should be preferred. Placing too many details on the same page, makes the CRF look cluttered and makes data entry difficult, which eventually leads to increase in data discrepancies. Case report form design should be standardized to address the needs of all those who handle the data such as investigator, data manager, biostatistician, clinical research monitor/coordinator, database developer/programmer and data entry personnel etc. An effective CRF design would always be user friendly. Moreover, it should capture legible, consistent and valid data, thereby, reducing query generations. While designing the CRFs, design standards should be adhered to for improving the quality of data collected. Hence, data should be organized in a format that facilitates data analysis and makes it simplified.

The following points are to be borne in mind while designing a CRF:

• Use of consistent formats, font style and font sizes throughout the CRF booklet • Selection of portrait versus landscape versus combination layouts.

• Use of clear and concise questions, prompts, and instructions • Visual cues, such as boxes that clearly indicate place and format of data to be recorded should be provided to the person recording the data as much as possible.

• Using the option of "circling of answers" should be limited as it's hard to interpret; instead check boxes would be appropriate • Clear guidance about skip patterns like what to skip and what not to skip should be mentioned at appropriate places.

• Skips (are instructions provided in the CRF page to maintain the connectivity between pages) should be kept to a minimum by the placement of questions to avoid confusions.

• Provide boxes or separate lines to hold the answers. This indirectly informs the data recorder where to write.

STANDARD CASE REPORT FORM TEMPLATES

Some of the data requirements such as demography, PE, AEs are same across studies, so standard CRF templates should be developed which can be customized accordingly. These templates are of great help while conducting multiple studies in the same research area. These templates will have the same design principles that help the user to enter data with ease since the design is familiar to them; there is no need for special training on these modules of CRFs. A "library" of standard templates should be established and maintained by the sponsor/contract research organizations, pharmaceutical companies in order to maintain uniformity in the CRF design and to save time. Most commonly used standard CRF templates are inclusion criteria, exclusion criteria, demography, medical history, PE, AE, concomitant medication and study outcome modules, whereas, the modules which captures efficacy data are not unique. Their design varies from study to study depending on the protocol specifications.

CHALLENGES IN CASE REPORT FORM DESIGNING

- Commonly encountered challenges in CRF designing are consistency in the design, collection of precise data and user-friendliness. These challenges can be overcome by proper planning by a team of data management personnel, biostatisticians, clinicians, and medical writers. Objectives should be defined clearly before designing.
- Consistent design is a crucial aspect as it reduces the number of mistakes in data entry. It is of great advantage when using them across various studies. Maintaining standard CRF templates would resolve this issue.
- Collection of extraneous data is another issue and measures should be taken to avoid it, as processing this becomes tedious. In such instances, ensuring accuracy and quality become major challenges. Attention should be paid to

avoid duplication.

- Design the CRF to avoid referential and redundant data collection. For example, collecting calculated fi elds/ derivable data should be avoided and to ensure that data collection is cost-effective. Designing user-friendly CRF to reduce data entry errors is again a challenge. Simple/standard designs should be incorporated wherever possible. User feedback mechanism should be built into the CRF design and maintenance process.

Best practices should be applied to improve the data quality and save time with CRF design. Providing CRF completion guideline aids in minimizing the challenges in data capture and data entry.

Guidelines to the preparation of Contracts and agreements

Definition

- **A clinical trial agreement (CTA) or clinical study agreement (CSA)** is a legally binding agreement that governs the conduct of a particular study and sets forth the obligations of each party to the agreement. Parties to clinical trial or study agreements include the participating site, the study sponsor, and/or the relevant clinical research organization (CRO).

Policies/guidelines

- CTAs and CSAs are processed by the Office of Clinical Trials (OCT). The assigned OCT contract and budget negotiator will facilitate review by all relevant UMMC departments and offices and signature by the OCT Director.
- CTAs and CSAs are not signed until the contract and budget are approved and UMMC IRB approval is confirmed via UMMC's internal routing system, called Radar.
- The bullet points below illustrate the CTA/CSA process for industry-sponsored clinical research studies:

  - OCT negotiator reviews and revises the agreement, which is uploaded to an electronic contract routing system (3 business days)
  - Office of Intellectual Property and Commercialization, Office of General Counsel, Office of Integrity and Compliance, Division of Information Systems, and Office of Information Security review and revise the agreement (15 business days)
  - OCT negotiator compiles changes and sends CTA/CSA response to sponsor or CRO (3 business days)
  - OCT negotiates the CTA/CSA with the sponsor or CRO until finalization (2 business days per party, not to exceed 30 calendar days)

Essential Components of a Clinical Trial Agreement

1. **Description of the Project**

This section of the agreement is often overlooked by sponsors, CROs and sites. The purpose of this section is to explicitly state the research project description. You want to document the overarching purpose of the agreement in this section.

In the United States, with the Sunshine Act, there is an increased scrutiny on payments made to health care organizations and health care professionals. The project description provides the necessary details on the nature of the agreement.

In the event there is a compliance audit questioning financial payments to the research site, the project description can provide clarity.

2. Payment Terms and Schedule

Sites want to get paid for their research services. In the case of a multi-year clinical trial, sponsors and CROs want to manage their budget and expense projections for current and future years.

This is where the payment schedule comes handy.

The payment schedule lists the project deliverables and expected payments for each deliverable.

Additionally, in some cases, payments are triggered when certain milestones are met. For example, once the site is activated for enrolment, a site start-up payment is triggered.

The payment terms and schedule will also state what the research site will NOT get paid for. For example, for a post-approval clinical study, the sponsor may not want to provide the medical device for free.

Finally, this section of the agreement should clearly state where the site needs to send invoices (name and contact information of the person), as well as the payment terms (example: payment will be made within 45 days).

3. Sponsor, CRO and Site Responsibilities

It's no surprise to us that clinical research is a regulated industry.

There is serious responsibility on the part of sponsors, CROs and sites to comply with the study protocol, government laws and regulations.

The purpose of this section is to document that the research site will comply with laws, the participating physicians and institution are qualified to conduct research, and the institution will inform the sponsor of Institutional Review Board (IRB)/Ethics Committee (EC) approval (or denial).

On the other hand, sponsors and CROs are required to notify the IRB/EC directly of any non-compliance that could impact the safety and well-being of trial subjects.

4. **Publication and Intellectual Property (IP) Terms**

A CTA must include the sponsor's take on publication and presentation of clinical trial data.

Sponsors are committed to reporting trial results on ethical grounds. Clinical site investigators, on the other hand, are excited with the idea of publishing research data.

Generally speaking, sites have to wait for the entire study results to be released before they can publish data on their subset of enrolled subjects. Also, sites would be required to submit the manuscript to the sponsor review prior to making a journal submission.

This section of the CTA will spell out how many days the sponsor has to review and comment on the manuscripts. Once the sponsor review period has lapsed, the site can go ahead and publish the results.

The data from a clinical trial is owned the trial sponsor, unless the agreement states otherwise.

5. **Indemnification and Insurance**

Indemnification may be a fancy word you've never heard before, but the concept behind this term is fairly straightforward.

If a third party, such as a clinical trial subject, is negatively affected as a result of the CTA that is between the sponsor and site, the sponsor will compensate for loss and assume full responsibility.

There may be limitations to the indemnification language. For instance, the sponsor may not agree to indemnify the site if it fails to follow the protocol or sells subject personal health information (PHI) to a third party.

Just like your auto or health insurance policy, sites, CROs and sponsors generally carry clinical trial insurance to protect themselves or the parties involved in a clinical trial.

6. **Record keeping and Inspection**

Generally speaking, the purpose of a clinical trial is to collect safety and effectiveness data on a given medical product.

But what happens if the clinical site provides incomplete or incorrect data to the sponsor? Or is hesitant to allow a CRO to monitor the data at the site?

That's where the recording keeping section of the CTA comes handy.

The purpose of this section is to document the agreement between the site and the sponsor on how long the trial data will be stored for after the trial is completed (typically two years at a minimum).

Additionally, this section includes other agreements, such as the sponsor's right to audit the site or verify data on a regular basis, and the site's responsibility to cooperate with the sponsor or a regulatory agency, such as the FDA.

7. **Guidelines for Dispute Resolution**

What happens if the sponsor or the site has a dispute?

The purpose of this section to explain how issues will be escalated and attempts will be made to resolve them through mutual resolution.

If either party to the agreement decides to take legal action, this agreement will specify under which jurisdiction the case will be handled.

8. **Grounds for Contract Termination**

As sponsor and site, you want to prepare yourself for contract termination.

Below are some reasons for which contract termination may be necessary:

- Fraud
- Non-compliance with national, state or local laws and regulations
- Change in business strategy requiring the sponsor to terminate a trial early
- EC or IRB may determine the trial is no longer safe for the subjects

All parties on the CTA could be required to provide 30–45-day notice depending on the reason for termination.

If agreed on a signed CTA, sponsors will have the right to data collected prior to contract termination and sites will receive compensation for trial activities performed by the research staff.

9. **Amendment of Contract Terms**

New and unexpected situations always arise.

Site may realize there is more work involved on a trial than they had anticipated. Or sponsors decide to revise the protocol, which in turn impacts the milestone payment schedule in the CTA.

Contract amendments are not fun. But they may be necessary. You want to have provisions in your CTA that allow you to request for an amendment of contract terms.

Site Feasibility Studies

clinical trial feasibility is a process of evaluating the possibility of conducting a particular clinical program / trial in a particular geographical region with the overall objective of optimum project completion in terms of timelines, targets and cost.

Types of feasibilities:

There can be three broad types of feasibilities:

a) Program level: this relates to the entire program of studies planned e.g. a program on antibacterial in a variety of infections

b) Study level: this is very specific to a particular study e.g., an antibacterial in skin and soft tissue infections

c) Site or Investigator level: this is most specific related to conducting the study in a particular hospital / clinic

a) Program level:

Program level feasibilities are broad based. They are mainly aimed towards finding prevalence of particular diseases or conditions in a particular region and hence include clinical and epidemiological information

• Ethical and Regulatory: Program feasibilities aim towards finding overall time for clinical trial approval, particular regulatory requirements which can affect decision related to placing of the study etc.

• Medical: Disease frequency, prevalence of programspecific patient population, nature of existing treatment patterns or guidelines, presence of alternative drugs and treatments. The broad objective of program level feasibilities is to identify which regions can be considered for the morespecific study level feasibilities.

a. **Study level:**
b. Study level feasibilities are more customized towards assessing whether a particular clinical study can be conducted in a country or region.

• **Clinical aspects**: This relates to the epidemiological data on the study specific population (more specific in terms of stage of disease, protocol based definition of study disease and population), availability of standard care (in terms of background therapy and comparators), specific agreement with inclusion and exclusion criteria and acceptance of study specific procedures in line with existing medical practices.

• **Regulatory:** This is one of the most important pieces of information in a study level feasibility. This would include the overall approval timelines to get the study ongoing, understanding specific regulatory requirements (e.g., translated protocol, export of biological materials, special requirements in case of biological samples etc)

• **Technical:** The usage of technology in clinical trials has increased significantly in recent times. This includes e-CRFs, tools for randomization, clinical supplies shipments, etc. Feasibilities can assess prior experience of usage of tools, any problems which are anticipated and exploring possible options to overcome these challenges

• **Operational**: As clinical trials are becoming more global, some countries (e.g., Eastern and Central Europe, Korea, Taiwan, India etc) have emerged as major destinations for clinical trials across therapeutic areas. This increases the chance of studies with similar patient population being conducted in the same country and actually competing with each other for recruitment affecting overall study and country performance. It is necessary to identify such a risk. Similarly assessing a general estimate of sites and numbers of patients helps in resource allocation and study planning. From a recruitment point of view, identifying recruitment strategies and exploring various options also helps in planning of the study.

a. **Site or Investigator level:**

This is actually the micro feasibility – deciding whether to work with an investigator or not and identifying challenges and probable solutions. Given the challenges above, selecting the right site is of paramount importance.4 While country offices have greater responsibility in this case, study teams provide overall oversight and guidance. It consists of the following

• **Clinical aspects**: Assessing the investigator's readiness in terms of standard care (e.g., type of drugs, dosage), actual study population vs. the patient population treated or seen by the potential investigator, readiness and acceptance of background and comparative therapy and familiarity with use of tools and technology is done in investigator level feasibility.

• **Site demographics**: Site demographics help us in assessing the type of clinical practice (hospital vs. outpatient), prior experience in clinical trials, and availability of study coordinators, pharmacists and nurses. This helps in assessing the 'competency' of the investigator/ site to conduct the clinical trial, not necessarily in terms of medical knowledge but more in terms of protocol related knowledge, personnel availability etc.

• **Recruitment and retention**: This is the most important section of the site feasibility. It helps us in finding the recruitment potential, specifically in anticipated subjects per month and in the entire trial. On one hand, it helps in deciding whether we want to explore other sites, on the other it helps in tracking site performance during study conduct. Other information collated includes ethical considerations, presence of competitive studies, prior experience in conducting similar studies etc.

• **Ethical aspects:** This also helps in site start-up and planning. It includes ethics committee requirements, requirements of translations etc and overall process of ethics clearance. • Site infrastructure: Most clinical studies have specific requirements related to drug storage, processing of biological samples e.g., refrigerated centrifuge etc. Hence it is important to assess site's capabilities related to such requirements, whether it is available at the site or needs to be procured, whether there are team members who have the relevant expertise to conduct these activities and use such tools. Most studies also will have e-CRFs, hence we can assess whether sites have capabilities to use electronic data capture and their familiarity with such tools.

• **Quality:** One more aspect which also needs to be evaluated is whether sites have undergone sponsor/ independent site audits in the past. Secondly, in the past few years, site inspections have been carried out by the FDA, EMEA and some other regulatory agencies in India and other emerging countries. It may be advisable to check whether the site had undergone any of these and if so, were any concerns raised. This also helps teams in allocating appropriate resources and providing adequate training in the start-up period.

Site selection for clinical trials

Site selection is a rigorous process in conducting clinical trials successfully, efficiently and in compliance with the regulatory guidelines.

Most clinical research recruiters are well aware of the dangers of choosing wrongly, but simply do not know what they should look for when evaluating potential research sites. Here are some of the essential criteria to consider:

Staff experience:

To ensure clinical protocol compliance, it's important to be sure that the right staff are available at each site. They should be experienced enough to be familiar with necessary compliance procedures, study conduct and clinical protocol. They should also be familiar with trial procedures such as the informed consent process, submissions to ethical and regulatory authorities and contracting.

Site history:

The screening of potential sites should always begin with a review of the site's history. The only way to truly be sure the site can meet the requirements of the trial is to ensure it has previously been involved in a study of a similar size or complexity. Recruitment statistics for previous trials, if available, are also a great indicator of expected performance and should be compared to the estimates the site has provided.

Site capabilities:

Any thorough pre-screening of potential research sites should ensure that the site is equipped to fulfil all the activities specified in the clinical protocol. It is also important to determine whether they currently possess all the necessary infrastructure themselves or if some equipment needs to be provided. In this case, extra costs may be incurred, and delays will be caused.

Pre-registered patients:

If a site already has registered patients who meet the study criteria, this could be a significant benefit when it comes to meeting enrolment targets. However, it's also important to ensure the site is not already involved in other similar studies which may compete for its patients and resources.

Site knowledge:

If a site specializes in a specific, target disease, they are more likely to be successful in recruiting patients and following protocol.

Locality:

Travel is often a significant burden on patient recruitment and retention, and a barrier to patient participation. It is important to select research sites that are as close as possible to the target population, in order to achieve desired targets for enrolment and retention. This is especially crucial for those studies that require frequent site visits.

Investigator selection for clinical trials

It is important for the principal Investigator (PI) or an investigator to play a key role in recruiting patients, analysing data, publishing the results and speaking at conferences. Therefore, PI selection is a matter of consideration for sponsor.

Investigator selection is based on

- Education
- Training
- Experience

- Investigator should provide a copy of: the curriculum and /or other relevant documents requested by the sponsor, the ethics committee, the CRO or the regulatory authorities.
- He/She should clearly understand the time and other resource demands the study is likely to make and ensure they can be made available throughout the duration of the study.

- The PI should be able to demonstrate potential for recruiting the required number of suitable subjects within the agreed recruitment period.
- The investigator should have sufficient time to properly conduct and complete trial within agreed trial period.
- The PI should have available an adequate number of qualified staff and adequate facilities for the forseen duration of the trial to conduct the trial properly and safely.
- The PI should be thoroughly familiar with the safety and efficacy, appropriate use of investigational product as described in the protocol, investigators brochure and other information sources provided by the sponsor.
- PI should aware of and comply with GCP,SOP and applicable regulatory requirements.

Pre study Visit

Pre-Study Site Visit (PSSV) will be conducted at the 'site selection stage', there are no clinical governance issues, ergo research office approval is not required.

Site Initiation Visits (SIV) should take place after R&D approval is in place. However, the Research Office will facilitates SIVs and allow them before R&D approval if everything is nearly in place e.g. if all R-PEAK tasks are completed and the only item outstanding is a signed contract which is getting authorized by the sponsor.

Pre study Visit/ Site Qualification Visit/Site Selection Visit (SSV)/Pre-Study Qualification Visit (PSQV)

The site qualification name itself indicates the qualification of the hospital site. CRA has to confirm whether the hospital infrastructure and setup are qualified/capable to conduct the clinical trials.

This visit also referred to as Site Selection Visit (SSV) or Pre-Study Qualification Visit (PSQV). The CRA will usually request a tour of the hospital and time to discuss the fundamentals of the protocol and how that relates to the feasibility of recruiting potential participants.

The sponsor representative (CRA) time to discuss the basic rules of the protocol and the way it's associated with the feasibility of recruiting potential participants with the site staff. The qualified Investigator and Research Coordinator are responsible for providing the required information to the sponsor.

Other topics of discussion during the SQV include:

- Investigator responsibilities
- Qualifications of the investigator or other site personnel

- Study objectives, endpoints, indication challenges, inclusion-exclusion criteria, protocol-required procedures, eligibility criteria, and patient recruitment
- IRB (e.g., informed consent requirements)
- Adverse event reporting, source documentation, and record retention
- Infrastructure, availability of a storage area to store investigational drug or devices, and availability of required equipment or instruments
- Reporting of the event, documentation source.

As a representative of a sponsor to the institution that is fully capable and equipped to make a specific clinical trial. SQV performs after feasibility Assessment (To evaluate the possibility to conduct a clinical trial in a proposed location based on a list of questions. The assessment will allow the sponsor and qualified PI to make a decision regarding the feasibility of the study at his/her site).

It is a 1-day visit. After the site qualification visit, CRA will prepare the SQV report and it will be reviewed by the project manager. CRA may ask for all the relevant documents from the site to verify the documents. Upon finalization of SQVR, CRA will share the follow-up letter along with the site selection letter (whether selected/rejected) for the clinical trials.

INVESTIGATOR MEETING

Investigator meeting is nothing but a group meeting conducted on behalf of sponsor/CROs to train investigators and their lead clinical trial staff on trial related activities, standard operating procedures and to discuss the applicable regulatory picture. The content of an investigator meeting is usually trial specific, nevertheless a common agenda, on SOP's, Adverse Event Reporting, Source Documentation etc are also discussed.

An Investigator Meeting is usually a sponsor's job, but a CRO may also be delegated with this task. For many from the industry, investigator meeting is much targeted and criticized for overspending. It is argued that these meetings are generally hosted to lure investigators in clinical trials but if we try to understand the need of such events, they are much more fruitful than being thought of.

The meeting has multiple sessions on each aspect of the clinical trial, wherein the pros and cons of trial related activities are discussed. The discussion is also extended towards highlighting the expected issues that investigators may face and how to deal with them.

An investigator meeting ensures to:

- Ensure that all investigators have an understanding of how to conduct the trial in strict compliance with the protocol, SOP's, guidelines and applicable regulations.
- To introduce the investigators with Case Report Forms (CRFs).
- Document the responsibilities of all participating investigators and its staff and train them prior to the start of the trial.
- Discuss the study protocol in detail.
- Facilitate communication between investigators.

The ICH guideline for GCP states that investigators "should ensure the accuracy, completeness, legibility, and timeliness of the data reported to the sponsor in the CRFs" (4.9.1).

It is the Investigator Meeting that provides a CRO a premier opportunity to present the clinical trial team to a sponsor. Hence effective execution of IM is perceived as a reflection of the team's capabilities.

Clinical Trial agreement execution

A clinical trial agreement ("CTA") is the legally binding agreement between a sponsor, usually a pharmaceutical laboratory that provides the drug or study apparatus and provides financial support, and the host institution, often an NHS hospital or trust, which provides data and results of interest.

Health Science Canter introduced new accounting and budget requirements; access to research.uthscsa.edu/ocr/clinical.shtml. This type of agreement can be initiated by a sponsor or reviewer. A clinical trial agreement, initiated by a sponsor, is required if the drug or device under review has financial support.

However, other parties may participate in the conduct of the trials, for example. B a contract research organization, clinicians, manufacturers, suppliers and, of course, volunteers for patients.

The roles and responsibilities, and perhaps especially the liabilities of each party, must be clearly defined before a judicial proceeding is conducted. In the case of company-based minutes, sponsors generally make payments on the basis of cost per patient, with a payment plan based on intermediate stones of certain treatments/visits.

Other study fees (for example. B Pharmacy fees, patient recruitment fees, patient grants or fees related to certain procedures, such as pregnancy tests or radiological procedures) may also be paid separately from standard costs per patient.

For minutes initiated by the investigator, sponsors usually indicate certain registration stones that must be reached before payment. Pay attention to the timing and requirements of the milestones. Payment plans can be attached to the contract as a table or narrative or as a paragraph in the contract. See below an example of a common payment plan for a study of 10 patients out of $2500/subject. If an examiner wishes to participate in an industry-sponsored clinical trial, preparation must be done on several fronts. On the other hand, sponsors and CROs are required to inform the IRB/EC directly of any infringements that may affect the safety and well-being of the subjects.

To obtain a Project/Grant number from the Health Science Center for a clinical trial, the following documentation is required: a completed and signed Certificate of Proposal (COP), a copy of the study protocol, a written agreement signed between the sponsoring company and the Health Science Center, the approval of the Institutional Review Board (IRB), the first payment received by the sponsor.

The project will be implemented as part of the PeopleSoft 48002 fund group. It is important that all parties understand the language used in the treaty. When the agreement is revised, capitalized terms, restrictive words and words that are not understood are sought. The contract should have a definition section. Lead investigators should discuss all aspects of the clinical trial with their contract officer before negotiations begin.

Questions

1.What are the Guidelines for the preparation of Protocols in clinical research?
2.What are the Guidelines for the preparation of Investigators brochure in clinical research?
3.What are the Guidelines for the preparation of Informed consent form in clinical research?
4.What are the Guidelines for the preparation of Case report form in clinical research?
5.What are the Guidelines for the preparation of contracts and agreement in clinical research?
6.What are site feasibility studies in clinical trial?
7.Write a note on site selection for clinical trial?
8.Write a note on Investigator selection for clinical trial?
9.Write a note on pre study visit for clinical trial?
10.Write a note on Investigators meeting for clinical trial?
11.Write a note on clinical trial agreement execution?

CHAPTER FOUR

Investigational Product

Procurement and Storage of Investigational Product

An investigational product refers to a preventative (vaccine), a therapeutic (drug or biologic), device, diagnostic, or palliative used in a clinical trial. An investigational product may be an unlicensed product or a licensed product when used or assembled (formulated or packaged) differently from the approved form, when used for an unapproved indication, or when used to gain further information about an approved use.

Storage and handling of investigational product

Considerations and Principles

Definition of study product

Study product is the general term for any of the following: study intervention, investigational product, investigational medicinal product, investigational drug, investigational device, study drug, or clinical trial material. Study product is that which is used in an interventional research project, whether or not the research is regulated, for example as a drug or device study, under FDA regulations.

Investigator responsibilities

For IND and non-IND studies alike and unless otherwise specified, the Investigator is responsible for managing and documenting all of the following: ordering, receiving, and tracking inventory; storing, dispensing, and returning study product properly; and, where necessary, labeling of study product prior to dispensing according to protocol guidelines and good manufacturing practices (GMPs) if applicable. In practice, a subset of these responsibilities is usually delegated to the research pharmacist. The Investigator is responsible for monitoring pharmacy activities to ensure all requirements are being met.

Accountability definition and principles

Study product accountability is the process of documenting all aspects of study product receipt, storage, use, and disposition so that a full accounting of each unit can be made. For IND-regulated studies, several regulations describe sponsor/Investigator obligations to manage study product appropriately. These can be found at 21 CFR Parts 312.57(a), 312.59, 312.61, and 312.62(a). Additional principles, for IND and non-IND studies alike, include the following: • All study product supplied for a protocol must be accounted for and tracked in a manual or electronic accountability log for the study. Accountability of the study product must be documented from the time of initial receipt through dispensation and final disposal of leftover study product.

The accountability log should indicate the date, amounts, batch numbers, and conditions at receipt for all materials received from the supplier.

• Each time study product is dispensed from the pharmacy to a participant, the occurrence should be thoroughly documented in the accountability log. The accountability log should be unique to a study and should indicate the date, batch number(s), expiration date, unique bottle or kit identifier (if applicable), and amounts dispensed to the participant and date, amounts, and condition of materials returned/destroyed/disposed by the participant. A balance of remaining study product should be maintained and documented in the study's accountability log.

• At study completion, remaining study product should be returned or destroyed as dictated by the protocol, specific Investigator instructions, or other documented instructions. The balance returned or sent for destruction should be recorded in the study's accountability log. Quality assurance reviews/inspections of study product accountability documentation will be performed at intervals during a study by a clinical monitor. Similar document reviews may be conducted at any time by an auditor.

Placebos For placebo-controlled studies

placebos should match the shape, color, burnish, smell, taste (if applicable), and any other defining characteristics of the active study product as much as possible. If the main supplier of study product does not have matching placebos on hand, an alternate manufacture strategy will be needed, with additional time set aside for planning and executing the manufacture; consult with Office of Clinical Trials Operations and Management (OCTOM) for additional specific advice. Special packaging considerations may apply if the study calls for administering a mixture of active and placebo study product (e.g., to achieve multiple blinded dose levels). Packaging, including masking, should be conducted by dedicated packaging staff unaffiliated with the Investigator or any clinical staff involved in the conduct of the study. Randomization codes should be generated by an impartial statistician likewise uninvolved in the study, and these codes should be maintained in sealed, tamper-evident packages or in an equivalent locked electronic form if the codes are maintained electronically.

Initial planning and ordering of study product

It is important to communicate early with the study product supplier to ensure that study product is delivered in time for planned study start; delivery can sometimes occur months after a request is made.

Sufficient quantities should be obtained to cover all possible study enrollment scenarios and should further allow for

(a) laboratory procedures such as dilutions or unit-dose preparation that may involve loss of material as well as

(b) accidental loss of, damage to, or destruction of finished material during the course of the study.

If study product is not being donated, provisions should be made to ensure the budget can cover costs for this larger quantity of study product. The frequency of study product shipments from the supplier should be calibrated with anticipated enrollment rates and the known stability of the drug. That is, products with short shelf lives should be ordered in frequent, small batches to ensure fresh material is always available for enrolled participants. Whenever possible, all shipments should come from the same manufacturing lot.

Operational Guidelines

Study product ordering and receipt

Study product may be ordered from the supplier, distributor, or manufacturer by the Investigator, study coordinator, or research pharmacist as designated by the Investigator. Arrangements should be made between the product supplier and the study site to determine the most appropriate time and place for study product delivery, particularly for products requiring special storage conditions. Additional considerations apply for shipments made from locations outside the United States; consult staff from the OCTOM for drug importation guidance. Upon receipt of study product, the Investigator or designee should ensure that the information on the packing slip matches the study product received.

At a minimum, the recipient should verify the following:

• Product identification

• Amount of product received

• Lot numbers

• Expiration dates

• Physical product is in good condition

• Maintenance of proper storage conditions Evidence of breakage, compromised storage, or product tampering should be reported to the supplier immediately. The study product should be quarantined and maintained under the correct storage conditions until further instructions are given. Accountability: Enter the amount received, lot numbers, expiration dates, and condition of the study product into the study's accountability log. Keep copies of shipping inventories and packing slips with the accountability records. Note: study products must not be dispensed to study participants until they are properly inventoried, the quality is verified and proper authorization has been received that the enrollment process can begin.

Study product storage

Study product should be stored in a limited-access location and according to instructions received from the supplier, distributor, or manufacturer.

Proper storage conditions should address the temperature, light, moisture, ventilation, and sanitation needs of the study product. A log of key environmental conditions should be kept (e.g., a manual log or an automated recording of temperature and humidity) to document that required conditions were maintained during the entire storage timeframe.

Environmental controls (e.g., for temperature or light) may also be needed during transport between the pharmacy and the dispensing area. Meeting these handling requirements should also be documented. Study products that are to be shipped offsite for a protocol must be packaged in containers that maintain the proper storage conditions during transport. Maintenance of proper storage conditions during transport should be documented if possible. Chain of custody documentation should also be maintained for the transport, handling, and receipt of study product.

If storage conditions have been compromised (e.g., temperature excursions from the allowable range), or if there is any suspicion that the study product has not been stored properly:

• Quarantine the study product.

• Maintain the study product under the correct storage conditions until further notice.

• Contact the Investigator immediately, providing the protocol number, the protocol name, description of the degree of temperature/storage violation, and the length of storage violation time.

• Document the occurrence and the action taken per Investigator input (e.g., return to general inventory, return to the manufacturer, onsite destruction).

Study product requisition and dispensation

Study product should be maintained under the control of pharmacy staff at all times until a request is made by an authorized Investigator for release to an authorized trial staff person for administering to a specific enrolled trial participant. A mechanism must be established to ensure that the study product is dispensed only upon the order of the Investigator or the licensed clinician directly responsible to the Investigator, as stated on Form FDA 1572 (IND studies) or the Investigator agreement (non-IND studies).

Form FDA 1572 is a binding and legal document, whereby in completing and signing the form the IoR has certified that the study product will be administered only to participants under his/her personal supervision or under the supervision of sub-investigators responsible to him/her.

Prescribers (investigators) must be licensed clinicians allowed to prescribe in the site jurisdiction. For intramural studies, study product delivery to the designated trial staff person is authorized by means of a study product order (e.g., a prescription) issued by the Investigator. For extramural studies, a similar process should be in place to document a request for study product from the Investigator for dispensing to a specific trial participant.

Study product orders are an important part of the accountability documentation chain for all study products, prescription or not.

In general, study product orders should include the following:

• Protocol number

• Date of the order

• Participant identification number

• Randomization number, if available

• Participant height and weight, if applicable

• Study product prescribed (if study is blinded, the study product will be labeled accordingly)

• Quantity or instructions to indicate appropriate amount to be dispensed • Route of administration

• Prescriber's signature The pharmacist should ensure that there is a current IRB-approved version of the protocol, Investigator's Brochure, and/or a product package insert on file for reference, and that the protocol is followed when dispensing the protocol-specific drug.

Additionally, the research pharmacist should receive and have on file all protocol amendments, study-specific manuals of procedures (SOPs), and study-related correspondence, as applicable.

If the study product is custom-compounded at the pharmacy for use in the study, specific procedures should be established (and verified/validated as appropriate) before study conduct gets underway. Such procedures may be defined in the protocol or in specific study product preparation instructions.

All preparation procedures must be fully documented, including details on specific equipment used, lot numbers for all ingredients, and initials of the person performing or reviewing each step. Specific procedures should be established to ensure appropriate allocation of active vs. placebo study product in the case of a blinded study.

Study product delivered by the pharmacy for use in a study must be labeled with the following information at minimum:

• Protocol number

• Participant number or identifier

• Amount dispensed

• Dosing and storage instructions

• Date of dispensing Accountability: Pharmacy staff should record in the study's accountability log the date of dispensing, participant number, amount, and lot number(s) of the study product dispensed.

Study product use and return

The date/time and amount of study product administration to an identified study participant should be documented in the case report form (CRF) for that participant.

If the participant is sent home with a supply of study product for use over a period of time, the amount given to the participant and the day/time that the study product was given to the participant should likewise be recorded in the CRF.

Any study product returned by a study participant should be returned to the pharmacy and may also be recorded on the CRF if it is so designed. Accountability: Pharmacy staff should record study product returned from a study participant in the study's accountability log.

Study product disposition

At the end of a study, the Investigator or designee should ensure that leftover study product is either destroyed with appropriate documentation thereof, donated as agreed to with the manufacturer (for marketed products only), or returned properly to the supplier, distributor, or manufacturer from where it came. Study product should be stored and shipped to the appropriate individual under conditions suitable to the product.

Accountability: Pharmacy staff should record in the study's accountability log the amount destroyed/donated/returned, lot numbers, expiration dates, and condition of product.

Essential documents for the conduct of a clinical trial

Essential Documents are those documents which individually and collectively permit evaluation of the conduct of a trial and the quality of the data produced. These documents serve to demonstrate the compliance of the investigator, sponsor and monitor with the standards of Good Clinical Practice and with all applicable regulatory requirements.

Essential Documents also serve a number of other important purposes. Filing essential documents at the investigator/institution and sponsor sites in a timely manner can greatly assist in the successful management of a trial by the investigator, sponsor and monitor. These documents are also the ones which are usually audited by the sponsor's independent audit function and inspected by the regulatory authority(ies) as part of the process to confirm the validity of the trial conduct and the integrity of data collected.

The minimum list of essential documents which has been developed follows. The various documents are grouped in three sections according to the stage of the trial during which they will normally be generated:

1) before the clinical phase of the trial commences,

2) during the clinical conduct of the trial, and

3) after completion or termination of the trial.

A description is given of the purpose of each document, and whether it should be filed in either the investigator/ institution or sponsor files, or both. It is acceptable to combine some of the documents, provided the individual elements are readily identifiable.

Trial master files should be established at the beginning of the trial, both at the investigator/institution's site and at the sponsor's office. A final close-out of a trial can only be done when the monitor has reviewed both investigator/ institution and sponsor files and confirmed that all necessary documents are in the appropriate files.

Any or all of the documents addressed in this guideline may be subject to, and should be available for, audit by the sponsor's auditor and inspection by the regulatory authority(ies).

The sponsor and investigator/institution should maintain a record of the location(s) of their respective essential documents including source documents. The storage system used during the trial and for archiving (irrespective of the type of media used) should provide for document identification, version history, search, and retrieval. Essential documents for the trial should be supplemented or may be reduced where justified (in advance of trial initiation) based on the importance and relevance of the specific documents to the trial. The sponsor should ensure that the investigator has control of and continuous access to the CRF data reported to the sponsor. The sponsor should not have exclusive control of those data. When a copy is used to replace an original document (e.g., source documents, CRF), the copy should fulfill the requirements for certified copies. The investigator/institution should have control of all essential documents and records generated by the investigator/institution before, during, and after the trial.

A. Before the Clinical Phase of the Trial Commences

During this planning stage the following documents should be generated and should be on file before the trial formally starts

1. Investigator's brochure

To document that relevant and current scientific information about the investigational product has been provided to the investigator

2. Signed protocol and amendments, if any, and sample case report form (crf)

To document investigator and sponsor agreement to the protocol/amendment(s) and CRF

3. Information given to trial subject-informed consent form

(including all applicable translations)

To document the informed consent

- any other written information

To document that subjects will be given appropriate written information (content and wording) to support their ability to give fully informed consent

- advertisement for subject recruitment (if used)

To document that recruitment measures are appropriate and not coercive

4. Financial aspects of the trial

To document the financial agreement between the investigator/institution and the sponsor for the trial

5. **Insurance statement**

(where required)
To document that compensation to subject(s) for trial-related injury will be available

6. **Signed agreement between involved parties**

e.g.:
- investigator/institution and sponsor
- investigator/institution and CRO
- sponsor and CRO
- investigator/institution and authority(ies) (where required)

To document agreements

7. **Dated, documented approval/favourable opinion of institutional review board (irb) /independent ethics committee (iec) of the following:**

- protocol and any amendments
- CRF (if applicable)
- informed consent form(s)
- any other written information to be provided to the subject(s)
- advertisement for subject recruitment (if used)
- subject compensation (if any)
- any other documents given approval/ favourable opinion

To document that the trial has been subject to IRB/IEC review and given approval/favourable opinion. To identify the version number and date of the document(s)

8. **Institutional review board / independent ethics committee composition**

To document that the IRB/IEC is constituted in agreement with GCP

9. **Regulatory authority(ies) authorisation / approval / notification of protocol**

To document appropriate authorisation / approval / notification by the regulatory authority(ies) has been obtained prior to initiation of the trial in compliance with the applicable regulatory requirement(s)

10**Curriculum vitae and/or other relevant documents evidencing qualifications of investigator(s) and sub-investigator(s)**

To document qualifications and eligibility to conduct trial and/or provide medical supervision of subjects

12. **Normal value(s)/range(s) for medical / laboratory / technical procedure(s) and/or test(s) included in the protocol**

To document normal values and/or ranges of the tests
12.medical/laboratory/technical procedures / tests

- certification or
- accreditation or
- established quality control and/or external quality assessment or
- other validation (where required)

To document competence of facility to perform required test(s) , and support reliability of results

1. **Sample of label(s) attached to investigational product container(s)**

To document compliance with applicable labelling regulations and appropriateness of instructions provided to the subjects

2. **Instructions for handling of investigational product(s) and trial-related materials**

(if not included in protocol or Investigator's Brochure)
To document instructions needed to ensure proper storage, packaging, dispensing and disposition of investigational products and trial-related materials

3. **Shipping records for investigational product(s) and trial-related materials**

To document shipment dates, batch numbers and method of shipment of investigational product(s) and trial-related materials. Allows tracking of product batch, review of shipping conditions, and accountability

4. **Certificate(s) of analysis of investigational product(s) shipped**

To document identity, purity, and strength of investigational product(s) to be used in the trial

5. **Decoding procedures for blinded trials**

To document how, in case of an emergency, identity of blinded investigational product can be revealed without breaking the blind for the remaining subjects' treatment

6. **Master randomisation list**

To document method for randomisation of trial population

7. **Pre-trial monitoring report**

To document that the site is suitable for the trial (may be combined with 8.2.20)

8. **Trial initiation monitoring report**

To document that trial procedures were reviewed with the investigator and the investigator's trial staff (may be combined with 19)

B.During the Clinical Conduct of the Trial

1.investigator's brochure updates

To document that investigator is informed in a timely manner of relevant information as it becomes available

2.any revision to:

- protocol/amendment(s) and CRF

- informed consent form
- any other written information provided to subjects
- advertisement for subject recruitment (if used)

To document revisions of these trial related documents that take effect during trial

3.dated, documented approval / favourable opinion of institutional review board (irb) / independent ethics committee (iec) of the following:

- protocol amendment(s)
- revision(s) of:
- informed consent form
- any other written information to be provided to the subject
- advertisement for subject recruitment (if used)
- any other documents given approval/favourable opinion
- continuing review of trial (where required)

To document that the amendment(s) and/or revision(s) have been subject to IRB/IEC review and were given approval/favourable opinion. To identify the version number and date of the document(s).

4.regulatory authority(ies) authorisations / approvals / notifications where required for:

- protocol amendment(s) and other documents

To document compliance with applicable regulatory requirements

5.curriculum vitae for new investigator(s) and/or sub-investigator(s)

6.updates to normal value(s) / range(s) for medical / laboratory / technical procedure(s) / test(s) included in the protocol

To document normal values and ranges that are revised during the trial (see 8.2.11)

7.updates of medical/laboratory/ technical procedures/tests

- certification or
- accreditation or
- established quality control and/or external quality assessment or
- other validation (where required)

To document that tests remain adequate throughout the trial period (see 8.2.12)

8.documentation of investigational product(s) and trial-related materials shipment

9. Certificate(s) of analysis for new batches of investigational products

10.monitoring visit reports

To document site visits by, and findings of, the monitor

11.relevant communications other than site visits

- letters
- meeting notes
- notes of telephone calls

To document any agreements or significant discussions regarding trial administration, protocol violations, trial conduct, adverse event (AE) reporting

12.signed informed consent forms

To document that consent is obtained in accordance with GCP and protocol and dated prior to participation of each subject in trial. Also to document direct access permission

13.source documents

To document the existence of the subject and substantiate integrity of trial data collected. To include original documents related to the trial, to medical treatment, and history of subject

14.signed, dated and completed case report forms (crf)

To document that the investigator or authorised member of the investigator's staff confirms the observations recorded

15.documentation of crf corrections

To document all changes/additions or corrections made to CRF after initial data were recorded

16.notification by originating investigator to sponsor of serious adverse events and related reports

Notification by originating investigator to sponsor of serious adverse events and related reports in accordance with 4.11

17.notification by sponsor and/or investigator, where applicable, to regulatory authority(ies) and irb(s)/iec(s) of unexpected serious adverse drug reactions and of other safety information

Notification by sponsor and/or investigator, where applicable, to regulatory authorities and IRB(s)/IEC(s) of unexpected serious adverse drug reactions in accordance with 5.17 and 4.11.1 and of other safety information in accordance with 5.16.2 and 4.11.2

18.notification by sponsor to investigators of safety information

Notification by sponsor to investigators of safety information in accordance with 5.16.2

19.interim or annual reports to irb/iec and authority(ies)

Interim or annual reports provided to IRB/IEC in accordance with 4.10 and to authority(ies) in accordance with 5.17.3

20.Subject Screening Log

To document identification of subjects who entered pre-trial screening

21.subject identification code list

To document that investigator/institution keeps a confidential list of names of all subjects allocated to trial numbers on enrolling in the trial. Allows investigator/institution to reveal identity of any subject

22.subject enrolment log

To document chronological enrolment of subjects by trial number

23.investigational products accountability at the site

To document that investigational product(s) have been used according to the protocol

24.signature sheet

To document signatures and initials of all persons authorised to make entries and/or corrections on CRFs

25.Record of Retained Body Fluids/ Tissue Samples (If Any)

To document location and identification of retained samples if assays need to be repeated

C.After Completion or Termination of the Trial

After completion or termination of the trial, all of the documents identified in sections A and B should be in the file together with the following

1.Investigational Product(S) Accountability At Site

To document that the investigational product(s) have been used according to the protocol. To documents the final accounting of investigational product(s) received at the site, dispensed to subjects, returned by the subjects, and returned to sponsor

2.Documentation Of Investigational Product Destruction

To document destruction of unused investigational products by sponsor or at site

3.Completed Subject Identification Code List

To permit identification of all subjects enrolled in the trial in case follow-up is required. List should be kept in a confidential manner and for agreed upon time

4.Audit Certificate (If Available)

To document that audit was performed

5.Final Trial Close-Out Monitoring Report

To document that all activities required for trial close-out are completed, and copies of essential documents are held in the appropriate files

6.Treatment Allocation and Decoding Documentation

Returned to sponsor to document any decoding that may have occurred

7.Final Report by Investigator to Irb/Iec Where Required, And Where Applicable, To the Regulatory Authority (Ies)

To document completion of the trial

8.Clinical Study Report

To document results and interpretation of trial.

Guidelines for the preparation of a

contract research organization master file

Background

1. General information
2. Quality management system of the contract research organization
3. Personnel
4. Ethics committee
5. Computer systems
6. Equipment and instruments
7. Documentation
8. Safety monitoring
9. Investigational medicinal products and comparator products
10. Pathology
11. Bioanalytical laboratory
12. Biostatistics
13. Study volunteers
14. Other information

Background

A contract research organization master fi le (CROMF) is a document

prepared by the contract research organization (CRO) containing specific and factual information about the CRO and the conduct of clinical studies as well as the analyses of samples and related operations (including clinical trials, clinical data management, pharmacokinetics and statistical analysis and regulatory affairs) carried out at the named site. If only some of the operations referred to below are carried out at the site, the master fi le (MF) needs to be presented only for those operations.

In a case where a CRO is responsible for activities pertaining only to bioanalytical procedures, then only sections in the CROMF relating to these should be described. Other sections may be marked as "not applicable". Where a CRO performs various activities, separate sections could be prepared for the different units, e.g. clinical pharmacology unit (CPU) and bioanalytical laboratory (BAL).

A CROMF provides information on the policies, approach and general activities of a CRO. It is not trial-specific as trial-specific data are submitted in a product dossier. It serves as general information to regulators and can be used during preparation for inspections by regulatory inspectors in addition to the trial-specific data and information submitted for assessment. It also provides an overview of the organization's approach to good clinical practices (GCP), good laboratory practices (GLP) and other guidelines pertaining to its activities.

A CROMF should be submitted to the national medicines regulatory authority (NMRA) where such a document is requested. It should be succinct and as far as possible not exceed 25 A4 pages (where appropriate, supportive documentation may be appended).

An updated CROMF should be submitted when requested by the NMRA, or if significant changes have been implemented by the CRO.

1. General information

1.1 Name and exact address of the CRO, including telephone, fax, 24-hour telephone numbers and e-mail address

1.2 Short description of the CRO (including size, location, number of beds, layout and plan, areas for handling samples and waste)

1.3 Activities as licensed/authorized by the national authority

1.4 Inspections and approvals

1.4.1 Inspections/approvals/accreditations by any regulatory agency

1.4.2 Audits of subcontractors

1.5 Type of studies (and indications, where appropriate) performed on site (a list of projects conducted at this site may be provided)

1.6 Provisions for insurance

1.6.1 Number of employees engaged in studies, quality, storage and distribution

1.7 Contract services employed

1.7.1 Use of outside scientific, analytical or other technical assistance in relation to studies and analysis (e.g. clinical laboratory, bioanalytical laboratory, X-ray facilities and caterers)

1.7.2 Services outsourced, e.g., contracts with tertiary care hospital for handling of medical emergencies, ambulance facility, nutrition, biomedical waste, chemical waste, caterers, pest control and pathology laboratory

2. Quality management system of the contract research organization (Short description including, e.g., responsibilities of the quality assurance unit. A list of quality system documents can be included)

2.1 Organization chart including the arrangements for quality assurance

2.2 Internal audits and self-inspection

2.3 Corrective and preventive action plans (CAPA)

3. Personnel

(A brief description can be presented in tabular format)

3.1 Qualifications, experience and responsibilities of key personnel as applicable

3.1.1 project manager

3.1.2 principal investigator

3.1.3 analytical investigator

3.1.4 biostatistician

3.1.5 clinical research associates

3.1.6 data manager

3.1.7 monitor

3.1.8 the study director(s)

3.1.9 person responsible for quality assurance

3.2 Training of personnel:

3.2.1 training policy and procedure (brief description)

3.2.2 training records

4. Ethics committee

4.1 Constitution and relation to CRO

4.2 Procedures including review and approval of protocols

5. Computer systems

(Short description)

5.1 Hardware

5.2 Software (and version number) used (e.g., in the bioanalytical laboratory, in pharmacokinetic and statistical analysis) and change control procedure

5.3 Data management systems (include a procedural fl ow chart and a brief description of query generation and resolution)

5.4. Security procedures

5.5 Electronic exchange of confidential information

5.6 Brief description of validation programme

5.7 Back-up and storage of electronic data

6. Equipment and instruments

6.1 Brief description of major equipment and instruments (a list of equipment is not required)

6.2 Qualification, maintenance and calibration programme, including the temperature recording systems

7. Documentation

7.1 Briefly describe document management systems

7.2 Project work flow including quality assurance and control process

7.3 Preparation of protocols

7.4 Preparation of informed consent forms and subject information forms

7.5 Preparation of report forms

7.6 Preparation of final report

8. Safety monitoring

(Brief description)

Adverse drug reaction reporting procedure Provisions made for emergencies, including protocols and equipment available

9. **Investigational medicinal products and comparator products**

(Brief description)

9.1 Acquisition, storage, handling, sampling and disposal

9.2 Pharmacy and dispensing

10. Pathology

10.1 Biological sample collection and storage

10.2 Handling and analysis of biological samples

11. Bioanalytical laboratory

(Brief description)

11.1 Method development and validation

11.2 Reference standard materials used for preparation of calibration standards and quality control samples

11.3 Biological matrix storage, and handling of matrix samples

11.4 Analysis of unknown samples

11.5 Preparation and labelling of reagents

11.6 Storage of samples

11.7 Stability procedures

11.8 Waste management

12. Biostatistics

12.1 Data processing and analysis

12.2 Data management

13. Study volunteers

13.1 Procedure for recruitment

13.2 Collecting information on volunteers (e.g. databank), while confidentiality is maintained

13.3 Procedure for obtaining informed consent

14. Other information

14.1 Power supply system — uninterrupted power supply and generator availability and capacity

14.2 Brief description of any other activities performed on site by the CRO

14.3 Any other information which the CRO may feel it appropriate to add

Investigator Site File (ISF)

An Investigator Site File (ISF) contains essential documents which shows that the clinical trial site and Investigator are following the regulatory requirements set out by the ICH GCP guidelines.

According to the International Council for Harmonisation (ICH) Good Clinical Practice (GCP) guidelines, essential documents are defined as "documents which individually and collectively permit evaluation of the conduct of the trial and the quality of the data produced."

The ICH GCP 4.9.4 guideline states that "the Investigator and Institution should maintain the trial documents as specified in the 'Essential Documents for the Conduct of a Clinical Trial' guidelines.

An ISF plays a crucial role in the outcome of the clinical trial and should be established once a Clinical Trial site has been confirmed by the Sponsor. The Principal Investigator (PI) or an appointed delegate is responsible for setting up, maintaining and completing the ISF.

It is the responsibility of the PI or the delegate to ensure that all the essential documents are collected before the trial begins and that the ISF is updated throughout the duration of the study and archived as part of the Clinical Trial Agreement with the Sponsor.

Essential Documents

All essential documents, including any correspondence should be placed in the ISF within 5 business days of the receipt. The essential documents are to be made readily available for monitoring, Sponsor audits and regulatory inspections.

The essential documents that should be included in the ISF include:

- Trial Protocol
- Participant Information Sheet and Consent Forms
- Investigator Brochure
- Regulatory documents, applications and approvals
- Delegation Logs
- Safety Reports
- Correspondence between delegated site staff and Sponsor

Pharmacy File

A Pharmacy Folder is also included in the ISF (when applicable). It lists the recruited participants, Investigational Product shipping details, receipts and accountability documents. An up-to-date Trial Protocol and Investigator's Brochure should also be included.

The Pharmacy File is kept at the site pharmacy and is maintained by the delegated pharmacist.

Paper and Electronic ISF (eISF)

Certain information should be included on the cover and spine of a paper ISF folder. This information includes:

- A Human Research Ethics Committee (HRECS) reference number and local project number
- Name of Principal Investigator
- Study name

If a document is removed from the ISF, there needs to be a note explaining why it was removed and where it was moved to.

The same controls should be put in place for using an electronic ISF. When converting paper ISF's to electronic copies, they should be validated and used with quality control checks to ensure that no data was lost during the conversion.

Investigator Site File Outline

Section 1: Contact Details

- Contact list of study personnel and site staff
- Contact details of external vendors

Section 2: Investigator's Brochure/Product Information

- Current versions of the Investigator Brochure and Product Information Forms
- Previous submitted versions

Section 3: Protocol

- Current approved version
- Previous approved versions and updates
- Signature pages

Section 4: Participant Information and Consent Form

- Current approved versions
- Previous approved versions
- Signed Informed Consent forms
- Signed Informed Consent Tracking Log

Section 5: Participant Tools

- Patient Card, Diary or Questionnaire (if applicable)
- Current approved versions
- Previous approved copies
- Translation certificates (if available)

Section 6: Advertisement for Trial Participant Recruitment

- Current approved version
- Previous approved versions
- Translation certificates (if available)

Section 7: Case Report Form (CRF)

- Current version (blank sample)
- Previous version (blank sample)
- Completion guidelines
- Signed, dated and completed CRFs
- Documentation of CRF edits made

Section 8: Source Documents
Section 9: Ethics

- Initial submission
- Amendments
- Progress Reports

- Ethics Composition
- Notification of Safety Reports
- Notification of Non-compliance and Protocol Deviations
- Correspondence

Section 10: Governance

- Site Authorisation Letter
- Post Authorisation Submission and Authorisation Letters

Section 10A: Regulatory Documents

- Clinical Trial Notification (CTN) or Clinical Trial Exemption (CTX) forms
- Therapeutic Goods Administration (TGA) acknowledgement letter
- Correspondence

Section 11: Study Personnel

- Delegation Log/Signature sheet
- Curriculum Vitae (CV) (including GCP and Medical License, etc)
- Training log and documentation

Section 12: Agreements

- Signed Confidentiality Agreement
- Signed Clinical Trial Agreement
- Other relevant agreements/contracts
- Insurance Certificate
- Indemnity

Section 13: Participant Logs

- Participant Screening Log
- Participant Enrolment Log
- Participant Identification Log
- Participant Visit Tracking Log

Section 14: Investigational Product (IP)

- Instructions for handling the IP
- Shipping and receipt records
- Dispensing and Accountability logs
- IP Destruction Logs
- IP Storage and Temperature Logs
- Decoding and Un-blinding Procedure
- Sample of labels attached to IP containers

Section 15: Randomisation

- Instructions
- Un-blinding process

Section 16: Monitoring

- Site Visit Log
- Visit Correspondence (appointment confirmation and follow-up letters)

Section 17: Laboratory

- Normal values and ranges for medical procedures and tests included in protocol
- Certification/Accreditation/Established Quality Control/Validation for medical procedures and tests

Section 18: Biological Samples

- Sample Log
- Sample Handling Manual
- Sample Shipping Record
- Laboratory Manual and Certification
- Shipping Materials
- Samples Destruction/Return Records

Section 19: Safety Reports

- Serious Adverse Event (SAE) Tracking Log
- SAE Reports which have been submitted to the Sponsor
- Safety Reports

Section 20: Study Reports/Publications

- Interim Report and Data Safety Monitoring Boards (DSMB) Reports
- Final Clinical Study Report
- Relevant Study Publications and References

Section 21: Study Meetings

- Investigator Meeting (agenda and presentation)
- Site Initiation Visit (agenda and presentation)
- Other relevant meeting documentation

Section 22: Correspondence

- Correspondence with Trial Sponsor
- Correspondence with Site Staff
- Correspondence with Laboratory/Vendors
- Other relevant correspondence

Section 23: Miscellaneous

- Newsletters

All essential documents found in the ISF are required to be filed and stored in a secure location (a locked office or an electronic filing system with password protection). After the clinical trial has ended, all essential documents need to be archived in accordance with the Clinical Trial Agreement and the NSW Health Record Retention Policies. A Sponsor must give their written permission before any older ISFs are destroyed and one copy must always be kept for archiving purposes.

Study Close-Out Visit

DEFINITION

- The **Study Close-out Visit** is a visit and process arranged by the sponsor of the research study to ensure that all necessary aspects of the study closure have been addressed, to include organization and completion of documentation and reporting.

Policies/Guidelines

- The study close-out visit occurs once participants are no longer receiving investigational treatment, all the data have been collected (there are no more outstanding adverse events & all outstanding queries/data clarification forms have been resolved appropriately), the database is locked and ready for statistical analysis, and the study conduct has ended.
    - This is the study monitor's final visit to shut down the study at the site.
- The study monitor will ensure that everything is neat and tidy at the study site and that the documentation is well organized and will remain intact and be accessible in the future as needed for regulatory reasons.
    - If it isn't documented, it didn't happen!

Templates/Forms

- Study Close-out Visit Checklist
    - Site Checklist (created by the National Center for Complementary and Integrative Health (NCCIH))

Site Checklist for NCCIH Closeout Visit

Scheduling/Logistics

- Query PI and relevant study staff (including pharmacy if applicable) regarding the monitor's proposed visit dates
- Confirm mutually-agreeable visit date with the monitor and study staff
- Confirm pharmacy appointment date and time and communicate to the monitor
- Reserve work space for the monitor
- Obtain access to necessary electronic records for the monitor, if applicable

- Provide logistics information to the monitor for first visit day: directions to site/room, time to meet, emergency contact/backup number as requested

Regulatory/Essential Documents

- NCCIH approval of protocol, CRFs, ICF, and DSMP
- Local IRB has been informed of the study closure, or the timeline to do so in accordance with local IRB reporting requirements
- Per the NCCIH regulatory summary sheet and checklist at nccih.nih.gov/grants/toolbox/resources, all required IRB and NCCIH approvals, documents of staff qualification and training, lab certifications, tracking and other logs are complete, up to date, and organized for review
- All ICFs signed to date are complete and on file, and the informed consent process is documented appropriately in participant records
- File visit confirmation letter received from the monitor in the regulatory binder

Study Data

- Provide a current list of enrolled participant ID numbers to the monitor upon request
- Progress note or checklist entry is included in each participant chart indicating that the end of the study participation was communicated to each participant
- CRFs and/or database records are complete with all data queries resolved (or a timeline for resolution)
- Study data have been reviewed for QC per the QC plan

Pharmacy, if applicable

- All study agents are accounted for and pharmacy documentation is in order
- Remaining study agents are returned/destroyed as outlined in the protocol or agreement with supplier

Specimens, if applicable

- All study specimens are accounted for and documentation is in order

Post-Visit Follow-up

- Return completed Action Item – Site Response Form to the monitor within 30 days of receipt, recording resolution of Action Item or plan for resolution if pending
- File visit report(s) received from the monitor, completed Action Item – Site Response Form in the regulatory binder
- Provides an overview of what will be reviewed by monitors during a site visit.

Questions

1. Explain in detail about procurement and storage of investigationalproduct in clinical research?
2. What are he investigator responsibilities in procurement and storage of investigationalproduct in clinical research?
3.What are the operational guidelines for study product ordering and receipt?
4.What are the essential documents to conduct clinical trial?
5.Enlist the documents before clinical phase is commences?
6.What are the guidelines for the preparation of a contract research organization master file?
7.Short note on Investigator site file?
8 Short note on Pharmacy file?
9.Short note on Study close out visit?

CHAPTER FIVE

Quality Assurance and Quality Control in Clinical Trials

Audit

A systematic and independent examination of trial related activities and documents to determine whether the evaluated trial related activities were conducted, and the data were recorded, analysed and accurately reported according to the protocol, sponsor's standard operating procedures (SOPs), Good Clinical Practice (GCP), and the applicable regulatory requirement(s).

Audit Certificate

A declaration of confirmation by the auditor that an audit has taken place.

Audit Report

A written evaluation by the sponsor's auditor of the results of the audit.

Audit Trail

Documentation that allows reconstruction of the course of events.

If or when sponsors perform audits, as part of implementing quality assurance, they should consider:

Purpose

The purpose of a sponsor's audit, which is independent of and separate from routine monitoring or quality control functions, should be to evaluate trial conduct and compliance with the protocol, SOPs, GCP, and the applicable regulatory requirements.

Selection and Qualification of Auditors

(a) The sponsor should appoint individuals, who are independent of the clinical trials/systems, to conduct audits.

(b) The sponsor should ensure that the auditors are qualified by training and experience to conduct audits properly. An auditor's qualifications should be documented.

Auditing Procedures

(a) The sponsor should ensure that the auditing of clinical trials/systems is conducted in accordance with the sponsor's written procedures on what to audit, how to audit, the frequency of audits, and the form and content of audit reports.

(b) The sponsor's audit plan and procedures for a trial audit should be guided by the importance of the trial to submissions to regulatory authorities, the number of subjects in the trial, the type and complexity of the trial, the level of risks to the trial subjects, and any identified problem(s).

(c) The observations and findings of the auditor(s) should be documented.

(d) To preserve the independence and value of the audit function, the regulatory authority(ies) should not routinely request the audit reports. Regulatory authority(ies) may seek access to an audit report on a case by case basis when evidence of serious GCP non-compliance exists, or in the course of legal proceedings.

(e) When required by applicable law or regulation, the sponsor should provide an audit certificate.

a) The Objective

As the audit is intended to verify what has taken place, its form depends on the mission of the auditor, i.e. on the objective in question. It can be a system audit of the promoter or an aspect of the trial such as the galenic files of the treatment units, the maintenance of records, the biometry, or the work of clinical research teams. Or the audit can be conducted on site by a systematic assessment of the work of the investigators, or by random sampling, or, in case of suspected fraud, by the service company in charge of the trial. Laboratories conducting biological or complementary examinations can also be audited. Thus, the choice is large and must necessarily be limited. System audits are most often performed regularly to assess the general situation without any specific reference to a clinical trial. However, onsite audits relate directly to a clinical trial and are conducted especially to improve the credibility and thus the admissibility of the trial by the state supervisory agencies.

Audit Rules

An audit cannot be performed secretly as it is an important act for firms. The question or questions raised by an audit must always be indicated in advance since they determine how it will be carried out:

1. The firm must advise all the teams concerned of the decision to perform an audit by an individual or a team.
2. The auditor must clearly understand the objective of his mission, i.e. what must be audited and why. He makes sure that the persons involved are clearly aware of the purpose of the audit.
3. The auditor familiarizes himself with all the information required for his work.
4. With the assistance of the sponsor, the auditor draws up an operating plan and an evaluation scale.

1. In practice, the auditor conforms to the accepted plan and evaluates compliance with the working rules (procedures).
2. The auditor keeps records of his meetings, draws up a general report of what he has observed and finally gives his opinion about compliance with the procedures he has investigated and their admissibility by state supervisory agencies. The auditor expresses a clear judgment but does not make a decision. His judgment should be factual since it may be contested by others. In addition to the audit itself, the firm can request advice and opinions about the effective operation of a department, although these observations must not be included in the report.

Types of audits

On-site audit

The on-site audit is performed to check the work of the investigators and often of the monitoring team in a particular trial. This audit is intended to provide the trial with an attestation of conformity and thus make it more credible in the eyes of the authorities. The auditor makes a judgment about the compliance of the teams with the rules initially set forth. The audit is announced and described during the meetings with investigators before the trial.When the plan of the audit is developed, the procedure will be described, indicating in particular what will be verified on-site. This procedure should be sent to all investigators before the audit takes place so that they can become familiar with the rules to be followed, the number of sites audited and the actual date of the audit.

The following elements define the plan of action of the audit:

- The protocol and the data sheets and binders;
- The procedures for starting up the trial, the meetings of investigators, the pre-investigation visits, the setting up of the trial, the follow-up and the closing of the centers, as well as the procedures for administrative management of the trial within the firm;
- The list of centres;
- For each center audited, the observations are already noted as well as the reports of visits.

The investigator is advised of the auditor's visit, which occurs independently of that of the monitoring team. The auditor checks all the data required and the way in which they were obtained. In particular, he ensures that the patients included in the trial exist, have given their informed consent and have been seen at the times indicated in the binders.He determines whether the investigator and his team are performing the clinical trial according to the protocol and the established rules of evaluation. If there are procedures specific to the trial, the auditor ensures that they are understood and followed.

After the visit, the auditor prepares a report which is sent to the promotor and, if previously agreed, to the investigator. In his report, the auditor indicates all the failings noted and evaluates patient by patient, and then in terms of the center, the degree of credibility that can be accorded to the trial data. After the audits of all the sites have been performed, the auditor writes a general report indicating his opinion on the credibility of the trial.

The system audits

The system audit is both easy and difficult. It is generally easy since most of the persons involved are present on the site, but it is difficult as well since all of the actions of the teams are not codified (unwritten practices are the rule). The persons in charge of quality assurance and control are overworked and generally do not concentrate on the essential elements expressed in official texts. Finally, the units or departments in a firm are not isolated, even if there is little communication among them (as is generally the case). Interdepartmental interfaces are vital and yet difficult to manage because of the overlapping of responsibility. System audits are generally intended to accomplish the following:

1. To check that all actions have been performed in accordance with the laws and regulations and that the administrative documents are complete.
2. To ensure that no document essential to the operation of a department is lost and that it is used, checked and filed in an acceptable manner.
3. To determine that it is impossible in the operation of the departments to modify an essential piece of information without leaving an explicit indication. Consequently, the auditor should verify that no fraud is possible or, if detected, that it is reported to the highest authorities concerned and given special attention.

It is not the role of the auditor to make a judgment about the organization of departments, which relates to another type of mission. However, it is his duty to indicate the inadequacy of procedures or their possible absence. The auditor should generally comment on the disparity between the description of the procedure and the true state of operations. In fact, procedures should reflect reality and may thus be modified. For this reason, the system audit is often used by managers to improve the operations of departments and check their adequacy in terms of the requirements of authorities, in the event of an official inspection of a particular trial.

Audit resolution and preparing for FDA inspections

CDM (Clinical data management) is the process of collection, cleaning, and management of subject data in compliance with regulatory standards.

Clinical trial is intended to find answers to the research question by means of generating data for proving or disproving a hypothesis. The quality of data generated plays an important role in the outcome of the study.

Clinical data management is a relevant and important part of a clinical trial. All researchers try their hands on CDM activities during their research work, knowingly or unknowingly.

Objective of CDM processes

- to provide high-quality data by keeping the number of errors and missing data as low as possible and gather maximum data for analysis.

To meet this objective, best practices are adopted to ensure that data are complete, reliable, and processed correctly.

This has been facilitated by the use of software applications that maintain an audit trail and provide easy identification and resolution of data discrepancies.

Sophisticated innovations have enabled CDM to handle large trials and ensure the data quality even in complex trials.

High-quality data should be absolutely accurate and suitable for statistical analysis. These should meet the protocol-specified parameters and comply with the protocol requirements. This implies that in case of a deviation, not meeting the protocol-specifications, we may think of excluding the patient from the final database.

It should be borne in mind that in some situations, regulatory authorities may be interested in looking at such data. Similarly, missing data is also a matter of concern for clinical researchers. High-quality data should have minimal or no misses. But most importantly, high-quality data should possess only an arbitrarily 'acceptable level of variation' that would not affect the conclusion of the study on statistical analysis. The data should also meet the applicable regulatory requirements specified for data quality.

Tools for CDM

Many software tools are available for data management, and these are called Clinical Data Management Systems (CDMS). In multicentric trials, a CDMS has become essential to handle the huge amount of data.

Most of the CDMS used in pharmaceutical companies are commercial, but a few open source tools are available as well.

Commonly used CDM tools are ORACLE CLINICAL, CLINTRIAL, MACRO, RAVE, and eClinical Suite.

In terms of functionality, these software tools are more or less similar and there is no significant advantage of one system over the other.

These software tools are expensive and need sophisticated Information Technology infrastructure to function.

Multinational pharmaceutical giants use custom-made CDMS tools to suit their operational needs and procedures.

Among the open-source tools, the most prominent ones are OpenClinica, openCDMS, TrialDB, and PhOSCo.

These CDM software are available free of cost and are as good as their commercial counterparts in terms of functionality. These open source software can be downloaded from their respective websites.

In regulatory submission studies, maintaining an audit trail of data management activities is of paramount importance.

These CDM tools ensure the audit trail and help in the management of discrepancies. According to the roles and responsibilities, multiple user IDs can be created with access limitation to data entry, medical coding, database designing, or quality check.

This ensures that each user can access only the respective functionalities allotted to that user ID and cannot make any other change in the database. For responsibilities where changes are permitted to be made in the data, the software will record the change made, the user ID that made the change and the time and date of change, for audit purposes (audit trail). During a regulatory audit, the auditors can verify the discrepancy management process; the changes made and can confirm that no unauthorized or false changes were made.

Regulations, Guidelines, and Standards in CDM

Akin to other areas in clinical research, CDM has guidelines and standards that must be followed. Since the pharmaceutical industry relies on the electronically captured data for the evaluation of medicines, there is a need to follow good practices in CDM and maintain standards in electronic data capture. These electronic records have to comply with a Code of Federal Regulations (CFR), 21 CFR Part 11. This regulation is applicable to records in electronic format that are created, modified, maintained, archived, retrieved, or transmitted. This demands the use of validated systems to ensure accuracy, reliability, and consistency of data with the use of secure, computer-generated, time-stamped audit trails to independently record the date and time of operator entries and actions that create, modify, or delete electronic records. Adequate procedures and controls should be put in place to ensure the integrity, authenticity, and confidentiality of data. If data have to be submitted to regulatory authorities, it should be entered and processed in 21 CFR part 11-compliant systems. Most of the CDM systems available are like this and pharmaceutical companies as well as contract research organizations ensure this compliance.

Society for Clinical Data Management (SCDM) publishes the Good Clinical Data Management Practices (GCDMP) guidelines, a document providing the standards of good practice within CDM. GCDMP was initially published in September 2000 and has undergone several revisions thereafter. The July 2009 version is the currently followed GCDMP document. GCDMP provides guidance on the accepted practices in CDM that are consistent with regulatory practices. Addressed in 20 chapters, it covers the CDM process by highlighting the minimum standards and best practices.

Clinical Data Interchange Standards Consortium (CDISC), a multidisciplinary non-profit organization, has developed standards to support acquisition, exchange, submission, and archival of clinical research data and metadata. Metadata is the data of the data entered. This includes data about the individual who made the entry or a change in the clinical data, the date and time of entry/change and details of the changes that have been made. Among the standards, two important ones are the Study Data Tabulation Model Implementation Guide for Human Clinical Trials (SDTMIG) and the Clinical Data Acquisition Standards Harmonization (CDASH) standards, available free of cost from the CDISC website (www.cdisc.org). The SDTMIG standard describes the details of model and standard terminologies for the data and serves as a guide to the organization. CDASH v 1.1 defines the basic standards for the collection of data in a clinical trial and enlists the basic data information needed from a clinical, regulatory, and scientific perspective.

Electronic data capture (EDC) system in clinical trials

An electronic data capture (EDC) system —also known as electronic case report form (eCRF)— is a web-based software application used to collect, clean, transfer, and process data in clinical trials.

There is no legal or regulatory obligation to use an EDC software in a clinical trial. Moreover, EDC systems are relatively new technologies and there was a time when clinical trials were conducted without EDCs.

For example, clinical data used to be collected using paper-based forms, something still done today (although less frequently). In any case, clinical data has to be collected by some means and nowadays EDC solutions are the best option.

Advantages of using an EDC system in clinical trials

- Utilizing an EDC solution streamlines data collection when compared to paper-based data collection. Clinical sites can access the EDC system from any computer and

enter data quickly and easily, making it immediately available to data reviewers. This avoids the hassle of writing and shipping paper forms.

- EDC tools accelerate the data cleaning process. Data managers can easily review the data entered in the system and issue queries to sites to solve discrepancies.
- EDC platform guarantees solid data authenticity, integrity, and security, since it integrates advanced mechanisms to manage access controls and data traceability.

Data collected in EDC systems

EDC systems collect different types of data depending on the therapeutic area of the clinical trial.

For instance, in oncology studies the following data forms are typically used: demographics, medical history, vital signs, ECOG performance status, electrocardiogram data, biochemistry, hematology, coagulation tests, urinalysis, pregnancy tests, adverse events, concomitant medications, tumor assessments, treatment data, survival follow-up, and death information, among others.

Data collected procedure in an EDC software

An EDC software usually comes in the form of a web-based application without the need of installing anything else in the computer.

This means that users only have to access the EDC system via a web browser using their usernames and passwords.

Once logged in the application, users will type the clinical data in the fields contained in the various data forms.

Therefore, data entry in an EDC tool is done remotely by local site users, who extract the patient data from the site's source documents (medical records).

Data cleaning in an EDC system

Once the clinical data has been entered in the EDC web-based platform by the hospital's personnel, it is time to refine this information by detecting and solving discrepancies.

The process of identifying and correcting missing or inconsistent information is known as "data cleaning".

Data cleaning in clinical trials is typically performed by data managers belonging to the vendor in charge of data management (e.g. CRO staff).

These data managers will periodically review the EDC information and will issue queries to sites, asking them to clarify and/or correct data discrepancies.

This process is repeated until all the data is complete, clear, and consistent, so that it can be exported and analyzed.

Data export for analysis in an EDC software

After the clinical data entered in an EDC system has been cleaned, the next step is to export this information for further analysis.

EDC applications normally integrate data export mechanisms to generate dataset files that can be in turn used in statistical software tools (e.g. SAS, SPSS).

The clinical information contained in EDC platforms is structured in datasets, and the details of the export processes are documented beforehand, in the early stages of the clinical trial.

How and how often will the data be exported? In what format? These questions are normally addressed in the Data Management Plan (DMP).

EDC systems designed and implementation

EDC systems require a specialized and strict design and implementation process for each clinical trial.

A number of plans have to be written to document the design and implementation procedures, including a Data Management Plan (DMP) and an annotated CRF (aCRF) document.

A DMP is a document that helps data managers and statistical programmers to understand the type of data that will be produced in a clinical trial, and how this data will be collected, stored, cleaned, exported, and analyzed.

An aCRF is a document that maps the clinical data collection fields used to capture patient data to the corresponding variables contained within the Study Data Tabulation Model (SDTM) datasets.

Essentially, the EDC system design and implementation process consists of developing the system specifications and then actually building the software system itself (implementing, testing, and validating the data forms and fields) according to such requirements.

These activities are performed by the data managers of the company in charge of building the EDC system (e.g. CRO staff).

Regulatory requirements for EDC solutions

The regulatory requirements that EDC systems must meet have been established in the United States through the part 11 of Title 21 of the Code of Federal Regulations; Electronic Records; Electronic Signatures (21 CFR Part 11).

To achieve regulatory compliance of EDC systems, the following technical controls must be in place:

- Technical controls: Measures that ensure the quality, accuracy, and integrity of data stored in the electronic systems.
- User authorization controls: Security measures to identify the person who accesses the application and submits the data, to prevent unauthorized access to the system.

- Audit trail controls: Measures to ensure that the system keeps a record about sources from which data originates, who made changes, when, and what information was changed.
- Attributability controls: Measures to ensure that data will be retrievable in such a way that all information regarding each subject in a study is attributable to that subject.
- Data validation controls: Checks performed by the computerized systems to ensure the validity and quality of clinical information.

Finally, system integrity measures must be implemented to guarantee the integrity of the system and protect against data loss (e.g. periodic backups).

Main security and data quality features EDC systems

EDC systems should at least have the following mechanisms to ensure data security and traceability: an internal clock (date and time), an access control module, and an activity registry.

The internal clock system should consistently show the current date and time, so that all the activity taking place in the system is recorded with the right time.

Secondly, an access control module should be available to track each user's access date and time, the user identity, the IP address used, and the type of access (e.g., login, logout, time out, login error).

Additionally, an activity registry must be in place to track the activity through the EDC pages. For each action in the system, data such as Subject ID, username, variable name, inserted value, form name, as well as the date and time of the action should be recorded.

Best EDC systems

Some of the best and most widely used EDC systems worldwide are Rave from Medidata, Inform from Oracle, and Trial Master from Anju Software.

The CDM Process

The CDM process, like a clinical trial, begins with the end in mind. This means that the whole process is designed keeping the deliverable in view. As a clinical trial is designed to answer the research question, the CDM process is designed to deliver an error-free, valid, and statistically sound database. To meet this objective, the CDM process starts early, even before the finalization of the study protocol.

Review and finalization of study documents

The protocol is reviewed from a database designing perspective, for clarity and consistency. During this review, the CDM personnel will identify the data items to be collected and the frequency of collection with respect to the visit schedule. A Case Report Form (CRF) is designed by the CDM team, as this is the first step in translating the protocol-specific activities into data being generated. The data fields should be clearly defined and be consistent throughout. The type of data to be entered should be evident from the CRF.

For example, if weight has to be captured in two decimal places, the data entry field should have two data boxes placed after the decimal.

Similarly, the units in which measurements have to be made should also be mentioned next to the data field. The CRF should be concise, self-explanatory, and user-friendly (unless you are the one entering data into the CRF). Along with the CRF, the filling instructions (called CRF Completion Guidelines) should also be provided to study investigators for error-free data acquisition. CRF annotation is done wherein the variable is named according to the SDTMIG or the conventions followed internally. Annotations are coded terms used in CDM tools to indicate the variables in the study.

In questions with discrete value options (like the variable gender having values male and female as responses), all possible options will be coded appropriately.

Annotated sample of a Case Report Form (CRF). Annotations are entered in coloured text in this figure to differentiate from the CRF questions. DCM = Data collection module, DVG = Discrete value group, YNNA [S1] = Yes, No = Not applicable [subset 1], C ...

Based on these, a Data Management Plan (DMP) is developed. DMP document is a road map to handle the data under foreseeable circumstances and describes the CDM activities to be followed in the trial

The DMP describes the database design, data entry and data tracking guidelines, quality control measures, SAE reconciliation guidelines, discrepancy management, data transfer/extraction, and database locking guidelines. Along with the DMP, a Data Validation Plan (DVP) containing all edit-checks to be performed and the calculations for derived variables are also prepared. The edit check programs in the DVP help in cleaning up the data by identifying the discrepancies.

Database designing

Databases are the clinical software applications, which are built to facilitate the CDM tasks to carry out multiple studies. Generally, these tools have built-in compliance with regulatory requirements and are easy to use. "System validation" is conducted to ensure data security, during which system specifications, user requirements, and regulatory compliance are evaluated before implementation. Study details like objectives, intervals, visits, investigators, sites, and patients are defined in the database and CRF layouts are designed for data entry. These entry screens are tested with dummy data before moving them to the real data capture.

Data collection

Data collection is done using the CRF that may exist in the form of a paper or an electronic version. The traditional method is to employ paper CRFs to collect the data responses, which are translated to the database by means of data entry done in-house. These paper CRFs are filled up by the investigator according to the completion guidelines. In the e-CRF-based CDM, the investigator or a designee will be logging into the CDM system and entering the data directly at the site. In e-CRF method, chances of errors are less, and the resolution of discrepancies happens faster. Since pharmaceutical companies try to reduce the time taken for drug development processes by enhancing the speed of processes involved, many pharmaceutical companies are opting for e-CRF options (also called remote data entry).

CRF tracking

The entries made in the CRF will be monitored by the Clinical Research Associate (CRA) for completeness and filled up CRFs are retrieved and handed over to the CDM team. The CDM team will track the retrieved CRFs and maintain their record. CRFs are tracked for missing pages and illegible data manually to assure that the data are not lost. In case of missing or illegible data, a clarification is obtained from the investigator and the issue is resolved.

Data entry

Data entry takes place according to the guidelines prepared along with the DMP. This is applicable only in the case of paper CRF retrieved from the sites. Usually, double data entry is performed wherein the data is entered by two operators separately. The second pass entry (entry made by the second person) helps in verification and reconciliation by identifying the transcription errors and discrepancies caused by illegible data. Moreover, double data entry helps in getting a cleaner database compared to a single data entry. Earlier studies have shown that double data entry ensures better consistency with paper CRF as denoted by a lesser error rate.

Data validation

Data validation is the process of testing the validity of data in accordance with the protocol specifications. Edit check programs are written to identify the discrepancies in the entered data, which are embedded in the database, to ensure data validity. These programs are written according to the logic condition mentioned in the DVP. These edit check programs are initially tested with dummy data containing discrepancies. Discrepancy is defined as a data point that fails to pass a validation check. Discrepancy may be due to inconsistent data, missing data, range checks, and deviations from the protocol. In e-CRF based studies, data validation process will be run frequently for identifying discrepancies. These discrepancies will be resolved by investigators after logging into the system. Ongoing quality control of data processing is undertaken at regular intervals during the course of CDM. For example, if the inclusion criteria specify that the age of the patient should be between 18 and 65 years (both inclusive), an edit program will be written for two conditions *viz.* age <18 and >65. If for any patient, the condition becomes TRUE, a discrepancy will be generated. These discrepancies will be highlighted in the system and Data Clarification Forms (DCFs) can be generated. DCFs are documents containing queries pertaining to the discrepancies identified.

Discrepancy management

This is also called query resolution. Discrepancy management includes reviewing discrepancies, investigating the reason, and resolving them with documentary proof or declaring them as irresolvable. Discrepancy management helps in cleaning the data and gathers enough evidence for the deviations observed in data. Almost all CDMS have a discrepancy database where all discrepancies will be recorded and stored with audit trail.

Based on the types identified, discrepancies are either flagged to the investigator for clarification or closed in-house by Self-Evident Corrections (SEC) without sending DCF to the site. The most common SECs are obvious spelling errors. For discrepancies that require clarifications from the investigator, DCFs will be sent to the site. The CDM tools help in the creation and printing of DCFs. Investigators will write the resolution or explain the circumstances that led to the discrepancy in data. When a resolution is provided by the investigator, the same will be updated in the database. In case of e-CRFs, the investigator can access the discrepancies flagged to him and will be able to provide the resolutions online.

Discrepancy management (DCF = Data clarification form, CRA = Clinical Research Associate, SDV = Source document verification, SEC = Self-evident correction)

The CDM team reviews all discrepancies at regular intervals to ensure that they have been resolved. The resolved data discrepancies are recorded as 'closed'. This means that those validation failures are no longer considered to be active, and future data validation attempts on the same data will not create a discrepancy for same data point. But closure of discrepancies is not always possible. In some cases, the investigator will not be able to provide a resolution for the discrepancy. Such discrepancies will be considered as 'irresolvable' and will be updated in the discrepancy database.

Discrepancy management is the most critical activity in the CDM process. Being the vital activity in cleaning up the data, utmost attention must be observed while handling the discrepancies.

Medical coding

Medical coding helps in identifying and properly classifying the medical terminologies associated with the clinical trial. For classification of events, medical dictionaries available online are used. Technically, this activity needs the knowledge of medical terminology, understanding of disease entities, drugs used, and a basic knowledge of the pathological processes involved. Functionally, it also requires knowledge about the structure of electronic medical dictionaries and the hierarchy of classifications available in them. Adverse events occurring during the study, prior to and concomitantly administered medications and pre-or co-existing illnesses are coded using the available medical dictionaries. Commonly, Medical Dictionary for Regulatory Activities (MedDRA) is used for the coding of adverse events as well as other illnesses and World Health Organization–Drug Dictionary Enhanced (WHO-DDE) is used for coding the medications. These dictionaries contain the respective classifications of adverse events and drugs in proper classes. Other dictionaries are also available for use in data management (eg, WHO-ART is a dictionary that deals with adverse reactions terminology). Some pharmaceutical companies utilize customized dictionaries to suit their needs and meet their standard operating procedures.

Medical coding helps in classifying reported medical terms on the CRF to standard dictionary terms in order to achieve data consistency and avoid unnecessary duplication. For example, the investigators may use different terms for the same adverse event, but it is important to code all of them to a single standard code and maintain uniformity in the process. The right coding and classification of adverse events and medication is crucial as an incorrect coding may lead to masking of safety issues or highlight the wrong safety concerns related to the drug.

Database locking

After a proper quality check and assurance, the final data validation is run. If there are no discrepancies, the SAS datasets are finalized in consultation with the statistician. All data management activities should have been completed prior to database lock. To ensure this, a pre-lock checklist is used and completion of all activities is confirmed. This is done as the database cannot be changed in any manner after locking. Once the approval for locking is obtained from all stakeholders, the database is locked and clean data is extracted for statistical analysis. Generally, no modification in the database is possible. But in case of a critical issue or for other important operational reasons, privileged users can modify the data even after the database is locked. This, however, requires proper documentation and an audit trail has to be maintained with sufficient justification for updating the locked database. Data extraction is done from the final database after locking. This is followed by its archival.

Roles and Responsibilities in CDM

In a CDM team, different roles and responsibilities are attributed to the team members. The minimum educational requirement for a team member in CDM should be graduation in life science and knowledge of computer applications. Ideally, medical coders should be medical graduates. However, in the industry, paramedical graduates are also recruited as medical coders. Some key roles are essential to all CDM teams. The list of roles given below can be considered as minimum requirements for a CDM team:

- Data Manager
- Database Programmer/Designer
- Medical Coder
- Clinical Data Coordinator
- Quality Control Associate
- Data Entry Associate

The data manager is responsible for supervising the entire CDM process. The data manager prepares the DMP, approves the CDM procedures and all internal documents related to CDM activities. Controlling and allocating the database access to team members is also the responsibility of the data manager. The database programmer/ designer performs the CRF annotation, creates the study database, and programs the edit checks for data validation. He/she is also responsible for designing of data entry screens in the database and validating the edit checks with dummy data. The medical coder will do the coding for adverse events, medical history, co-illnesses, and concomitant medication administered during the study. The clinical data coordinator designs the CRF, prepares the CRF filling instructions, and is responsible for developing the DVP and discrepancy management. All other CDM-related documents, checklists, and guideline documents are prepared by the clinical data coordinator. The quality control associate checks the accuracy of data entry and conducts data audits. Sometimes, there is a separate quality assurance person to conduct the audit on the data entered. Additionally, the quality control associate verifies the documentation pertaining to the procedures being followed. The data entry personnel will be tracking the receipt of CRF pages and performs the data entry into the database.

Data-Mining

Data-Mining (CDM) involves the conceptualization, extraction, analysis, and interpretation of available clinical data for practice knowledge-building, clinical decision-making and practitioner reflection. Depending upon the type of data mined, CDM can be qualitative or quantitative; it is generally retrospective, but may be meaningfully combined with original data collection. Any research method that relies on the contents of case records or information systems data inevitably has limitations, but with proper safeguards these can be minimized. Among CDM's strengths however, are that it is unobtrusive, inexpensive, presents little risk to research subjects, and is ethically compatible with practitioner value.

Data mining:

Data mining is a multidisciplinary field at the intersection of database technology, statistics, (machine learning) ML, and pattern recognition that profits from all these disciplines. Although this approach is not yet widespread in the field of medical research, several studies have demonstrated the promise

Application of data mining

- Disease-prediction models,
- Assessing patient risk, and
- Helping physicians make clinical decisions

Data-mining models

Data-mining has two kinds of models:

1. **Descriptive**

   descriptive models are often used to find patterns that describe data that can be interpreted by humans.

1. **Predictive.**

   Predictive models are used to predict unknown or future values of other variables of interest, whereas.

Data-mining tasks

A model is usually implemented by a task, with the goal of description being to generalize patterns of potential associations in the data.

Therefore, using a descriptive model usually results in a few collections with the same or similar attributes.

Prediction mainly refers to estimation of the variable value of a specific attribute based on the variable values of other attributes, including classification and regression.

Medical public database

1. Surveillance, Epidemiology, and End Results (SEER)

   https://seer.cancer.gov/

2. Medical Information Mart for Intensive Care (MIMIC)

   https://mimic.physionet.org/

3. National Health and Nutri- tion Examination Survey (NHANES)

   https://wwwn.cdc.gov/nchs/ nhanes/

4. Global Burden of Disease (GBD)

   http://ghdx.healthdata.org/

5. UK Biobank (UKB)

   https://www.ukbiobank.ac.uk/

6. The Cancer Genome Atlas (TCGA)

   http://cancergenome.nih. gov/

7. Gene Expression Omnibus (GEO)

   https://www.ncbi.nlm.nih. gov/geo/

8. International Cancer Genome Consortium (ICGC)

https://dcc.icgc.org/

9. China Kadoorie Biobank (CKB)

   https://www.ckbiobank.org/ site/

10. Comparative Toxicogenomics Database (CTD)

    Free http://ctdbase.org/

11. Paediatric Intensive Care (PIC)

    http://pic.nbscn.org/

12. Biologic Specimen and Data Repositories Informa- tion Coordinating Center (BioLINCC)

    https://biolincc.nhlbi.nih.gov/

13. China Health and Nutrition Survey (CHNS)

    http://www.cpc.unc.edu/ projects/china

14. China Health and Retirement Longitudinal Study (CHARLS)

    http://charls.pku.edu.cn/

15. eICU Collaborative Research Database (eICU-CRD)

    https://eicu-crd.mit.edu/

16. Health and Retirement Study (HRS)

The data-mining process

The data mining process is divided into several steps:

(1) database selection according to the research purpose;

(2) data extraction and integration, including downloading the required data and combining data from multiple sources;

(3) data cleaning and transformation, including removal of incorrect data, filling in missing data, generating new variables, converting data format, and ensuring data consistency;

(4) data mining, involving extraction of implicit relational patterns through traditional statistics or ML; (5) pattern evaluation, which focuses on the validity parameters and values of the relationship patterns of the extracted data; and

(6) assessment of the results, involving translation of the extracted data-relationship model into comprehensible knowledge made available to the public.

Examples

A previous study identified sepsis as a major cause of death in ICU patients.

The authors noted that the predictive model developed previously used a limited number of variables, and that model performance required improvement. The data-mining process applied to address these issues was, as follows:

(1) data selection using the MIMIC III database;

(2) extraction and integration of three types of data, including multivariate features (demographic information and clinical biochemical indicators), time series data (temperature, blood pressure, and heart rate), and clinical latent features (various scores related to disease);

(3) data cleaning and transformation, including fixing irregular time series measurements, estimating missing values, deleting outliers, and addressing data imbalance;

(4) data mining through the use of logical regression, generation of a decision tree, application of the RF algorithm, an SVM, and an ensemble algorithm (a combination of multiple classifiers) to established the prediction model;

(5) pattern evaluation using sensitivity, precision, and the area under the receiver operating characteristic curve to evaluate model performance; and

(6) evaluation of the results, in this case the potential to predicting the prognosis of patients with sepsis and whether the model outperformed current scoring systems.

Data-mining methods

- The data mining method depends on whether or not dependent variables (labels) are present in the analysis.
- Predictions with dependent variables (labels) are generated through **supervised learning**, which can be performed by the use of linear regression, generalized linear regression, a proportional hazards model (the Cox regression model), a competitive risk model, decision trees, the random forest (RF) algorithm, and support vector machines (SVMs).
- In contrast, **unsupervised learning** involves no labels. the learning model infers some internal data structure. Common unsupervised learning methods include principal component analysis (PCA), association analysis, and clustering analysis.

Supervised learning

Supervised learning is the partitioning of datasets.

To prevent overfitting of a model, a dataset can generally be divided into two or three parts:

1. a training set,
2. validation set, and
3. test set.

Ripley defined these parts as a set of examples used for learning and used to fit the parameters (i.e., weights) of the classifier, a set of examples used to tune the parameters (i.e., architecture) of a classifier, and a set of examples used only to assess the performance (gen of a fully-specified classifier, respectively.

Training set is used to train the model or determine the model parameters, the validation set is used to perform model selection, and the test set is used to verify model performance. In practice, data are generally divided into training and test sets, whereas the verification set is less involved. It should be emphasized that the results of the test set do not guarantee model correctness but only show that similar data can obtain similar results using the model.

The applicability of a model should be analysed in combination with specific problems in the research. Classical statistical methods, such as linear regression, generalized linear regression, and a proportional risk model, have been widely used in medical research.

Classical statistical methods have certain data requirements or assumptions; however, in face of complicated clinical data, assumptions about data distribution are difficult to make. In contrast, some ML methods (algorithmic models) make no assumptions about the data and cross-verify the results; thus, they are likely to be favoured by clinical researchers. For these reasons, this chapter focuses on ML methods that do not require assumptions about data distribution and classical statistical methods that are used in specific situations.

Decision tree

A decision tree is a basic classification and regression method that generates a result similar to the tree structure of a flowchart, where each tree node represents a test on an attribute, each branch represents the output of an attribute, each leaf node (decision node) represents a class or class distribution, and the topmost part of the tree is the root node.

The decision tree model is called a classification tree when used for classification and a regression tree when used for regression.

Studies have demonstrated the utility of the decision tree model in clinical applications.

In a study on the prognosis of breast cancer patients, a decision tree model and a classical logistic regression model were constructed, respectively, with the predictive performance of the different models indicating that the decision tree model showed stronger predictive power when using real clinical data.

Applications of decision tree model

- diagnosis of kidney stones
- predicting the risk of sudden cardiac arrest,
- exploration of the risk factors of type II diabetes.

A common feature of these studies is the use of a decision tree model to explore the interaction between variables and classify subjects into homogeneous categories based on their observed characteristics.

Advantages

- strong interaction between variables,
- it is more suitable for use with decision algorithms that follow the same structure.
- In the construction of clinical prediction models and exploration of disease risk factors and patient prognosis, the decision tree model might offer more advantages and practical application value than some classical algorithms.

Disadvantages

It recursively separates observations into branches to construct a tree; therefore, in terms of data imbalance, the precision of decision tree models needs improvement.

The RF method

The RF algorithm was developed as an application of an ensemble-learning method based on a collection of decision trees.

The bootstrap method is used to randomly retrieve sample sets from the training set, with decision trees generated by the bootstrap method constituting a “random forest” and predictions based on this derived from an ensemble average or majority vote.

advantage of the RF method

- Random sampling of predictor variables at each decision tree node decreases the correlation among the trees in the forest, thereby improving the precision of ensemble predictions.
- RF minimizes overfitting in classification and regression and improves predictive accuracy.
- Correctly differentiating in-hospital mortality in patients experiencing sepsis after admission to the emergency department.
- Predictive performance of the RF method was superior to that of traditional emergency medicine methods and the methods enabled evaluation of more clinical variables than traditional modelling methods, which subsequently allowed the discovery of clinical variables not expected to be of predictive value or which otherwise would have been omitted as a rare predictor.
- Another study based on the Medical Information Mart for Intensive Care (MIMIC) II database found that RF had excellent predictive power regarding intensive care unit (ICU) mortality.

These studies showed that the application of RF to big data stored in the hospital healthcare system provided a new data-driven method for predictive analysis in critical care.

Random survival forests have recently been developed to analyse survival data, especially right-censored survival data, which can help researchers conduct survival analyses in clinical oncology and help develop personalized treatment regimens that benefit patients.

SVMs

The SVM is a relatively new classification or prediction method developed by Cortes and Vatnik and represents a data-driven approach that does not require assumptions about data distribution.

The core purpose of an SVM is to identify a separation boundary (called a hyperplane) to help classify cases; thus, the advantages of SVMs are obvious when classifying and predicting cases based on high dimensional data or data with a small sample size.

Example

In a study of drug compliance in patients with heart failure, researchers used an SVM to build a predictive model for patient compliance in order to overcome the problem of a large number of input variables relative to the number of available observations.

Additionally, the mechanisms of certain chronic and complex diseases observed in clinical practice remain unclear, and many risk factors, including gene–gene interactions and gene-environment interactions, must be considered in the research of such diseases. SVMs are capable of addressing these issues.

Yu et al. applied an SVM for predicting diabetes onset based on data from the National Health and Nutrition Examination Survey (NHANES).

Advantages

- strong discrimination ability
- making SVMs a promising classification approach for detecting individuals with chronic and complex diseases.

Disadvantage of SVMs

- Number of observation samples is large,
- the method becomes time- and resource-intensive, which is often highly inefficient.

Competitive risk model

Kaplan–Meier marginal regression and the Cox proportional hazards model are widely used in survival analysis in clinical studies.

Classical survival analysis usually considers only one endpoint, such as the impact of patient survival time.

However, in clinical medical research, multiple endpoints usually coexist, and these endpoints compete with one another to generate competitive risk data.

In the case of multiple endpoint events, the use of a single endpoint-analysis method can lead to a biased estimation of the probability of endpoint events due to the existence of competitive risks.

The competitive risk model is a classical statistical model based on the hypothesis of data distribution.

Advantage

- Accurate estimation of the cumulative incidence of outcomes for right-censored survival data with multiple endpoints.

In data analysis, the cumulative risk rate is estimated using the cumulative incidence function in single-factor analysis, and gray's test is used for between group comparisons.

Multifactor analysis uses the Fine-Gray and cause specific (CS) risk models to explore the cumulative risk rate.

Difference between the Fine-Gray and CS models

Fine Gray is applicable to establishing a clinical prediction model and predicting the risk of a single endpoint of interest, whereas the CS is suitable for answering etiological questions, where the regression coefficient reflects the relative effect of covariates on the increased incidence of the main endpoint in the target event-free risk set.

Currently, in databases with CS records, such as Surveillance, Epidemiology, and End Results (SEER), competitive risk models exhibit good performance in exploring disease-risk factors and prognosis.

Examples

A study of prognosis in patients with oesophageal cancer from SEER showed that Cox proportional risk models might misestimate the effects of age and disease location on patient prognosis, whereas competitive risk models provide more accurate estimates of factors affecting patient prognosis.

In another study of the prognosis of penile cancer patients, researchers found that using a competitive risk model was more helpful in developing personalized treatment plans.

Unsupervised learning

In many data-analysis processes, the amount of usable identified data is small, and identifying data is a tedious process.

Unsupervised learning is necessary to judge and categorize data according to similarities, characteristics, and correlations and has three main applications: data clustering, association analysis, and dimensionality reduction. It includes clustering analysis, association rules, and PCA.

Clustering analysis

The classification algorithm needs to “know” information concerning each category in advance, with all of the data to be classified having corresponding categories.

When the above conditions cannot be met, cluster analysis can be applied to solve the problem.

Clustering places similar objects into different categories or subsets through the process of static classification. Consequently, objects in the same subset have similar properties. Many kinds of clustering techniques exist. Here, we introduced the four most commonly used clustering techniques.

1. **Partition clustering**

The core idea of this clustering method regards the centre of the data point as the centre of the cluster. The k-means method is a representative example of this technique. The k-means method takes n observations and an integer, k, and outputs a partition of the n observations into k sets such that each observation belongs to the cluster with the nearest mean. The k-means method exhibits low time complexity and high computing efficiency but has a poor processing effect on high dimensional data and cannot identify non spherical clusters.

2. **Hierarchical clustering**

The hierarchical clustering algorithm decomposes a dataset hierarchically to facilitate the subsequent clustering. Common algorithms for hierarchical clustering include BIRCH, CURE, and ROCK. The algorithm starts by treating every point as a cluster, with clusters grouped according to closeness. When further combinations result in unexpected results under multiple causes or only one cluster remains, the grouping process ends. This method has wide applicability, and the relationship between clusters is easy to detect; however, the time complexity is high.

3. **Clustering according to density**

The density algorithm takes areas presenting a high degree of data density and defines these as belonging to the same cluster. This method aims to find arbitrarily-shaped clusters, with the most representative algorithm being DBSCAN. In practice, DBSCAN does not need to input the number of clusters to be partitioned and can handle clusters of various shapes; however, the time complexity of the algorithm is high. Furthermore, when data density is irregular, the quality of the clusters decreases; thus, DBSCAN cannot process high dimensional data.

4. Clustering according to a grid

Neither partition nor hierarchical clustering can identify clusters with nonconvex shapes. Although a dimension-based algorithm can accomplish this task, the time complexity is high.

To address this problem, data-mining researchers proposed grid-based algorithms that changed the original data space into a grid structure of a certain size.

A representative algorithm is STING, which divides the data space into several square cells according to different resolutions and clusters the data of different structure levels.

Advantage

- high processing speed and its exclusive dependence on the number of units in each dimension of the quantized space.

In clinical studies, subjects tend to be actual patients. Although researchers adopt complex inclusion and exclusion criteria before determining the subjects to be included in the analyses, heterogeneity among different patients cannot be avoided.

Application of cluster analysis

- In clinical big data is in classifying heterogeneous mixed groups into homogeneous groups according to the characteristics of existing data (i.e., "subgroups" of patients or observed objects are identified).

This new information can then be used in the future to develop patient-oriented medical management strategies.

Docampo et al. used hierarchical clustering to reduce heterogeneity and identify subgroups of clinical fibromyalgia, which aided the evaluation and management of fibromyalgia.

Guo et al. used k-means clustering to divide patients with essential hypertension into four subgroups, which revealed that the potential risk of coronary heart disease differed between different subgroups.

Density- and grid-based clustering algorithms have mostly been used to process large numbers of images generated in basic research and clinical practice, with current studies focused on developing new tools to help clinical research and practices based on these technologies.

Cluster analysis will continue to have extensive application prospects along with the increasing emphasis on personalized treatment.

Association rules

Association rules discover interesting associations and correlations between item sets in large amounts of data. These rules were first proposed by Agrawal et al. and applied to analyse customer buying habits to help retailers create sales plans.

Data-mining based on association rules identifies association rules in a two-step process:

1) all high frequency items in the collection are listed and

2) frequent association rules are generated based on the high frequency items.

Therefore, before association rules can be obtained, sets of frequent items must be calculated using certain algorithms.

The Apriori algorithm is based on the a priori principle of finding all relevant adjustment items in a database transaction that meet a minimum set of rules and restrictions or other restrictions. Other algorithms are mostly variants of the Apriori algorithm.

The Apriori algorithm must scan the entire database every time it scans the transaction; therefore, algorithm performance deteriorates as database size increases, making it potentially unsuitable for analysing large databases.

The frequent pattern (FP) growth algorithm was proposed to improve efficiency. After the first scan, the FP algorithm compresses the frequency set in the database into a FP tree while retaining the associated information and then mines the conditional libraries separately.

Examples

Association-rule technology is often used in medical research to identify association rules between disease risk factors (i.e., exploration of the joint effects of disease risk factors and combinations of other risk factors).

For example, Li et al. used the association-rule algorithm to identify the most important stroke risk factor as atrial fibrillation, followed by diabetes and a family history of stroke. Based on the same principle, association rules can also be used to evaluate treatment effects and other aspects.

For example, Guo et al used the FP algorithm to generate association rules and evaluate individual characteristics and treatment effects of patients with diabetes, thereby reducing the readability rate of patients with diabetes.

Association rules reveal a connection between premises and conclusions; however, the reasonable and reliable application of information can only be achieved through validation by experienced medical professionals and through extensive causal research.

PCA

PCA is a widely used data-mining method that aims to reduce data dimensionality in an interpretable way while retaining most of the information present in the data.

The main purpose of PCA is descriptive, as it requires no assumptions about data distribution and is, therefore, an adaptive and exploratory method.

During the process of data analysis, the main steps of PCA include standardization of the original data, calculation of a correlation coefficient matrix, calculation of eigenvalues and eigenvectors, selection of principal components, and calculation of the comprehensive evaluation value. PCA does not often appear as a separate method, as it is often combined with other statistical methods.

In practical clinical studies, the existence of multicollinearity often leads to deviation from multivariate analysis. A feasible solution is to construct a regression model by PCA, which replaces the original independent variables with each principal component as a new independent variable for regression analysis, with this most commonly seen in the analysis of dietary patterns in nutritional epidemiology.

In a study of socioeconomic status and child-developmental delays, PCA was used to derive a new variable (the household wealth index) from a series of household property reports and incorporate this new variable as the main analytical variable into the logistic regression model.

Additionally, PCA can be combined with cluster analysis. Burgle et al. used PCA to transform clinical data to address the lack of independence between existing variables used to explore the heterogeneity of different subtypes of chronic obstructive pulmonary disease.

Therefore, in the study of subtypes and heterogeneity of clinical diseases, PCA can eliminate noisy variables that can potentially corrupt the cluster structure, thereby increasing the accuracy of the results of clustering analysis.

Coding dictionaries in clinical trial

Coding dictionaries serve as a solution to unify spelling, abbreviation, or other common errors that occur in the data collection process.

As an example, if one researcher reports an adverse event one way and another researcher inputs the same adverse event in a slightly different way, they can both utilize medical coding software to adjust the data to meet the standardized terminology. Additionally, if there are common terms being reported which do not have exact matches to a standard dictionary, coders can grow their own synonym dictionaries for using across studies.

Medical coding prevents common problems such as spelling errors, incorrect abbreviations, or non-standardized terms. Medical coding prevents common problems such as spelling errors, incorrect abbreviations, or non-standardized terms.

For example, say a handful of participants mention they are feeling a potential side effect from the trial therapy. One participant may report suffering from head discomforts, while another report experiencing dizziness. Standard coding dictionaries will help organize those otherwise scattered terms into a standard parent category, which can help identify important trends within the trial.

Latest version releases of the industry's popular coding dictionaries are MedDRA and WHO Drug, and what it means for users.

MedDRA dictionary version

The purpose of the MedDRA dictionary is to classify and code adverse events (AEs) and serious adverse events (SAEs). This dictionary experienced a version release on March 1st, 2019 – Version 22.0. MedDRA Version 22.0 incorporated 1,333 user change requests. This includes approved changes to Standardized MedDRA Queries (SMQs) and added new a SMQ for Hypokalaemia. Additionally, the SMQ spreadsheet was updated.

Proactivity requests resulted in a more optimal placement for anesthesia terms in the dictionary, as well as more consistent placement for existing chemical burn and corrosive injury terms. Lastly, updates were made in relation to the rename provision, which allows for the modification of preferred terms (PTs) and lowest level terms (LLTs).

WHO Drug dictionary version

The purpose of the WHO Drug dictionary is to classify and code concomitant medications. On March 1st, 2019, the B2/C formats were completely phased out and replaced by B3/C3 formats. WHO Drug launched this new and improved dictionary format to better comply with CDISC SDTM standards. According to the Uppsala Monitoring Centre (UMC), the B3/C3 formats are introduced to facilitate regulatory submissions of WHO Drug data in a format meeting regulatory CDISC SDTM expectations, without the need of any workarounds.

UMC has made this recommendation for WHODrug dictionary users: companies planning to submit study data (to the U.S. FDA or other regulatory agencies) are recommended to make use the B3/C3 formats as soon as possible, to meet regulatory SDTM expectations and benefit from the improvements of the new formats. So, it is crucial for medical coding professionals to have a tool that is compatible with the most up-to-date WHODrug format.

UMC's WHO Drug Koda is an automated coding engine that leverages machine learning to achieve more efficient and accurate coding. Not only will Koda be available as a web application and as an add-on to WHO Drug subscriptions, it also boasts an API, which will allow for integration with existing coding tools.

Replacing ds Navigator, a popular medical coding tool

Users of ds Navigator, the coding platform created by Cerner, learned that this tool would stop receiving updates and support after 2017, thus making it defunct. Since B2 and C WHODrug formats are officially unavailable for use (and not adopting new MedDRA versions), ds Navigator can no longer be considered an accurate and effective solution for coding professionals. This has led many companies to transition to a new coding platform that is certified with the medical dictionaries they need for their data collection and analysis.

Trial Kit Coder, our medical coding solution

The team behind the Trial Kit platform has created a medical coding solution that makes the process secure and swift. Trial Kit Coder is a fast and powerful coding platform functioning entirely in the cloud. Trial Kit Coder is available on any web browser or iOS device. This gives medical coders the ability to code and approve at any time, from any place.

Trial Kit Coder also operates in two ways:

1. Automatically integrated with Trial Kit, the data collection and study management platform, and
2. As a standalone platform for those who do not have a need for electronic data capture (EDC) technology, or who have data from any external source that is now in need of coding and standardizing. Trial Kit Coder is a certified vendor with both MedDRA and WHO Drug (B3 format) and adheres to CDISC STDM standards.

Clinical Data Warehousing

Clinical Data Warehousing is a technological approach that allows clinical research departments to link, merge and re-use the clinical data from previous studies to answer new clinical questions concerning drug efficacy and/or safety.

Clinical business intelligence tools such as clinical data warehouse enable health care organizations to objectively assess the disease management programs that affect the quality of patients' life and well-being in public.

Objectives

The purpose of these programs is to reduce disease occurrence, improve patient care, and decrease health care costs.

Therefore, applying clinical data warehouse can be effective in generating useful information about aspects of patient care to facilitate budgeting, planning, research, process improvement, external reporting, benchmarking, and trend analysis, as well as to enable the decisions needed to prevent the progression or appearance of the illness aligning with maintaining the health of the population.

Questions

1.Explain in detail about audit in clinical trial?
2.Explain in detail about the quality control and quality assurance in clinical trial?
3.Types of audit in clinical trial?
4.Short note on on site audit?
5.Short note on system audit?
6.Define clinical data management? Objectives of CDM Process?
7.Tools for CDM?
8.Explain about Electronic data capture system in clinical trial?
9.Explain about clinical data mining?
10.What are medical data bases for data mining ?
11.What are data mining methods?
12.Short note on decision tree, RF method, Svms
13.Explain about coding dictionaries in clinical tril?
14.Short note on MedDRA?
15.Short note on WHO Drug Dictionary version?
16.Explain about Clinical Data warehousing?

CHAPTER SIX

References

1. World Health Organization. Guide for writing a Research Protocol for research involving human participation; 2014. Available from: http://www.who.int/rpc/ research_ethics/guide_rp/en/index.html.

2. https://www.who.int/docs/default-source/medicines/norms-and-standards/guidelines/regulatory-standards/trs957-annex7-guidelinespreparationcontractresearchorgmasterfile.pdf?sfvrsn=958aef39_2

3. https://pubmed.ncbi.nlm.nih.gov/34380547/

4.https://ichgcp.net/

5.Conducting Feasibilities in Clinical Trials: An Investment to Ensure a Good Study by Dr Viraj Rajadhyaksha.

6.MedDRA Introductory Guide Version 12.1, September 2009, MSSO-DI-6003-12.1.0 2.

7.WHO Drug Dictionary Sample Getting Started © UMC Products & Services, 2006.

9 798889 518679

Printed by Libri Plureos GmbH in Hamburg,
Germany